THE STATUS OF WOMEN

Psychoanalysis & Women Series
Series Editor: Frances Thomson-Salo

THE STATUS OF WOMEN

Violence, Identity, and Activism

edited by

Vivian B. Pender

A volume in the Psychoanalysis & Women Series
for the Committee on Women and Psychoanalysis
of the International Psychoanalytical Association

KARNAC

First published in 2017 by
Karnac Books Ltd
118 Finchley Road, London NW3 5HT

British Library Cataloguing in Publication Data

A C.I.P. for this book is available from the British Library

   ISBN 978 1 78220 305 6

Edited, designed and produced by The Studio Publishing Services Ltd
www.publishingservicesuk.co.uk
email: studio@publishingservicesuk.co.uk

www.karnacbooks.com

CONTENTS

34.
———
/ 33

ACKNOWLEDGMENT AND PERMISSIONS *28*

I owe gratitude to University Professor Gayatri Chakravorty Spivak of Columbia University, New York for her prolific writing, teaching, and tireless generosity to women, girls, and humanity.

Permissions

Reprinted by permission to use the following illustrations from *One! Hundred! Demons!* by Lynda Barry © 2002 granted by Darhansoff & Verrill Literary Agents: Panel 1: "Is it autobiography if parts of it are not true?" Panel 2: "Is it fiction if parts of it are?"

Reprinted by permission to use scattered graphics from *The Essential Dykes to Watch Out For* by Alison Bechdel © 2008 granted by Houghton Mifflin Harcourt.

Reprinted by permission to use the illustrations Captain Marvel and Ms. Marvel granted by © Marvel Entertainment.

Reprinted by permission to use *Ms. Magazine* covers © July 1972 and Fall 2012.

Reprinted by permission to use "Fighting supervillains is a cinch—fighting misogyny is the real challenge" by Tom Toro, from The Cartoon Bank, New Yorker Collection, Condé Nast Collection.

Vera J. Camden, PhD, is Professor of English at Kent State University, Clinical Assistant Professor of Psychiatry at Case Western Reserve University and Clinical Faculty of Social Work at Rutgers University. She is a training and supervising analyst at the Cleveland Psychoanalytic Center. A member of the Committee on Research and Special Training at the American Psychoanalytic Association, she is co-editor of *American Imago*, and on the editorial board of *The American Psychoanalyst and Bunyan Studies: A Journal of Reformation and Dissent*. She specializes in seventeenth-century British literature, psychoanalysis, and comics and graphic narratives.

Ruth S. Fischer, MD, Clinical Professor of Psychiatry of the University of Pennsylvania School of Medicine, Department of Psychiatry, is an adult and child psychiatrist and psychoanalyst, and a training/supervising analyst at the Psychoanalytic Center of Philadelphia. She spearheaded an unprecedented joint meeting of the Psychoanalytic Association and the University of Pennsylvania on female psychology and aggression. She was an original National Woman Scholars of the American Psychoanalytic Association. She received the 2015 Earl Bond award from the University of Pennsylvania, and the lifetime achievement award from the Psychoanalytic Center of Philadelphia. She teaches at the University of Pennsylvania, Jefferson University, and the Psychoanalytic Center of Philadelphia.

Adrienne Harris, PhD is a member of the faculty of the New York University Postdoctoral Program and the Psychoanalytic Institute of Northern California. In 2009, she co-established the Sandor Ferenczi Center, New School University. She co-edits the Relational Book Series. Her books include *Gender as Soft Assembly*. She co-edited *Rocking the Ship of State: Women and Peace Politics*; *Storms in her Head*; *First Do No Harm: Psychoanalysis, War-making and Resistance*; *The Legacy of Sandor Ferenczi: From Ghost to Ancestor*. She is on the editorial board of the IPA ejournal, *Psychoanalytic Dialogues*, *Studies in Gender and Sexuality*, and the *Journal of the American Psychoanalytic Association*.

Sargam Jain, MD, is a Clinical Instructor and Assistant Attending Psychiatrist at Weill Cornell Medical College and has worked internationally in Mexico, Brazil, and Tanzania with marginalized populations. Following a public psychiatry fellowship at NYS Psychiatric Institute, she developed an integrated care program for homeless individuals and became interested in a psychoanalytic approach to the politics of displacement and exclusion. She is a candidate in the Adult Psychoanalysis program at Columbia University and a member of the International Psychoanalytical Association Committee to the UN. She continues public work as a consultant to the Legal Aid Society regarding the impact of welfare policy on psychiatric disabilities.

Alexander D. Kalogerakis, MD, is a Clinical Associate Professor of Psychiatry at Weill Cornell Medical College. He is a child/adolescent supervising analyst of the American Psychoanalytic Association and a member of the Faculty at the New York Psychoanalytic Society and Institute, where he teaches Technique of Child and Adolescent Analysis and Adult Development. He is a member of the United Nations Committee of the International Psychoanalytical Association. He has written book chapters on adolescent identity and culture, and is a contributor to Auchincloss and Samberg's *Psychoanalytic Terms & Concepts*. He has a private practice in child, adolescent, and adult psychiatry and psychoanalysis in New York.

Vivian B. Pender, MD, is a Clinical Associate Professor of Psychiatry at the Weill Cornell Medical College and a training psychoanalyst at Columbia University. At the UN, she represents the International Psychoanalytical Association and the American Psychiatric Association. Until 2011, she chaired the NGO Committee on the Status of Women. She is the current Chair of the NGO Committee on Mental Health. She is a volunteer Asylum Evaluator for Physicians for Human Rights. She is the author of journal articles and a book chapter on affect, motivation, pregnancy, female psychology, and women's health. She produced four documentaries of conferences at the United Nations on mental health, human rights, and violence.

Shabnam Shakibaie Smith, MD, is an Assistant Professor of Psychiatry at Columbia University Medical School. She is the liaison psychiatrist in the Obstetrics-Gynecology Department at the New York Presbyterian Hospital, where her focus is perinatal mental health issues. She started practicing medicine as a primary care physician in underserved areas in the Persian Gulf. She is the co-chair of the Women's Committee of the New York County Psychiatric Society. She is a candidate at the Columbia University Psychoanalytic Center for Training and Research and a volunteer Asylum Evaluator for Columbia University Human Rights Initiative, Asylum Clinic. At the UN, she is a consultant on the treatment of addiction in pregnancy.

Johanna Mendoza Talledo, MA, is a clinical psychologist and was granted a Masters in Theoretical Studies in Psychoanalysis at the Pontificia Universidad Católica del Perú, where she also completed her coursework in Philosophy. She is a training analyst of the Peruvian Psychoanalytic Society. She was the Scientific Secretary of the Peruvian Association of Psychoanalytic Psychotherapy for Children and Adolescents, and Psychoanalysis and Gender Professor in the Master of Theoretical Studies in Psychoanalysis. She is a co-editor of *Motherhood and its Vicissitudes Today* (2006). Lima: Sidea. She has written articles on early identification, early bonding, gender, and Greek tragedy.

Isaac Tylim, PsyD, is a training analyst at the Institute for Psychoanalytic Training and Research and New York University Postdoctoral Program. He is a former Vice-chair of the NGO Committee on the

Mental Health, member of the IPA UN Committee and Cultural Committee. He is the co-founder of the Trauma and Disaster Specialization Program, NYU Postdoc, and the Art, Psychoanalysis and Society Project at IPTAR. A journalist at the *Buenos Aires Herald*, he has been on the Editorial Board of the *Journal of the American Psychoanalytic Association*, a co-editor of *Film and Psychoanalysis*, co-editor of *Terrorism and the Psychoanalytic Space*, and *Home Sweet Home: Revisiting the Psychoanalytic Frame*.

Sverre Varvin, MD, Dr. Philos, is a training and supervising analyst, Norwegian Psychoanalytic Society and Professor, Oslo and Akershus University College for Applied Sciences. He has worked clinically with severely traumatised patients for more than twenty-five years and has written articles and books on this subject. Main research areas are: traumatisation and treatment of traumatised patients, treatment process, traumatic dreams, and psychoanalytic training. He is the Past President of the Norwegian Psychoanalytical Society. He has been IPA Vice President, Board representative, and member of research committees. He has worked for many years with psychotherapy training programs in China and is presently Chair of the IPA China Committee.

Niamey P. Wilson, MD, MSHP, obtained her medical degree from Columbia University and her training in general surgery and breast surgical oncology at the University of Pennsylvania. She was selected as a Robert Wood Johnson Clinical Scholar, obtained a Masters degree in Health Policy Research and researched surgical decision making. She is currently the Co-Director of the Breast Center at Saint Francis Hospital in Hartford, Connecticut. Dr. Wilson is a member of the American College of Surgeons, American Society of Breast Surgeons, and the American Society of Clinical Oncology. She holds an appointment as Assistant Professor of Surgery at the University of Connecticut School of Medicine.

SERIES EDITOR'S FOREWORD

It gives me great pleasure to write this foreword for the latest book in Karnac's Psychoanalysis and Women series, exploring issues of gender and sexuality, scientifically, culturally, and politically. This book has been edited by Vivian Pender, who, for the past fifteen years, has chaired the United Nations committee of the International Psycho-analytical Association. This committee is charged with making psychoanalysis visible and heard in the United Nations, and assessing the discipline and practice of psychoanalysis in the light of inter-national concerns such as conflict prevention and resolution, effects of prejudice and ethnicity, violence, and child abuse, and, from this vantage point, Pender has selected supremely relevant topics for this book.

Women as a large heterogeneous group, correspondingly experi-ence huge variations of status, and the authors, with their knowledge of the multi-faceted aspects of women's status, have made a psycho-analytic contribution to this area a reality.

In a wide sweep, the book includes chapters that use the powerful lens of development in the life of a girl baby from preconception towards adulthood and motherhood, and, in doing so, highlights conditions for, and the position of, women and daughters. The book culminates in a dispassionate study of disadvantage and abuse. Throughout, exploration of why abuse has been perpetrated and condoned by male family members and societal representatives has not been neglected. In this way, the book provides an informed exploration of many sectors, historical, political, affective, and intersubjective, to come closer to an understanding of the abuse always endured by women and girls.

As Vivian Pender writes, the scale of abuse towards women is staggering. The authors bring us time and again to ask why progress is so slow and what it will take to redress all forms of abuse. On everyone's behalf, I thank them, as analysts and writers, for what they have endured and contributed to bring us their understanding.

Frances Thomson-Salo
Series Editor for Psychoanalysis and Women series

Introduction

This book would not exist were it not for my work with the United Nations (UN) over the past twenty years. The impetus for writing and gathering contributors derives from that experience. In 1997 the International Psychoanalytical Association (IPA) became accredited with the UN as a non-governmental organization (NGO) with special consultative status. For that innovative connection we owe thanks to Afaf Mahfouz and Otto Kernberg. Since then, I have had the privilege of representing the IPA at the UN, especially as Chair of the NGO Committee on Women and Chair of the NGO Committee on Mental Health. Fifty years before, in 1947, the first UN Commission on the Status of Women met and was mandated to meet yearly to examine and monitor the advancement of women in the areas of women's rights, inclusiveness, and global awareness of discrimination and disproportionate effects of poverty and laws on women. I have witnessed UN Women document disparities such as lack of equal pay, or child marriage, or control of family planning. I have helped women avoid imprisonment and torture. I have lobbied governments to decriminalize same-sex relationships, as well as prohibit children from being used as soldiers ordered to commit murder. I have worked for a decade to raise awareness of human trafficking. Members of several non-governmental organizations have engaged and urged stakeholders at the UN to intervene and implement their policies. I have realized that progress has been inordinately slow, and sometimes followed by backlash and regression. Presently, to many at the UN, the status of women is ultimately unacceptable. Too many attitudes towards girls and women in all areas of the world are deeply destructive, not only to them, but to all of humanity. Why are girls not being educated at the same rate as boys? Why are there so few women in leadership positions? Why are governments and UN agencies more concerned about the physical consequences than the life-long psychological effects of the state-sponsored rape of fourteen-year-old girls? What justification is there for a thirty-five-year-old man to marry an eight-year-old girl? When is it morally acceptable to institutionalize sexual slavery to serve the sexual needs of military men? How does a culture accept a law that allows only half of the population to vote? Who is the most frequent victim of domestic violence? When do resistance and repercussion have a worsening effect on the status of women? Who writes and enforces the laws that we all adhere to? When did sexism become a structural identification? Why do women default to using their sexual bodies as a method of income and resign themselves to sexual performance for men? What defenses are girls taught in order to survive in a male environment?

These questions and many others came to mind over the years with increasing awareness of women's status and, with this book, the reality of a psychoanalytic contribution. This book examines the status of women in different eras and in different areas of society. It consists of a collection of papers that focus on the challenges that confront women worldwide. The contributors, from the International Psychoanalytical Association's United Nations Committee and from a variety of disciplines, draw on their international experience to consider how women are viewed, treated, and represented in society today. They offer perspectives on why the status of women and girls has not changed in some areas of the world since the beginning of recorded history, while in other areas there has been discrete and noteworthy progress and improvement in women's status. The emphasis is on how and why the status of women has either stalled or evolved to its present place. This exploration of the different aspects of the status of women should offer new perspectives to the broad scope of psychoanalytic theory and practice. At a time when women's rights are in peril through the regimes of fundamentalist religions and extremist cultures, there is a risk of trivializing the threat of sexual assault of vulnerable women on every continent and at every socio-economic level.

The contributing authors were asked to reflect on the realities of the status of women and, perhaps, find psychoanalytic understanding. Because women are a large heterogeneous group, the chapters of the book are similarly diverse. Although the word status could mean privileged, it is used to denote state, condition, or position. The first four chapters examine the conditions that women experience, or have experienced in the past, in the USA and in the Middle East, in the office and on a college campus. In Chapter One, Wilson shares with the reader an in-depth and personal view of her experience as she traverses the masculine world of surgeons. She reveals insight into her internal changes that must occur for a singular exceptional woman to thrive in an almost entirely male universe. Although eventually successful, the report of her path is wrenching at times.

In Chapter Two, Jain describes a somewhat similar experience for de Beauvoir one hundred years ago and a psychoanalytic understanding of her trajectory. She has only belatedly been acknowledged as a philosopher in her own right, apart from Sartre.

In Chapter Three, Camden provides insight into the rich thinking and interests of college students. Graphics of current comics for young women are included to illustrate the struggles and the playful media vehicles that have evolved.

In Chapter Four, Shakibaie Smith illustrates her experience in the Middle East with pregnant women and gives clear evidence that female sexuality is not an open topic of discussion. As a result, the delivery of a child after denial of pregnancy can be a terrifying event.

The next three chapters review the position of girls in different societies. In Chapter Five, Kalogerakis examines the effects of migration on children, those who move and those who stay behind. He emphasizes the special vulnerability of girls.

In Chapter Six, Fischer explores the developmental path for female power from the perspective of a child and adolescent psychiatrist and psychoanalyst. Illustrating how current cultural icons saturate the girl's environment and both reflect and inform development, she reminds the reader that there is a separate normal line of development for girls.

Mendoza Talledo, in Chapter Seven, demonstrates clearly the transmission of denigrating female values traversing several generations. Without her clinical interpretations, unconscious attitudes would have prevailed.

The following three chapters discuss the devolution of the status of women. In Chapter Eight, Pender explores six factors related to abuse of women and girls and their relation to a universal maternal representation. They cover several areas of society that have either failed to provide human rights or have actively removed them. Equality and difference are denied to them.

In Chapter Nine, Varvin presents clinical experiences with mothers who have been imprisoned and tortured. He expresses both the difficulty and the necessity of such treatments.

Tylim grapples with the subject of masculinity as an identity and a defense in Chapter Ten. One might wonder how the mother functions to suppress her boy's masculinity and terrify him in the process.

In the final chapter, Harris takes a long view of history and feminist movements, how they furthered activism and how they hindered advancement. She ends with questions for the reader that could be construed as a call to action.

*This volume is in memory of my mother, and all mothers,
and in honor of my daughters and granddaughters,
and all daughters and granddaughters.
It is also dedicated to all women and men
who have served as models and who will provide
new models for new futures.*

CHAPTER ONE

A woman surgeon: her story

Niamey P. Wilson

"Surgery made a man out of me," she chuckled.

I paused. We were nearing the end of an operation, closing the skin. I was holding a needle driver with a loaded suture in one hand, and a tweezer-like instrument eponymously named Adson forceps in the other. The words had been spoken by a female attending surgeon with whom I had been working during my eighth and final surgical training year my fellowship year. We were exchanging stories about the grueling yet awesome experiences of surgical residency. We kept going. Surgeons are excellent multi-taskers; the fluidity with which a surgeon can carry on a conversation while also, say, deftly maneuvering a liver out of the way can be remarkable. But it is a learned skill, not entirely dissimilar to the parent who can carry on a heated argument about politics while simultaneously holding a child, typing on a computer, and preparing a meal. Except the life of the patient is at stake. To relieve the tension of that heavy responsibility without disengaging from the task is a delicate and simultaneous mental operation.

As all surgeons know, discussions during the course of an operation can be about anything, and vary wildly depending on the mood in the room. The mood might depend on how smoothly the operation is proceeding and if any emergent findings call for focus above the usual strict attention. But if all is well, topics of conversation may range from international monetary policy in Greece to incredibly personal details of one's life. And, without question, the many hours spent in the operating room are particularly opportune moments to learn the real dirt about your fellow surgeon standing across the OR table. There is a curtain of pretense that is lifted once a surgeon is gowned, gloved, and masked for surgery, and somehow honesty ensues. Oscar Wilde (1891) once wrote, "Man is least himself when he talks in his own person. Give him a mask, and he will tell you the truth". In no other setting would I have heard from my fellow surgeons such a cathartic divulging of secrets, bizarre suppositions about religion, intimate habits, and how they really felt about their spouses—all from behind the blue guise of operating room attire. The gravity of the situation, the fatigue, and the necessary dissociation offered by the mask seems to allow for psychological regression to take place. Since most of the surgeons were men, the kind of regression might have reflected the topics and gender. In fact, the conditions in the operating room may demand that this regression take place.

Narratives aside, these were very precious times that I remember with great fondness, these moments captured with my attending surgeons in the operating room. Nearly all surgeries require two sets of hands, and over the eight years I had spent in surgical residency, there was a gradual shift towards my hands carrying more and more responsibility for the actual performance of the operation. After a while, "muscle memory" becomes installed and surgical skill is, thus, usefully unconscious and automatic, and slowly the resident gains the training necessary to be an attending surgeon. Attending surgeons are faculty; the residents are those in training. Surgeons and residents often develop close relationships as master and pupil, and time spent together is invaluable and intense. While your patient sleeps, you have a captive audience with these near-parental figures. Those hours are labile with emotion while they teach you the painstaking skill of performing meticulous surgery: a mix of fear, determination, egotism, self-loathing, frustration, accomplishment, and pure satisfaction. The reward of curing a patient or fixing a mechanical problem surely must involve endorphins and dopamine receptors in the brain.

My attending surgeon did not need to explain this masculinization that occurred through her surgical residency; I totally understood.

Hers had certainly been a more difficult experience, as a female surgeon twenty-five years my senior. At that time, she was one of only a few women in the entire seven-year general surgery residency program, which held over fifty residents at that time. More notably, not every resident graduated to the following year. Up until the 1970s, the structure of surgical residency was pyramidal: only the best from each year were allowed to progress. This process had been designed by William Stewart Halsted, one of the most innovative surgeons in the past two centuries and a founding professor of the Johns Hopkins Hospital in Baltimore, Maryland. By the final or "chief" year of surgical residency, often there were only 1–2 individuals who survived this grueling challenge from the original, several-times larger pool. It was the definition of cut-throat meant to foster the most aggression. Edward Churchill, former chief of surgery at Massachusetts General Hospital in Boston, was the first to propose the current "rectangular" system of resident training to supplant Halsted's long-standing pyramidal system. It took years to adopt, but, by the 1980s, most training programs had converted to Churchill's design. It was in this rectangular system that I had matriculated. Every member of my generation of surgical residents progressed slowly but surely to the next year. Yet, I was the only woman in my graduating class of surgical residents.

She was discussing her brave and also decidedly preposterous decision to have children during residency as a woman in her early thirties. She revealed that her male colleagues (despite some of them having children of their own) did not appear to fully appreciate the extraordinary difficulty of first growing, then birthing, and finally raising a child as a female surgical trainee. How could they? A female surgical resident having a child meant more work for them—more call nights to cover, more operations to do with an already stretched-thin crew, and literally one less body around to handle the routine busy-work of managing the surgical patient list. They voiced their unhappiness to her and their superiors without hesitation. Such words would be considered grounds for a sexual discrimination lawsuit in the current training climate, but she took it in her stride, repaid her maternity leave (a measly four weeks) and raised her daughter in that toxic environment. She is the definition of tough. Today, she is a highly successful surgeon in her field. If there was a note of cynicism or resentment in her voice, I never heard it. When she said that surgery made a man out of her, the intended commentary was not missed.

It could be said that her training environment was harmful to her and her family. That assimilation into the highly aggressive male structure forced her to bend (or even distort) her natural inclinations to nurture a child, but did not stop her from trying. One could wonder about the strength of her maternal instincts that outweighed the influence of her environment. I wondered, at what personal cost?

I took the opportunity to ask why she chose surgery as a profession; to be more specific, if she understood her reasons for choosing surgery. She provided me with answers that I had heard in my own answer to that question: she enjoyed the operating room, she had natural dexterity and skill, she gained satisfaction from being able to "fix" something in a single instance. But we had more in common than that. There was a desire to prove that she could handle it, that she had the right materials to make an outstanding surgeon, that she was decisive and strong. She described herself as hardened through surgical training, but that she was thankful for it. She knew it would be the most difficult thing she would ever do with her life, and did not want to back away from that calling. And she knew that the emotional rewards would outweigh the personal sacrifices. Perhaps we both had the need to think that we could handle any situation and take care of anyone who needed our help. Whether because of anxiety or guilt, we could imagine that we would know what to do with our fears and we would do the right thing in the most difficult and stressful of situations. Being a surgeon could at least give us the internal illusion that we were strong and good people. We could fantasize that we were doing "God's work", members of a community that sacrificed and worked for the greater good.

By history and convention, surgery is a man's field. Despite growing numbers of women applying to surgical residency, there are far more practicing male surgeons today than female surgeons. The number of women in leadership positions in surgery can be pitifully counted on two hands. In 2008, Freischlag reported that she was ". . . one of only three women Department Chairs in Surgery in the country—and one of only six ever." Primarily, this stems from past restrictions on women in the field of medicine. Historically, the participation of women in the profession of medicine and surgery was significantly limited. Although women have always been caretakers of the sick, these were more often in other roles, such as nurses or nuns in convents. A few notable women have appeared in historical texts as the first women in surgery. Merit Ptah, an Egyptian woman in the second or third dynasty of Egypt, was described by her High Priest son as "chief physician", and is the earliest named woman in the history of science. In 3500 BCE, there were flint and bronze surgical-type instruments found buried with Queen Shubad of Ur in Mesopotamia. Leto, wife of Zeus in 500 CE, helped heal the wounds of Arneas, the founder of Rome. The Middle Ages were very disappointing for women in the medical field; women were actively banned from practicing medicine and surgery, unless they were taking over their deceased husband's practices. Miranda Stewart (1795–1865), a Scottish female surgeon disguised as a man, graduated from medical school age seventeen. She worked as an army surgeon for many years under the pseudonym Dr. James Barry. In fact, she is credited as performing the first cesarean section in 1820. Only at the time of her death was she discovered to be a woman. Elizabeth Blackwell (1821–1910) is well known as the first female physician in the USA. She was rejected from twenty medical schools in the USA, and ultimately attended Geneva Medical College. She could not find work as a surgeon, and became an obstetrical nurse in France. She returned to North America after several years, and along with her sister, Emily Blackwell, and Marie Zakrzewska, opened the New York Infirmary for Women and Children in 1857. Dr. Blackwell then opened the Women's Medical College of New York, which she oversaw in part from 1862 to 1899. Emily Jennings Stowe (1831–1903) was the first female physician in Canada, and also encountered sexual discrimination.

Given this back story, it is not surprising that women have struggled to gain a foothold in the world of surgery in the modern era. Societal sex stereotyping has been prevalent throughout history, and women have been fighting to overcome this perception of inability for many years. Life as a female surgeon in today's society has been a challenge for a variety of reasons, some of which overlap from a historical perspective. All surgical trainees, male and female, have similar expectations initially. I was expected to be tough, smart, and capable. I was expected to be fierce and determined. I was expected to handle the insurmountable, unending number of tasks assigned to me on a daily basis without becoming burnt out. I was expected to be able to stand through a ten-hour operation without succumbing to the physical needs of my body. I was expected to handle the unique interpersonal experience of cutting into another human being while maintaining composure and authority, yet suppressing the sheer momentousness of that occasion every single time.

Yet, there were additional expectations of me as a woman, which I was unable to appreciate until my later training years. In addition to being unapologetic in my pursuit to be a great surgeon, I also felt the need to express a higher level of empathy than my male counterparts. There was a subtle undercurrent of understanding throughout residency that I would be more compassionate, warmer, more kind and maternal. The expectation came from, and was expected by, the same people, and it was ubiquitous: patients, surgeons, nurses, pharmacists, and other clinicians throughout the hospital. I heard, over the years, "I can tell you this, you're a woman," or "You're a mom, you can understand," or even "Your hands are so petite and steady, I'm glad you'll be helping with the surgery." Attending male surgeons could achieve a certain level of this type of connection when confident in their masculinity, but the hospital hallways expected a certain amount of mothering when it came to their female doctors. The male surgical residents had empathy, but it was distinctly unattached from a paternal vibe. They practiced their art more often with a tough kind of love, with no sympathy for perceived weakness. They were expected to represent the hands of the cure, no matter how difficult; I was expected to be those hands as well, but with warm cotton gloves on.

I cannot possibly explain in a few words what I went through for the eight years of training, more than two thousand nine hundred days, both the highs and the lows. The highs were magnificent. I once saved a man's life by cutting his neck open while he was wide awake. He was bleeding pressurized blood into his neck, thereby constricting his trachea and suffocating him. Lucky for him that I walked around with an 11-blade scalpel in the pocket of my white coat. I watched a man walk out of the hospital after he suffered a gunshot wound to the chest; three months earlier, at 2.00 a.m. on a Friday night, I had held his bare heart in my gloved hands and had literally squeezed the life back into it during an eight-hour operation. I observed a master surgeon operate on a pregnant mother, open her uterus and remove a tumor from the back of her fetus, and close her uterus and abdomen again. Both recovered uneventfully and the baby was born later without even a scar. I fixed holes in the intestine, stopped internal bleeding, and cured abdominal infections. I removed tumors the size of cantaloupes. I removed blood clots to bring cold pulseless legs back to life. The adrenaline from these experiences is reason enough to pursue surgery as a field. It is magical; it is complex. Understanding the nature of the ways in which the human body can be altered by infection, inflammation, tumors, and trauma is completely addictive; being able to reverse those processes in a single day is even more so. It can be all consuming and, for many surgeons, it is the pursuit of these experiences that gives meaning to their lives. Even when there is no more adrenaline, only practiced hands performing the same operation again and again, there is immense satisfaction in replacing adrenaline with wisdom and expertise.

The lows were very difficult; being a doctor means dealing with suffering and death. I took care of a nineteen-year-old girl who choked on dinner on a random Sunday evening; she was brought into the hospital unconscious and became brain dead within hours. Her family was inconsolable. When they decided to donate her organs, I saw the beauty of human nature in the face of agony. I could not stop picturing her father, crying and holding his other children, while operating to help remove her heart, lungs, liver, and kidneys to be donated to six grateful recipients, six patients whose lives she saved. I watched, helplessly, as a severe abdominal infection slowly took the life of a two-month-old boy despite our attempts at surgical removal of the infection. I opened chests in the trauma bay on young men with gunshot wounds who died in front of my eyes. I took care of a seven-year-old girl who was a victim of a school shooting who had gunshot injuries to both her hand and her head, because she put her hand up in self-defense when the gun was fired. I took care of children whose injuries could only have been from child abuse. I called family members to come in to see their relative for the last time. I pronounced people dead. I filled out death forms and paperwork. I hugged strangers while they said their last goodbyes to their husbands, wives, moms, dads, sons, daughters, babies.

My co-residents and I would silently mourn these tragedies that faced us on a routine basis. We swallowed the pain and moved on, dealing with despair in our own ways, because it was necessary for survival. I rarely cried. Over the years, I slowly developed a barrier to grief, a force-field of toughness that became rather impenetrable. This was not a lack of empathy, but, rather, a methodology for coping with frequent pain and loss. The men seemed to have this more built in; I had to develop it. Over the years, I felt the rise of tears less and less frequently. I suppressed my emotions, and by the end actually believed that I was not feeling the pain of these experiences.

When I had children, everything changed. I had heard this sentiment many times before, that children will change your life. But it held new meaning for me as a surgeon. I had my daughter and my son during residency, and took only six weeks off for each maternity leave. My appreciation for the significance of human illness fundamentally changed once I became a mother. I experienced my patient's illnesses with new eyes, from a new vantage point. Over the last few years of my training, my force-field of toughness began disintegrating. I felt more emotional, and work became harder.

It slowly became obvious to me that it was impossible to keep a schedule that would satisfy my need to be a good surgeon, wife, and mother simultaneously. My experience as a female resident without children was most comparable to the experience of the male resident with children. Although not ideal, most of my male colleagues with children had wives at home with their children, and they were able to take comfort in knowing that their babies were with their mothers. However, once I had children of my own, my co-residents could not relate anymore to my particular struggle to balance a life at work and home. It was my choice to build a family, and I do not blame my residency or husband or anyone else for the challenges I faced as a new mother. But it was difficult, for myriad reasons.

I rarely saw my children during the last two years of training. I spent far more hours with my patients and my colleagues than I spent with my children. I cannot describe how I felt not seeing them for days in a row, because I left the house before they woke up and arrived home after they were asleep. During the months that I breast-fed my children, especially my son, most days I never nursed them even once; I used a breast pump in the resident call rooms, and called it quits because a difficult rotation was coming up. I saw my son most often only during overnight wake-ups, rocking him back to sleep. I was not there for his first steps. I did not participate in my children's school events because I was expected to be at work, and I never made it to the school moms'-nights-out. I missed all of their doctor's appointments, other children's birthday parties, and celebrations. My children would cry when our nanny left for the day, but not for me. I drove to and from work in the dark, morning and night. My phone was on 24/7, and anything relating to patient care took precedence over everything else, regardless of time, location, or company.

The trouble stemmed from the fact that I simultaneously loved surgery. I loved my work. And so I struggled with my identity as a surgeon, a wife, and a mother. Internally, I was becoming unhappy and stressed, gradually becoming unable to balance my opposing life interests, and I had tremendous guilt. The guilt arose from my lack of physical and emotional presence in my family's lives, and from my desire to be a well-trained surgeon. I was selfish in my pursuit to be the best, and I allowed surgery to take over my life. I was letting surgery win, slowly becoming more aware that it was causing my marriage and family to suffer, and there had to be a breaking point. Towards the second half of residency, when I disclosed that I was considering a career in breast oncologic surgery, which is known to be more lifestyle-friendly, but perhaps less technically challenging, some of my attending surgeons were visibly disappointed in my choice. When I told one of my former female attending surgeons that I had submitted my application for a breast surgery fellowship, she slumped her shoulders and said "Oh really? That's a shame." I felt very conflicted—that somehow I was betraying myself and them, while in the same breath I knew I was doing what was right for me and my family. This served only to add to my confusion and stress.

I have spent a long time examining my choices, trying to determine the reasons I chose medicine as a career, and surgery as a specialty. In part, my choice had to do with my upbringing. Both of my parents are physicians, my father a surgeon. They provided me with role models and mentorship. My mother did part of her residency half-time and took a leave from her work for about four years. She returned to full-time work when I was four years old. Although we had full-time childcare, I do not think I experienced my mother's absence the same way that my children experienced mine. And, as grandparents, they have often been there with my children. My parents have always encouraged academic pursuit in their children. All of my siblings have postgraduate degrees. I vividly remember a father–daughter day one year, when I had just turned fourteen years old. I joined him in the operating room, watching him use a microscope to place tiny tubes into a six-month-old infant's eardrums to help battle recurrent ear infections. It was incredible; I was hooked. I also will not deny that I gained some internal satisfaction from being the only one of four children to follow in my parents' footsteps. But it was more than that. I wanted to prove that I was smart. Both my parents and I pursued academic achievement. And so my greatest fear was that I was not smart enough. This might sound like a ridiculous statement coming from an Ivy League trained surgeon, but probably one that is familiar to many—that they are not smart enough, funny enough, good enough. Somewhere in my youth, I was imbued with a terrible and overwhelming desire to prove that I was capable of anything, and it had been there for a very long time. I went to a world-renowned public high school in New York City, where academics were rigorous, and where I was the captain of two varsity athletic teams. In college, I majored in theoretical mathematics with a minor in English literature. I went to a top ten medical school for my medical degree, where I met my husband, a Harvard man. I matched at a highly competitive general surgery program and fellowship program. I was selected to be a Robert Wood Johnson Foundation Clinical Scholar and obtained a Masters degree during my research years. On paper, I looked incredible—intimidating, even. Boxes checked. Internally, I had fear and self-doubt.

My husband jokingly diagnosed me with Imposter Syndrome. This is a psychological phenomenon whereby a person's feelings of inadequacy persist in spite of credible evidence to the contrary. These people are typically high achievers, and, interestingly, the syndrome tends to be prevalent in highly successful women. Despite outstanding academic and professional accomplishments, women who experience the imposter syndrome persist in believing that they are really not bright and have fooled anyone who thinks otherwise. Numerous achievements, which one might expect to provide ample objective evidence of superior intellectual functioning, do not appear to affect the impostor belief. There are two general themes in early family dynamics that contribute to this. One situation describes the syndrome whereby the girl has a sibling who was known as the "smart" one, whereas the girl is the "sensitive" one. As a result, there is an implication that she can never prove that she is as bright as the other sibling; hence, she both believes the myth and simultaneously tries to disprove it. Despite outstanding academic achievement and intellectual praise from others, the family maintains the other sibling as the "bright" one. On the one hand, the woman who feels she is an impostor is driven to find ways of getting validation for her intellectual competence; on the other hand, she thinks her family might be correct, secretly doubts her intellect, and begins to wonder if she has been successful through sensitivity to teachers' expectations, social skills, and feminine charms. Thus, the impostor phenomenon emerges. The other family dynamic is when indiscriminate praise is given to the young girl, who is told throughout early life that she is perfect and everything comes naturally to her. She is told numerous examples of precocity as a child, such as early reading or writing, and that she never has to try to be outstanding at anything she attempts. As she grows older, however, she learns that she cannot do everything perfectly, but feels obliged to fulfill the high expectations of her family. She then begins to distrust her family's perceptions of her, and begins doubting herself. These women often have outstanding academic achievements, but having internalized a vision of perfection in themselves, they must be imposters because they had to work hard to accomplish those achievements.

A more culturally oriented analysis would not be surprised that these feelings were actually quite out of place. After all, I was trying to fit myself into a male oriented world, one that is unapologetic for its roles, characteristics, and expected identities. The magnitude and gravity of the work drives the rigor with which it must be pursued. However, more empathy for the surgeons might result in more empathy for the patients. The male orientation did not supply me with enough understanding and support to progress through training comfortably. Instead, I felt that I was an outsider who had to perform as if I were one of the insiders. The culture is so large, unacknowledged, unquestioned, and pervasive that I could not change it. I had to change myself internally. This kind of vertical split made me feel dissociated from my true self. It was exceedingly unpleasant and distressing; fortunately, it was not permanent.

Towards the end of training, I took a step back and reassessed my life and what I wanted out of it. Together, my husband and I evaluated our relationship and life together as a family, our friends, and our careers. We spent time with our children; we spent time with our families. We grew very close with our friends. My husband and I were honest with each other about our behaviors, and we learned more about each other and our relationship than we thought possible. I confronted myself and tried to gain a better understanding of my motivations for my choices in life. Although we have some regrets, there is not much we would change. After almost ten years of marriage, my husband and I experienced a second honeymoon of sorts. We relocated to new careers and new lives after surgical training, and we are now expecting our third child. I consider myself extraordinarily lucky to have such an understanding and supportive companion in life, and I am proud of what we have accomplished as a family.

I am honored to leave my legacy as a working mother to my children. I have worked exceptionally hard in my life to reach the point where I am now, not only on a professional level, but, more recently, on an emotional level as well. While getting a pedicure with my daughter, another small girl asked her if her mommy was a nurse—I was in scrubs. Her reply, "No, my mommy is a surgeon", kindled some pride in my academic and professional accomplishments. But, in reality, my children are my greatest achievements, and I do not regret for a single moment my decision to have children during residency and the subsequent difficulties of being a mother and a surgeon. As my father always tells me, children are life's greatest rewards. It is not lost on me to whom this statement is directed. I have always felt my parents' unwavering love for me, and it is easy for me to do the same with my children. They are kind, creative, and well-adjusted youngsters. They are naturally joyous and sweet and empathic. Of course, there are tantrums about school and arguments over which kind of cereal to buy, but, in general, they are thriving in the environment that my husband and I provide because it is defined by unconditional love, trust, and understanding (and we choose our battles). We struggled with this during residency, but now it is much easier to provide this environment for them as we have come to a better understanding of ourselves and each other, and how we have chosen to define ourselves as working parents.

I am now the attending surgeon. I am a breast surgical oncologist; that is, a breast cancer surgeon. The treatment of breast cancer is mind-bogglingly complex and patient care can be an emotional rollercoaster. I am part of a team that includes medical oncologists, radiation oncologists, plastic surgeons, and several other therapists. My days are filled with telling women that, unfortunately, the biopsy came back as a breast cancer. Without question, they are the hardest words I have ever spoken to another person. It is the sentence they will never forget. Often the first question I hear is "Am I going to die from this?" To be expected, it is emotional, and I deal with a lot of fear. But I also have a weapon against it—I can offer them my hands, steady and well trained, and me. I will be with them while they go through their surgery. This time in my career, I can be emotional, too. As a result of my training, I also get to deliver the best news. I have the privilege of telling them after the operation that it is gone, it is out, the margins are all clear, and they are cancer free. My personal satisfaction from helping another human being in this way is profound, and their appreciation is immeasurable. Being a woman gives me a profound understanding of the women I treat. I can acknowledge the significance that the cancer is in their breast, a symbol of their femininity and femaleness. I am allowed extraordinary insight into their experience of having treatment for a cancer that is de-feminizing by its very nature. My role in this profession is not only to cure a woman of her breast cancer, but to comfort and empathize, and be a source of strength for her. The rewards from this ability make the years of personal sacrifice worth it, and any lingering imposter syndrome is quelled by the fact that I know I am doing something tangible to help other people.

Young female medical students and surgical residents often ask me about my choices, and what it was like to raise a family as a female surgeon during such a challenging time. They look to me for a glimpse into their own futures, to determine if they have the ability to balance a surgical career and a life. I do not minimize my experience. I tell them that they were the hardest years of my life, and, although I am finally at ease these days, of course I have some regrets. But I consider myself very lucky—I have never been one to live in the past, and I have learned from my mistakes. My strongest attribute is my resilience, which affords me my ability to forgive, including forgiveness for myself. It is my genuine optimism about the future that allows me to have truly reached a contented and peaceful existence, and perhaps what helps me to be a good surgeon. I advise my students that they might not understand the reasons they chose surgery until they can confront their own shortcomings and gain perspective. It is very difficult; it was for me. But, ultimately, true happiness comes from accepting responsibility for your choices in life. I am no victim in this life; I take responsibility for my actions. The balance of a career and family has been rocky and challenging, but it is precisely that challenge that has defined me. My choice to become a surgeon was the right one for me. I am totally honest with my students. For a period of time I was part of the male surgery culture: hyper-aggressive, unemotional, unwavering at work, denying internal needs. Temporarily, I gave up on my maternal wishes and feelings. I was not nurturing or warm. I denied that I felt an inner meaning. But, finally, I remembered who I was and returned to the reality of who I had always been. So I tell them what I think: I believe that surgery made a woman out of me.

References

Freischlag, J. (2008). Women surgeons—still in a male-dominated world. *Yale Journal of Biology and Medicine, 81*(4): 203–204.

Wilde, O. (1891). *"The Critic as Artist"*, *Intentions*. (p. 185). London: Heineman and Balestier.

CHAPTER TWO

Simone de Beauvoir and the trauma of sexism

Sargam Jain

S imone de Beauvoir's portrait of the ideal independent woman in *The Second Sex* offers a grim view of the emancipated woman's sexual choices in pre-war Europe. She could pursue her own career, engage in fleeting liaisons, and find lonely sexual disappointment: an intelligent woman, Beauvoir argued, could not authentically engage in the seduction narrative of the time, in which a virile, confident man sweeps away a charming, passive girl. A working woman simply interacted with men too much to maintain them in the idealized omnipotence necessary for a mutually gratifying sexual fantasy. In marriage, she could succumb to her social grooming and become man's diminished and resentful mirror, bearing his children, keeping his house, and lazily dismissing ambitions of her own. Or, the economically and intellectually independent woman who chooses to marry becomes burdened by the dual roles she believes she must play:

> ... she does not want her husband to be deprived of the advantages he would have had in marrying a "real woman": she wants to be elegant, a good housekeeper and a devoted mother as wives traditionally are. ... she insists ... on fulfilling every aspect of her destiny as woman. She will be a double for her husband at the same time as

being herself; she will take charge of his worries, she will participate in his successes just as much as taking care of her own lot ... split between the desire to affirm herself and self-effacement, she is divided and torn. ... independence won through work is not enough to abolish her desire for a glorious abdication ... she needs a gaze from above to reveal and consecrate her worth. (de Beauvoir, 2011, p. 734)

Within both of these scenarios, de Beauvoir notes, a cerebral, independent woman is doomed to enact sadistic or masochistic roles because of the narcissistic deprivations of an upbringing that put ambition, creativity, and intelligence into conflict with femininity. The kept wife becomes tyrannical with her children, obsessively controlling of the home, and nags her husband to compensate for her passivity. Meanwhile, the professional woman kills herself with double work and dual roles, always divided.

Maternity, too, is an ambivalent enterprise for de Beauvoir. It is both the historical source of woman's subjugation to man and also the fundamental activity that could inform and support her as a productive and independent subjectivity. In *The Second Sex*, de Beauvoir relies heavily on psychoanalytic theory to describe the little girl's descent into passivity and objectification. She describes the capacity to bear children as a "wonderful fairy power" (p. 299) and equates this with the powerful feelings a boy derives from having penis that can produce powerful jets of urine while standing up, dominating the world with his stream. However, for a girl, her generative power remains hidden until puberty and without an external, incarnating organ for the girl to use as an affirming object. Until then, she has instead a doll, or the tools of housework. Both are socially imbued with the idea of passivity and servitude, eventually to be incorporated into the idea of femininity, and then into maternity. With menstruation and its constructed connotations of wound, filth, and handicap, maternity is cast even further from autonomy. Once the baby comes, archaic desires for autonomy re-emerge and the new mother grasps at the female infant for the selfobject she never had:

... for the mother, the daughter is both her double and an other, the mother cherishes her and at the same time is hostile to her; she imposes her own destiny on her child: it is a way to proudly claim her femininity and also to take revenge on it ... success is made more difficult for her as another kind of accomplishment is demanded of her: she must at least also be a woman; she must not lose her femininity. (de Beauvoir, 2011, p. 295)

Such is the fate of a woman as mother and wife, de Beauvoir argues, until both sexes demand release from this master–slave dialectic. In psychological terms, one could say that such sexism is traumatizing because any narcissistic gratification for a woman is dependent on her ability to be a reflection; that is, she obtains approval from her family and her social sphere for obliterating herself. Thus, because independent women are doomed to suffer from narcissistic injuries in both their failure to be feminine enough and the lack of social recognition for their achievements, they will compensate for these by acting out sadomasochistically in marriage and motherhood.

*   *   *

Famously, *The Second Sex* began as Simone de Beauvoir's attempt to write about herself. In this manner, the book is as much about her own oppression as it is about the historical subjugation of all women—this itself is an oft-leveled criticism about the generalizability of *The Second Sex*. As a result, however, and taken together with her autobiographical works, it provides a stunning document of the personal impact of institutionalized oppression. Whether or not Simone de Beauvoir was able to describe the plight of all women does not matter in this case— she, perhaps accidentally, described the painful psychic consequences of social subjugation. Sexism traumatized *her*, particularly so in the absence of foremothers from whom she might have taken solace and direction. In consequence of this, while she avoided marriage and motherhood, she certainly did not escape the sadomasochistic fate she predicted for such women because she *internalized* the conflicts between gender, femininity, and ambition. Thus, she herself developed a sadomasochistic attitude towards relationships—masochistic with Sartre and sadistic towards other women.

This pattern did not reveal itself until the publication of Simone de Beauvoir's personal correspondence after her death in 1986. Until then, Beauvoir was the public exemplar of an independent and fulfilled woman in work *and* love and an idol for the women of feminism's second wave in the 1970s. In a polyamorous relationship with her intellectual partner, Jean-Paul Sartre, she had sex with whomever she wanted, with full control of her reproductive functions. Waiting for the advent of a socially equal world, she chose not to marry and not to have children in the meantime, writing fervently about her own life, her "original project," refusing any semblance of conventionality. But, as her letters revealed, her lived solution to the problem of woman's oppression had not brought her the equality and freedom she claimed such a life could bring. Rather, her freedom had come at the cost of truth, the mental health of her students, and her own sexual loneliness.

Simone de Beauvoir always publicly denied having sex with her students and women. In her diaries, she speaks often of these liaisons, beginning with her student from Marseilles, Olga Kosakewicz, in 1935. Indeed, de Beauvoir admitted late in life that her novel *She Came to Stay*, was a close depiction of the reality of de Beauvoir and Sartre's relationship with the young Olga and of de Beauvoir's jealousy of the erotic obsession Olga inspired in Sartre (Rowley, 2005, p. 62). Sartre and de Beauvoir's relationship with Olga became the first of subsequent "trios," in which the attractive, well-dressed de Beauvoir initiated sexual relationships with her students whom the fat, balding Sartre would desperately seduce and conquer. In 1943, she was permanently suspended from teaching in France after she was accused of seducing seventeen-year-old student Nathalie Sorokine, which she publicly denied, but which was, in fact, true. Another former student, Bianca Bienenfield, suffered from psychological breakdown after Sartre and de Beauvoir abruptly ended their affairs with her when the Nazis invaded France. De Beauvoir confessed to Sartre, "She's suffering from an intense and dreadful attack of neurasthenia, and it's our fault, I think. It's the very indirect, but profound, after-shock of the business between her and us" (Rowley, 2005, p. 157). Rowley writes,

> In the late 1940s, Bienenfield's psychoanalyst, Jacques Lacan, would come to the same conclusion. It was his view that Sartre and Beauvoir had had a quasi-parental relationship with Bienenfield, and Bienenfield's traumatized reaction was partly because they had broken the incest taboos by sleeping with her. (p. 157)

As she grew older, she continued to set Sartre up with her young female friends, probably "knowing what would happen" (Rowley, 2005, p. 223).

Simone de Beauvoir also publicly maintained that she was honest with her lovers, but her letters revealed that she often lied to them, and, in one instance, was having an affair with both halves of a couple without either knowing. These lovers, enthralled by the couple's charisma, eventually grew into a community called "The Family," perpetually shadowed by, and dependent on, Sartre and de Beauvoir. "The Family" was never privy to the pact that de Beauvoir and Sartre had made in 1929: that their relationship was to be primary, absolute while all others were secondary and that Sartre and Beauvoir would tell each other everything. Simone kept her promise; Sartre flouted it. While Sartre methodically divided his time between his various lovers, Beauvoir would often wait, sometimes desperately, for him. He proposed marriage to a lover, Dolores Vanetti, for whom he would have ended his relationship with de Beauvoir. By 1937, she and Sartre no longer had a sexual relationship, yet de Beauvoir would sacrifice her passionate romance with Nelson Algren, returning to Sartre when he ended his relationship with Vanetti in 1950. One could say Sartre even betrayed her in the end, leaving his literary estate to a young former lover he adopted, Arlette Elkaim, instead of to de Beauvoir, his lifelong partner, collaborator, and friend.

*   *   *

How did this split come to pass? As previously mentioned, Simone de Beauvoir's autobiographical works might hold clues about the nature of her trauma, which not only produced her masterful book, *The Second Sex*, but also her sexual exploitation of young women and surprising deference to Sartre. The aim is not to arrive at the truth of Simone de Beauvoir's psychological life through her autobiography— her writing and public life were performative, rather than reflective. However, in performance is the self: fantasized, expressed, disguised. In Simone de Beauvoir's autobiographical works, one might find themes, thoughts, facts, and recollections that possibly add up to a psychologically coherent explanation for her contradictory behaviors. To the question of what happened, we might be able to point to parts of her life and say well, maybe this could explain it. And it seems that the foundation for her "splits" might have been laid early on, in child-hood and adolescence.

The upbringing Simone de Beauvoir describes in her first auto-biography, *Memoirs of a Dutiful Daughter*, would predict the develop-ment of what is psychoanalytically known as the false self. Winnicott (1990, p. 140) describes the false self as a defensive psychological organization that serves to protect a child's authentic, true self against attack. The false self develops in response to the mother's needs at the expense of the child's needs and self-expression. To continue to obtain care, the child becomes compliant with the attitudes of the mother and environment: the false self is created and takes over, appearing as the child, but, in actuality, protecting the child's true tender core. In the case of a person with high intellectual ability, the false self, Winnicott explains, can co-opt a life of the mind to avoid the problem of unmet needs and its pursuant emotional consequences of anger, sadness and despair: a dissociation develops between psychosomatic being and intellectual activity. The person complains of feeling increasingly inauthentic the more successful they become as the wrong self is lauded. Eventually, this success must be destroyed, somehow, to rid oneself of phony feelings. The trauma of sexism, in the case of Simone de Beauvoir, could be the development of such a split self, insofar as it facilitated feelings of inauthenticity and destructive interpersonal relationships.

Simone de Beauvoir was the elder of two girls and was born in 1908 to a family in between the aristocracy and the *bourgeoisie*. Her father, Georges, reluctantly worked as a lawyer, the family estate having gone to his older brother. He preferred to spend most of his time as a dandy, amusing high society as an amateur actor. He needed an audience, and it appeared to Simone that he used acting to "escape from himself," referring to the split between the reality of his life as a working man and his conviction that he ought to live a life of idle, hedonistic privilege. He was a monarchist, anti-intellectual, anti-Semitic, disdained hard work, and believed in the

> cult of the family; woman, in her role as mother, was sacred to him; he demanded the utmost fidelity from married women and all young girls had to be innocent virgins, but he was prepared to allow great liberties to men. (de Beauvoir, 1959, p. 35)

As his fortune declined after the First World War, the family entered into near poverty, and he reluctantly announced to his daughters that "My dears, you'll never marry; you'll have to work for your livings" (p. 176). She chose to become a teacher. But, in their social class, working was both defeat and unusual; Simone stopped idealizing her father after recognizing his angry disappointment in his life, lack of responsibility for his fate, and his shame in his decline. Sadly, her embrace of a career in philosophy represented his own failure to her father; begrudgingly, he applauded her academic successes while withdrawing from and punishing her for her burgeoning love of ideas and non-conformity.

Her mother, Françoise, eight years younger than her father, was from a provincial family, the daughter of a once-wealthy banker who also lost his money during the First World War. She was raised strictly Catholic by a cold, distant mother. Her rigid moral values were in opposition to her husband's aristocratic dismissal of religious ritual and embrace of pleasure. She "willingly took second place. It was he who had introduced her to life and the world of books" (de Beauvoir, 1959, p. 36). She obeyed her husband in everything, but with her daughters and servant, she was "dictatorial and overbearing" (p. 37). If a close friend or relative irritated her, "she often reacted with anger and outbursts of violent frankness," but socially, she was anxious and timid. This attitude alternated with warmth and affection in the total care Françoise dedicated to her daughter. Questions about sex and puberty were particularly disgusting to Simone's mother, who categorically refused to answer questions about the body. When pressed by Simone in adolescence, she told Simone and her sister that babies were painlessly delivered through the anus.

It is unlikely, then, that Françoise de Beauvoir provided caregiving that encouraged autonomy, insight, freedom, or expression of self. Simone appears to have had a willful, curious, and intelligent disposition as a girl. She describes intense and rageful tantrums as a three-year-old, particularly when she was being deceived or manipulated by adults. She was the star pupil at her conservative, Catholic girls' school, Le Cours Desir, and overshadowed her younger sister, Poupette, in just about everything. Poupette, as well as a variety of young cousins, appear to have indulged Simone's dominating, somewhat sadistic tendencies during playtime. In this way, Simone's early tendencies towards aggression and ambition would have been decidedly against her strict, Catholic mother's ideals of conventional morality in a girl. Winnicott notes that:

> The mother who is not good enough is not able to implement the infant's omnipotence, and so she repeatedly fails to meet the infant gesture; instead she substitutes her own gesture which is to be given

sense by the compliance of the infant. This compliance on the part of the infant is the earliest stage of the False Self, and belongs to the mother's inability to sense her infant's needs. (1990, p. 145)

Simone's psychologically conflictual compliance with the attitudes of her socially conformist mother seems apparent in her adolescence. Neither of her parents questioned their various conflicting orthodoxies and, as a young girl, Simone often felt herself torn in trying to reconcile not only the inconsistencies in her parent's behaviors, but also hypocritical bourgeois attitudes towards sex, religion, and class. She writes,

> I saw greys and half-tones everywhere . . . Whatever I beheld with my own eyes . . . had to be fitted . . . into a rigid category: the myths and stereotyped ideas prevailed over the truth: unable to pin it down, I allowed the truth to dwindle into insignificance. (1959, p. 17)

As a result, Simone was an earnest child and adolescent, conformist, fervently Catholic, and patriotic, perfectionistic and high-achieving in school, curious but unthinking, a point her friend Zaza routinely teased her about.

As predicted by Winnicott, this façade evolved in response to a need for care and approval–she craved it from both of her parents and felt lost and devastated without it. She adored her father with "a romantic fervor" (1959, p. 72). Her father "raised me to his level, and then I was proud to feel myself a grown-up person. When I fell back to my ordinary level, I was dependent upon Mama" (p. 37). However, this dependence came at great cost to Simone: she lived in fear of her mother's anger, often directed towards her for minor mistakes. As Simone noted,

> I sensed that careless words and sudden changes of plan easily troubled her serenity. My responsibility towards her made my dependence even greater. And that is how we lived, the two of us, in a kind of symbiosis. She inculcated in me a sense of duty as well as teaching me unselfishness and austerity. My father was not averse to the limelight, but I learnt from Mama to keep in the background, to control my tongue, to moderate my desires, to say and do exactly what ought to be said and done. I made no demands on life, and I was afraid to do anything on my own initiative. (1959, p. 41)

As she grew older, she was increasingly torn by a sense of duty to her mother, and her resentment at her mother's arbitrary, controlling conformity:

> I believed that ... God expected me to be dutiful. ... My mother's whole education and upbringing had convinced her that for a woman, the greatest thing was to become the mother of a family; she couldn't play this part unless I played the dutiful daughter. ... I held it against her for keeping me so dependent upon her and continuing to impose her will upon me. In addition, I was jealous of the place she held in my father's affections because my own passion for him had continued to grow. (p. 106).

This would be an apt description of the pain of a growing divide between Simone de Beauvoir's two selves and of the longing for the impossible. She wanted the love her parents' perfect woman would have, without having to be this woman. But the conditions required for an independent woman to be loved in this way did not yet exist. The result appears to have been a "flattening" of Simone's capacity for intimate attachments—her relationship with Zaza, her first real friend, was a profound awakening because she could share a "real" world with someone for the first time. But even in this relationship, Simone was guarded, and somewhat distant. Throughout her life, even with Sartre, she refused to address anyone with the familiar "tu" and noted in an interview with Alice Schwarzer that

> I've always found it very difficult to address people in the familiar. I don't know why. My best friend Zaza always addressed her girl-friends in the familiar, but she used the polite form with me because I did so with her. (Rowley, 2005, p. 215)

Sartre commented, "The Beaver ... doesn't like saying tu. ... So even today we say vous. We have never said tu to each other. Not once ..." (Rowley, 2005, p. 215).

When Simone decided she would take the agregation (the French competitive examination for public secondary school teachers) in the subject of philosophy, the nuns at the Cours Desir told her mother "the study of philosophy morally corrupts the soul". Instead, she agreed to study mathematics and classics at the Catholic school for a year, before finally insisting on preparing for her entrance exams to the Sorbonne at age eighteen. This required reading literature of which her French Catholic bourgeois parents did not approve and Simone was caught between her beloved father's inability to provide a dowry and his increasing resentment that she was to become a professional woman, and, thus, a discredit to his name and legacy. He distrusted intellectuals, despised notions of democracy and class equality, and began to resent Simone even more for espousing these ideas. Her lack of social grace, refusal to participate in dinners and tea parties only made the situation worse—the more she deviated from her father's ideal of a "well bred lady," the more she was shunned, rebuked, and criticized. Simone was pushed from grace, a pariah in her family, a symbol of both their failures.

In response, Simone became withdrawn into her studies, taking them more seriously than her schoolmates and other young women in her social sphere because she would eventually need to depend on her education to make a living. Her parents found her ungrateful and irritating. It was a time of great pain and she writes that,

> I was cornered; my parents could neither bear what I had to say, nor my dogged silence. . . . But if I withdrew into my shell, my father would complain that I had no heart, that I was all brain and no feel-ing. I tried to put on protective armour by exhorting myself not to be afraid of blame, ridicule or lack of understanding. . . . But then I would feel so utterly cut off from my fellow-beings; I would gaze in the look-ing-glass at the person *they* could see: it wasn't *me* . . . Life is a lie I would tell myself in a fit of depression. (de Beauvoir, 1959, p. 193)

It is conceivable that such pain and anger led to an intellectual flight as much as necessity drove it. One can only imagine the esca-lating anxiety that Simone must have felt as she moved towards an unknown life, independence, and away from the approval of her family and social sphere. By the time she met Sartre in 1929, while studying for the agregation as a third-year student at the Sorbonne, she already felt her path would condemn her to loneliness and was convinced that there were parts of her no man could accept (Rowley, 2005, p. 17), maybe because these were parts her parents could not accept. She wrote that, "I speak mystically of love. I am too intelligent, too demanding, and too resourceful for anyone to be able to take charge of me entirely. No one knows me or loves me completely. I have only myself" (Rowley, 2005, p. 18).

Jean-Paul Sartre entered Simone de Beauvoir's life just as she was embarking on her lonely path—her best friend Zaza had just died that same year, officially of encephalitis, but to de Beauvoir, fighting against an arranged, oppressive marriage. Sartre listened to her as no one else ever did, interested and curious about her thoughts, encouraging of her drive and ambition—perhaps it seemed that the impossible was possible after all: she could be loved as an independent woman and would not suffer as a spinster or be destroyed as Zaza had been. He would provide approval, guidance, and reassurance as her parents and other love interests never had. Unfortunately, there was a catch: Sartre was not interested in marriage or monogamy and had little patience for dependency, jealousy, or the emotional needs of others. He envisioned living separate lives, for years at a time, meeting at intervals before separating again. He needed liberty and was not particularly concerned about how this affected people close to him; their emotions were their problem, a weakness to be overcome by willpower and choice. Although de Beauvoir had already set down her own path before she met Sartre, his need for an open relationship, and for her, too, to have her own affairs, would require a difficult psychological compromise. As Rowley notes,

> Beauvoir did not share Sartre's lone-hero dreams. She would have much preferred to undertake exotic adventures with him at her side. Her dream was the "Grand Amour," and she dreaded the idea of long separations. But for the time being . . . she did her best to suppress her fears. She knew Sartre would regard them as weakness. (2005, p. 27)

Thus began their famous pact of sexual freedom and transparency; for de Beauvoir, it began in a crucible of anxiety, uncertainty, loss, and abandonment. It is unclear whether at the time she had wanted children and marriage—Rowley notes that she had wanted both, and, until meeting Sartre, was in love with her cousin Jacques and had wished to marry him (2005, p. 29). Many years later, friends would note de Beauvoir's and Sartre's disgust with pregnant women and babies. When she first met Sartre, she disdained sexual promiscuity in a woman, and was horrified by not only her father's sexual indiscretions with prostitutes, but by the sexual escapades of friends outside of marriage. Of course, she famously went on to publicly have various male lovers. To maintain Sartre's interest and love, de Beauvoir would have to renounce, deny, or change her point of view on all these matters and it appears she did. Rowley notes,

> Beauvoir did not like to complain. From the beginning of their rela-
> tionship she made a supreme effort to see things from Sartre's
> perspective. It was partly because she felt she owed him everything. It
> was also because she was convinced that she loved him more than he
> loved her. She rationalized she could not make a grievance out of an
> objective fact. (2005, p. 35)

Psychological contingency had no place in Sartre's existentialism and, at the time, de Beauvoir's status as a woman meant fundamentally that she had fewer choices than he did. In this way, perhaps she traded one false self for another; perhaps it was a bargain to trade her emotional needs once more, as she had always done, for philosophical morals, a façade of freedom, for Sartre's approval, and for her writing. If she would never be loved completely, maybe it was be better to be loved as an independent woman than as a feminine one.

Psychoanalytic theory holds that emotions do not disappear; rather, the mind represses them when they become problematic, as they would have for de Beauvoir. She was not allowed to be jealous, needy, or even sexually gratified by Sartre. In a letter to Nelson Algren in 1951, she admitted that that Sartre no longer desired her and that, at age thirty-three, their sexual relationship had been over because of Sartre (Rowley, 2005, p. 127). She wrote,

> It was rather a deep friendship than love . . . Love was not very
> successful. Chiefly because [Sartre] does not care much for sexual life.
> . . . I soon felt it, though I had no experience; and little by little, it
> seemed useless, and even indecent, to go on being lovers. (Rowley,
> 2005, p. 128)

It is maybe not an accident that her first affair with a student, Olga Kosakewicz, began during her first major separation from Sartre, while she was teaching in Marseilles in 1932. She was depressed, lonely, missing Sartre terribly, and going on obsessional dangerous hikes to distract herself from her painful thoughts (Rowley, 2005, p. 47). During this time, Sartre carried on affairs with various women in Paris. As a teacher, she was intensely idealized by female students for her wit, charm, and beauty. In Olga she saw a smart but timid girl and, in time, as Sartre had done for her, de Beauvoir did for Olga. De Beauvoir was attentive, encouraging, and provided mentorship, and the relationship eventually became sexual. From Olga, as from her other affairs, she received the physical love and emotional appreciation denied to her by Sartre.

It would be hard to believe that de Beauvoir did not feel some anger at the compromises she had made to remain the object of Sartre's attention, and the resultant emotional neglect that came of these. Olga, and de Beauvoir's other students, would have been an easy target upon whom to vent her unconscious rage. When the "trios" began to develop, first with Olga, and subsequently with other female students, de Beauvoir must have known what Sartre would do: he would seduce, lose interest, and then move on to the next woman. De Beauvoir's intellect and strength were exceptional—these other women would never be as independent or as tolerant of Sartre's attitudes as she was. They would suffer, and de Beauvoir would win. She dominated them, with Sartre, financially and psychologically. Her rage would have found expression in these destructive triumphs, and her false self, with the self-denial it required, could endure. And, as time went on, fame might have replaced Sartre: their public relationship was as important to their philosophy of existentialism as their written works. It is conceivable that the legend of their relationship became the source of the ongoing approval for her false self while *The Second Sex* rationalized her sacrifices in its particularly dismal portrayal of marriage and motherhood. Both were doomed to divide a woman's self and cause pain; why not shoot for the moon instead? Or, at least, avoid both until the world did away with domination and submission forever. When considered alongside the possibility of de Beauvoir's suffering as an unlovable woman, her loud cries for pure autonomy in *The Second Sex* begin to feel like a reaction formation against the whispered desire for unconditional love.

* * *

Ultimately, cultural values held by Simone de Beauvoir's parents, particularly ideals around femininity, led de Beauvoir's ego to become split between her own drives and ambitions and needs for love and dependency. Contributing to this split might also have been a great deal of conflict over superseding her own parents; while more professionally successful than any of her family, one might wonder how much of this success felt authentic given the values with which she was raised. Another function of her pact with Sartre, in addition to obtaining approval and support for her intellectual strivings, might have fulfilled her own unconscious wishes for submission, bathed as she had been in the mythos of a submissive feminine ideal as a child. It is likely that this "split" was made all the more possible by existentialism's insistence on only free will and conscious choice in the construction of an authentic self, to the exclusion of the unconscious mind and emotional life as drivers of choice and motivation. It is in this way that Simone de Beauvoir was perhaps waylaid by the psychological damage of sexism, which twisted her relationships to people and probably left her with an indelible sense of inner defect.

Nevertheless, de Beauvoir is a foremother: her work has been essential to creating a world in which women are raised to pursue professional ambitions and in which they can still remain women. Of course, this world is still far from perfect: while social conceptions of femininity still compel women to become objectified and exist only in the gaze of men, there are at least now manifold role models of the sort Beauvoir lacked. In this legacy, she gave to two generations (and counting) of women what her own mother was never able to give to her—she demonstrated the multitude of ways in which women can live as the physical, moral, and intellectual equals of men. One can only wonder at how lonely and frightening it must have been for de Beauvoir, with no compass, to leave a familiar path, lonely and harshly judged for her efforts. Perhaps if she had been able to admit her vulnerabilities, she might have found more love and compassion along her way.

References

De Beauvoir, S. (1959). *Memoirs of a Dutiful Daughter*. New York: HarperCollins.

De Beauvoir, S. (2011). *The Second Sex*. New York: Vintage Books.

Rowley, H. (2005). *Tete A Tete: The Tumultuous Lives and Loves of Simone de Beauvoir and Jean-Paul Sartre*. New York: Harper Perennial.

Winnicott, D. W. (1990). *The Maturational Processes and the Facilitation Environment: Studies in the Theory of Emotional Development*. London: Karnac.

CHAPTER THREE

"Pure heroines" on campus: new wave feminism and popular culture

Vera J. Camden

W hen I was invited to contribute a chapter to this volume on psychoanalysis and the contemporary status of women around the globe, my first response was to demur. After all, I was not in a position to generalize on such an important topic from a global perspective: I teach within an American Midwestern public university, and my psychoanalytic practice draws largely from an academic setting. After some discussion, however, I became persuaded that this setting itself might be of interest within a volume on the status of women, if written from, precisely, the campus vantage point. Why not take up the status of college women in America?

I have taught women's literature for three decades within a curriculum largely shaped by the vast field that is called feminism: this work has influenced much of what I know as a psychoanalyst about the human unconscious—whether in the clinic, in the culture, or in the classroom.[1] As it happened, when I learned of this volume, I was in the midst of preparing a course entitled "Pure Heroines: Historical Feminism and Popular Culture" on the very topic of the "new wave" of feminism on the contemporary scene. The focus of this course was to be "Neo-feminism," "Fourth wave feminism," "Feminism redux," "Popular feminism" and "New Wave feminism", all phrases meant to categorize the phenomena of an indisputable rise in awareness of feminist issues in the past few years—especially among young adults—evidenced strikingly in popular culture and social media. When I began teaching in the university setting in the early 1980s, Women's Studies programs, feminism, and psychoanalysis were key contenders in many departmental debates, campus commit-tees, academic conferences, and, eventually, the literature classroom (see Hartman, 2015). Since then, academic culture wars have worn down and worn out, and psychoanalysis, once the darling of human-ities departments, has taken rather a back seat to the cognitive and neurosciences as a favored grid theory through which to run the study of literature and the arts.[2] And in the popular imagination, psycho-analysis has all but receded, only revived occasionally by its loyal remnant of practitioners who demonstrate its efficacy as a therapeutic alternative to bio-psychiatry. Feminism, by contrast, both in the culture at large and among college age students, has remained *au courant* and undergoes "waves" of relevance. We are now in the midst of a new wave in which feminism resurges with urgency and even panache. The "new feminism" among young women in our culture and on our campuses—grounded less in academic instruction and inquiry and more from within popular culture—is fueled in large part by web based social media and mass cultural production.[3] College students and young people, less concerned with the "cool" discourse of academic theory, are increasingly more invested in activism, populist social causes, and a feminism that promotes equality and sexual agency among women across race, class, gender, and sexuality.

It is worth noting that the feminist debates of the sort that domi-nated academic journals, conferences, and other publications in the 1980s and 1990s has been missing from the popular feminism of the past decade. The gender specialists who wielded so much power in the culture wars of the previous decades have perhaps moved on from the debate over whether the "category" of woman exists, and are now wondering whether we are in a post-feminist era, or whether popular feminism is so "haunted" by its predecessors as to be limited in scope or action: fiddling while popular feminism catches fire.[4] The rape victims catalogued and given voice in the best selling *Missoula*, the campus activists who are taking action to establish practical codes of consent, the followers of Emma Sulkowicz's Mattress project, and the scores of young women who follow websites and blogs too numerous to count that virtually patrol sexism in the media are dialoging what it means to live in a female body in the twenty-first century. They are motivated by a social activism that seeks to insure self-protection, self-actualization, economic/career achievement and, therefore, equal rights and equal pay. They sound, therefore, much like the early feminists of the 1960s and 1970s who took to the streets in protest. For these neo-feminists, for instance, Gloria Steinem remains a heroine very much in demand as a college speaker.

Perhaps the greatest distinction between the action heroine that has become integral to this new feminism and the academic feminists still debating is no better displayed than in our discussion of the business world in our class. For example, Ellen Pao, who claimed gender discrimination against Kleiner Perkins in the Silicon Valley empires in the USA,[5] propelled students in the class to read Sheryl Sandberg's best-selling book *Lean In: Women, Work, and the Will to Lead*, and to visit her website leanin.org. Empirically based studies were also daily being cited in the classroom about the dilemmas of women in the board rooms of business and other centers of power whose voices are not heard or whose ideas are ignored and then later appropriated. Students were invested in this discussion precisely for its practical and immediate implication for their own work, whether in the academy, the business world, or in politics, as well as in the arts and culture. The point is that the sort of academic high road assumed by bell hooks (2013) in her disavowal of popular feminist discourse as "faux feminism" does not have much currency in business, politics, or other worlds outside of the privileged halls of the academy. The concept of "Faux Feminism" seemed to ignore the urgency all my students felt to bring what they were learning into their worlds, which obviously included jobs in business, government, and social agencies, as well as teaching, health care, and culture. We agreed that we did not have the luxury to exclude active feminist enterprises however we might debate their "credentials."

Pure heroines in class and culture

T. S. Eliot (1975) wrote,

> It is just the literature that we read for amusement, or purely for pleasure that may have the greatest and least suspected influence on us.

... Hence, it is that the influence of popular novelists, and of popular playwrights of contemporary life, requires to be scrutinized most closely. (p. 103)

It seems *apropos*, therefore, to discuss the "status of women" on American college campuses through the content and context of American popular culture. Popular culture is the soup in which American students daily swim. In what follows, therefore, I offer examples from the "Pure Heroines" course, stressing how popular culture mobilizes shared feminist discourse, and insight into class members' unique identities, and creative expressions. I further hope that my interpretation, as professor and psychoanalyst, of the place of college women in America might contribute to the ongoing discussion of how to make psychoanalytic knowledge that was once so revolutionary not only available, but also relevant to the next generation. I take Freud at his word when, in "The question of lay analysis" (1926e), he proclaims that analysis offers perhaps the greatest contribution to human society.[6] The aspirations of the present volume are precisely to intervene, as psychoanalysts, into the social and cultural forces of our lives today.

Our course title played off the album title, "Pure Heroine" (2013), by New Zealand pop star, "Lorde" whose very name is a feminization of the noble noun, defined as a righteous female leader. At the age of seventeen, Lorde identified herself with ethical activism—cultural heroism—and burst on the pop–rock scene with an explicit feminist message in her songs and in her signature style. At the same time, the pun in her album title parodies the scourge of drug and other addictions so prevalent in youth culture, a trend she has openly decried, even as she has, with equal fervor, identified herself with socially conscious movements around the globe and the need for girls and women to stand up for human rights and equality. "I'm speaking for a bunch of girls when I say that the idea that feminism is completely natural and shouldn't even be something that people find mildly surprising, its just part of being a girl in 2013" (Lorde, 2013). For those of us who grew up with the so-called second wave feminism of the 1960s and 1970s, such alert and activist articulation through music is familiar and welcome. Not only Lorde but a whole host of other young feminists in popular culture were returning to the practical activism that had characterized Simone de Beauvoir, Gloria Steinem, Betty Friedan, Germaine Greer, and others of previous generations.

Our class probed how Beyonce's banner "Feminist" drapes as back-drop to her songs and as she incorporates the "Ted Talk," "We should all be feminists" (2013) by Chimamanda Ngozi Adichie. Yet, Beyoncé's feminism is not "your mother's feminism." The sixty-year-old singer–songwriter, Annie Lennox, for instance (who herself was once a cutting-edge rocker), in an interview on NPR with Steve Inskeep (2014), now criticizes the blatant, sexual parade that seems to propel the popularity at least some of the current pop icons.[7] Lennox trumpets a feminism that mutes lived experience of women of color, and does not fully consider the lives of young girls today. The concept of intersectionality reminds us that race, class, gender, and sexuality are active participants in the formation of our identities.[8]

It was clear from class discussion and student writings that the range of media thus brought to bear under the rubric of contemporary feminism would allow students to recognize the ubiquity of cultural production and the impact of a constantly revolving flux of messages and information from countless sources. The popular feminist renais-sance in social media, comics, television, film, music, fashion, and even politics, assumes a refreshing pragmatism that side-steps the enervating academic debates about essentialism, and frankly addresses economic, psychological, cultural, political, and social advance-ment of women. This new feminism leaves the academy behind in many ways and is impatient with the deliberations even of that branch of psychoanalysis that seeks to limit, prescribe, and diagnose the ener-gizing sexuality and aggression that fuels the progress so eagerly sought by young women today. For this reason, women's activism on campus is often more visible in Women's and LGBTQ Centers, which sponsor popular stars like Laverne Cox. Other more politically charged commentary, such as racially competitive debates around the performances of Iggy Izalea and the transgender surgery of Olympian athlete turned middle-aged vamp—formerly known as Bruce—Caitlyn Jenner (just to scratch the surface of internet intensity around sexual politics), fostered conversation and controversy in our class-room. The point is this: we made space for the swirling, lightning speed circulation of cultural controversy because every iota of this largely web-based information sustains an undeniable impact on the identities of the young people who daily absorb it.

So the debate roils regarding what is truly feminist, what is truly empowering, and what is truly healthy in the on-rush of women-centered media and culture. Such myriad performances, protests, and provocations constantly coming from popular culture are now more powerful than ever in the lives of girls and women. Our objectives, fundamentally Socratic, were to provoke inquiry, critique, and appreciation, while grounding our discussions in history, logic, and even introspection.[9] Our course thus sought to explore and even, to some extent, to explain where we are going as feminists and where we have been.[10]

The Dropbox and the syllabus

A key feature of the "Pure Heroines" course that I instituted to capture the peculiar immediacy of the emergence of the new feminism was our establishing of a constantly expanding "Dropbox". Students were invited to "drop" into this shared online storage space any materials from their social media, blogs, news articles, research, or virtually any other source that related to course discussion. Such contributions became a persistent context for personal identification, contribution, and controversy. Student responses reflected their own lives, relationships, family, and evolving sense of beliefs and values. Thus, primary texts were paired with other items from their worlds in ways that allowed students to create their own associations and contribute to class dynamics. Furthermore, the constant additions to this Dropbox allowed us all to have at our disposal an ongoing archive of relevant materials to which we might turn for further research, browsing, or other investigations. Fundamentally democratizing, the fluidity of our Dropbox allowed every student to offer relevant readings to which we might all turn as class discussion dictated: contributions that took me by surprise included the Syrian teenage activist Amil Kassir's slam poetry, and the performances of "Sister Outsider" slam poetry held at Kent State University during the semester the class was held.[11] Our course sought not only to recognize the confusion of tongues represented by the onslaught of examples of women's conflicts in our culture, we sought also to present figures of resistance, recovery, and triumph, whether from idealized fictions or recognizable, everyday realities. The Dropbox became a repository of media the students were encountering, accumulating evidence of the rising tide of contemporary feminism, which they analyzed in period reflective essays.

The Hunting Ground: *Rape on Campus*

Many of the texts we read, therefore, took up the vexed subject of rape on campus: the University of Virginia *Rolling Stone* rape article was just circulating during this class; Emma Sulkowicz was daily hoisting in prolonged performance-based protest, the mattress upon which—as she declaimed—she had been raped; the investigation of rape on campus, *Missoula*, by Jon Krakauer, was just being published and reviewed in advance articles, and the film *The Hunting Ground* was being shown at our Kent State University's Women's Center. As it happened, I had placed the Indian web-based graphic narrative *Priya's Shakti* (2014) as a culturally diverse contribution to bring the subject of rape and religious redemption into our class discussions. Although we struggled to channel both anxiety and outrage as the subject of campus rape seemed to dominate discussion, the Indian narrative, though mythically based and narratively naïve, did provide respite from grim and gritty Western media displays. Another place the subject of rape appeared was through the blockbuster novel, *Fifty Shades of Grey* (James, 2012), the movie of which was just coming out the semester of our class. Thus, we were forced to reckon not only with rape as a crime and a trauma, but also with fictional representations of rape as a prevailing female fantasy.

Here, I introduced students—in a Dropbox addition of my own—to the work of American psychoanalysts Nancy Kulish and Deanna Holtzman's *A Story of Her Own: The Female Oedipus Complex Reexamined and Renamed* (2008) to bring a much needed, if condensed, discussion of female sexuality into our debates about feminism, sexual agency, and sexual experience. We summarized how Kulish and Holtzman revisit and rename the female Oedipus complex in order to redress some of the unconscious (and conscious) sexism that has plagued psychoanalysis since its Victorian beginnings, and well into its contemporary politics and practice. Traditional psychoanalytic veneration of the oedipal theory not only elides clinical evidence of women's experience, but its prescriptive orthodoxy in psychoanalytic practice ends up distorting the very processes it is meant to illuminate. Thus, the very backbone of psychoanalytic theory—the Oedipus complex—just does not quite fit the story of the girl and the woman.

These new psychoanalysts, therefore, offer the myth of Persephone's abduction and rape as a peculiarly female-focused counterpoint to the "universal" myth of oedipal rivalry and destruction. I presented the work of these analysts as characteristic of an unfortunate normal-ization/hetero-normative inscription of rape as "seduction" or initia-tion for the young girl's nascent sexuality that, ironically, might help us understand the popularity of E. L. James' sadomasochistic fantasy. Here, my introduction to this psychoanalytic debate took an impor-tant turn in our class readings and discussion as we debated whether this myth of rape and abduction really fits a universal model of female sexuality or, rather, ends up normalizing trauma because of how ritu-alized female sexual initiation is so often linked to being forced. Our discussion centered around the prevalence of rape in the lives of girls and women, and how, through repeated and culturally normalized, even ritualized experiences of traumatic sexual initiation, the adoles-cent girl is forced into actions that end up refusing her any chance at "normal" development.

Then I introduced the students to D. W. Winnicott's (1953) illustra-tion of how intrusions and traumatic impingements in the normal development of the infant prevent the infant from becoming his or her "true self." Winnicott's literal illustration of the impact of what he calls environmental impingement on the developing infant bear explication here as an analogue to the kinds of intrusions in the lives of girls and young women that preclude the inner-directed exploration of sexual-ity which would foster sexual agency and identity. What has been called, by feminist theorists and cultural critics, the culture of rape bears out the impact of such impingements; it further illustrates the familiar Freudian psychological pattern whereby the repetition of trauma becomes a tragic substitution for the kind of reckoning that remembering and therapeutic working through offers the victim. The failure of the teenager to achieve this progression accounts for a sub-mission to a masochistic position within the patriarchy, a masculin-ization of sexual knowledge and practices, a dissociation from identi-fication with the inner genital and knowledge of connectedness within a feminine sensibility.

I dwell on this ambitious but incomplete alternative mythos for feminine sexual development because it highlights, I think, the ways that psychoanalysis continues to struggle to answer Freud's enigmatic question of what women want and to describe female desire in ways that are recognizable to real women.[12] Kulish and Holtzman's female-oriented psychoanalytic project attempts the kind of vast cultural intervention Freud imagines in his treatise on lay analysis, in which he accurately posits that true psychoanalytic change will come when the entire culture, as it were, goes on the couch, and not just individuals. That they posit of myth of Persephone to articulate female development ironically facilitated our discussion of E. L. James' literal capitalization on fantasies of rape and submission.

Here again the Dropbox came to our aid. Leslie Bennetts, a longtime writer for *Vanity Fair* and author of the bestseller *The Feminine Mistake: Are We Giving Up Too Much?* (2008), takes up the theme of sexual imposition in a review article on the normalization of the violence against women that inspires the phenomenon of the novel *Fifty Shades of Grey* (Taylor-Johnson, 2015). She outlines the culture of sexual imposition and "initiation" and the ways that fantasies of rape construct alternative avenues to sexual enjoyment in a world in which female sexuality cannot evolve (as Winnicott imagines the infant's exploration of a benign, good enough environment) without impingements that preclude agency or autonomy. Although she avers that "we all prefer not to acknowledge this, of course", the truth of "what it actually means to live life in a female body" in this and virtually every culture in the world is "so dark it makes Christian Grey's Red Room of Pain seem as innocuous as a backyard sandbox" (2015, p. 43). And, in terms that again bring us back to Winnicott's formula for childhood psychoses (1953), Bennetts catalogues "everyday" impingements of harassment, abuse, and criminal acts from the personal histories of herself, her family, and friends—not even mentioning the thousands of women that she has interviewed over the years—that may well suggest Persephone's abduction and rape, while not normal in any developmentally healthy terms, are experiences so familiar to women across time and the globe as to be "intrinsic to our experience," and merely taken for granted. "It was just life," as Gloria Steinem has sighed (Steinem, in Bennetts, 2015, p. 43). And, says Bennetts, it still is, as the merest glance at the headlines will attest. What Bennetts concludes concerning "true" or normal female sexual desire is that it remains covered over: an unknown because forbidden topography. What Winnicott would call "true" desire of the true self remains undiscovered.[13]

> From earliest childhood, women's experience of sex is so inextricably intertwined with all forms of male control that submission is forever eroticized in more ways than we can possibly unravel . . . The deepest truth about female sexuality may be that it has never, in all recorded history, been something we ourselves had the freedom to shape.
> (Bennetts, 2015, p. 46)

One of the most remarkable things about Bennetts' original and challenging article is that it appears in the popular periodical *Entertainment Weekly*: like so many of the resources brought into the "Pure Heroines" class, it became as central and evocative a text as any of the assigned pieces; her article modeled an informed critique of a film and book that virtually all of my student had either read or heard about, to their great excitement and confusion. *Fifty Shades of Grey*, Bennetts writes, "may represent the ultimate appropriation for capitalist consumption of themes that have resonated throughout history, but one thing its popularity can't tell us is the truth about female sexuality" (2015, p. 46). Her contextualizing this narrative in terms of the ubiquity of sexual harassment and rape within the everyday lives of girls and women not only opened up discussion of how sexual identity and desire are dictated by experience but also the very complex notion that unconscious repetition and seemingly dissonant fantasies can play out social, sexual, and psychological conditioning that is more complex than one can readily acknowledge. The vivid detailing from a first-person account by Bennetts herself of her own experience, that of her daughter, her friends, and colleagues in the most matter-of-fact course of days and years rang absolutely true to all of the young women in the classroom: this was, in that sense, one of the texts that fostered the most explicit processing of memory and the search for creative and constructive ways to capture the personal stake in the content and context of the course readings during this semester.

My own direction of these phases of the class was not directive, I must say: my impulse was to keep the class above water as we experienced a nearly constant influx of material and to keep students thinking about how they might themselves, in the end, create a graphic narrative of their own stories, however they chose, or, alternatively, how they might offer a feminist analysis of some key text from the class materials or the Dropbox. My goal, as the class began to come to a conclusion, was that each student would experience some sort of integration of class material and create some expression that would offer insight, a creative remedy, or, at least, an articulation of what they had seen, felt, and understood about feminism in our world today. Again, the point to stress in this summary description of the "status" of young women on campus and what I and others call the new feminism is that such articles, filled with complex, familiar, and yet fresh theories of women's experience in the context of feminist critiques are occurring in fashion magazines, entertainment blogs, comics, and web-based media that are instantly available and instantly disseminated.

Many of the personal narratives of these young students concerned their experience of feminism as it speaks to their emerging sexual lives. It needs to be stressed, perhaps, that college age women are especially vulnerable sexually: for most it is their first time away from home, they are mature young women of the age of consent, they are surrounded in most cases by young men who expect sexually active partners, and yet, many are still very sexually inexperienced and uncertain of themselves or what they should or should not be doing, experiencing, expecting of themselves and their sexual partners. Many are confronted with sexual choices and variations of partners and activities that they have precious little guidance in negotiating. Traditional sources of guidance from parents, churches and other religious institutions, medical resources, and schools have, in many ways, been subverted by advertising and media that seeks to market, provoke, and propel them into frantic sexual activity. Most of the young women in my class (as well as other classes where such matters might have been discussed) are confused: is sexual activity empowering? Is it merely a matter of appetite? Is it a bridge toward intimacy and love? Is it healthy or is it harmful? These and many other questions remain unanswered and, what is more, unexplored in their classes, and often even within their friendship and family circles. Yet, these questions pervade contemporary feminist discourse and provide a forum for young college age women: neo-feminism does not offer definitive answers so much as questions, narratives, confessions, testimonies, and even diatribes.

"Catching Fire"[14]

To catch the fire of the new feminism, we started the formal syllabus based readings of our course with the blockbuster books and films of the past year, *The Hunger Games* and *Divergent*: these are both young adult narratives with strong, even militant, female heroines who have become iconic in part because of their athletic and survivalist skills. The popularity of these films belies the otherwise startling failure of Hollywood to appeal to the young female audience. Central to our discussion of these films and the novels upon which they are based is the simultaneous recognition that even though they were blockbusters at the movie theaters, they are, in fact, the exceptions that prove the rule of Hollywood's systematic, even criminally discriminatory, exclusion of women from roles as actors, directors, producers, and writers of major studio films. From these examples, students were forced to grapple with the impossible double binds exposed by such hypocrisy and market manipulation: they discussed coming to grips with the cloying depiction of girls and women they had all grown up with through a culture imbued with sexism and discrimination; at the same time, they eagerly embraced the sheer pleasure in identifying with dynamic and active female heroines such as Katniss Everdeen from the *Hunger Games*. The dearth of such roles propelled an almost giddy gratitude for the roles celebrated by Hollywood in these novels, while, at the same time, provoking a profound resentment for "growing up absurd" in a culture whose dominant images of girls and women demeaned even their capacity to speak. Our course, thus, was designed to bring young women into the "speaking parts" that, rather notoriously, are being elided by mainstream Hollywood: an ironic last bastion, and, with any luck, a last gasp of an anxious patriarchy.[15]

Indeed, the ever-present spiritual guide in our course was the voice of Virginia Woolf, whose *A Room of One's Own* is arguably the fountainhead of the entire field of Women's Studies in the Western curriculum in English. Her ironic and yet still radically daring notion that two women might exist in fiction who genuinely liked each other and who worked together in a laboratory became a kind of default working paradigm of the course. For, she proclaimed, as she read the lines of one of the "new women" novelists of her era, "Then I may tell you that the very next words I read were these—Chloe liked Olivia . . .' Do not start. Do not blush. Let us admit in the privacy of our own society that these things sometimes happen. Sometimes women do like women" (2005, pp. 80–81). The radical notion here put forward, of course, is that in this laboratory and in the society of each other and their mutual enjoyment, men were not the sole focus of Chloe and Olivia's attention as they worked together. The contemporary cartoonist, Alison Bechdel, has followed Woolf in her now famous "Bechdel Test" (2008) for movie going: she will only go to a movie in which there are (1) two women, (2) who talk to each other (3) about something besides men (Figure 1).[16]

We therefore sustained our analysis of the new feminist heroine upon two premises: the first historical observation was that the new wave of feminists today have, again to quote Woolf, many "mothers":

Figure 1. "The Rule" from *The Essential Dykes to Watch Out For* (reprinted by permission).

"We think back through our mothers if we are women." (2005, p. 75). The second premise of the course that emerged from this initial embrace of the paramilitary heroines of these blockbuster films was that our course would define the heroine not in terms of romance, not in terms of the familiar "marriage plot," but in terms of action. I made it clear to the students that, as a scholar of the early English novel, I readily "laid down my pen"[17] at the genius of Jane Austen, her predecessors and heirs—those myriad narrators of classical "marriage plots" who have defined the history of the novel in English. That female heroine is the subject of a different course! I stressed that this course was taking a different tack: here, our encounter with the female heroine would concern women who variously left the domestic sphere. The point for our discussion was not to exclude romance, marriage, home, or family, but, rather, to extend the reach of female identity and orientation to include and embrace action outside: in the world. Thus, the thrust of the course was to offer different definitions and types of female identification and action in culture and society. Rather than focusing on problems of female identity within the familiar framework of romance, we examined the lives of girls and women primarily in relation to power and action in the world. Thus, as the title of this article suggests, the female "action" heroine today may be a construct of popular culture and pop icons, but she is also, I conclude in hope, a new feminist who aspires to gender equality and personal agency in uniquely twenty-first century ways.

My determination, however, was to demonstrate that this action heroine is based in history. As a scholar of early modern women, therefore, I was delighted to introduce the class to the historical achievement of Joan of Arc, as depicted in George Bernard Shaw's *Saint Joan*, the recently discovered silent film from 1928, *The Passion of Joan*, and recent historical novels, films, albums, and comics.[18] Similarly, we considered the military and political genius of Queen Elizabeth I, as dramatized in the recent film starring Cate Blanchett (Kapur, 1998, 2007), most interesting recently in the new comic series of *Catwoman*, who, as we shall discuss further below, intones in internal monologue quotations from the archives of Elizabeth's own speeches and letters. Once introduced to historical heroines in the context of contemporary depictions of action heroines, even the lesser known legion of women artists and actors on the historical stage—the vast numbers of silent "Judith Shakespeares" imagined by Virginia Woolf—were embraced by students with the fascination their stories deserve. For instance, when students read *The Narrative of the Persecution of Agnes Beaumont* (Camden, 1992), the seventeenth-century Puritan farm girl who fought for her life and her right to inherit her father's farm upon his death, or study the startling painting of Italian Renaissance artist Artemesia Gentileschi, whose resilience in the face of rape ultimately inspired her painting of *Judith and Holfernes* (hanging today in the Uffitzi gallery), class members were able to understand how action in the face of persecution and injustice has a deep history. It is this history that is being consciously referenced, even resurrected dramatically, by today's feminist activists.

The conscious identification with female predecessors is, we came to understand, an essential ingredient in the resurgence of female action heroes in popular culture today. In this regard the new feminists are countermanding the oedipally inflected theories of creativity under the "anxiety of influence" that have become, in my estimation, the false, even masculinist, doctrines of literary critics in past decades, led by Harold Bloom and his followers.[19] Rather than compete in murderous rivalry with dominant figures of the past, the new feminist heroines have embraced historical predecessors according to Virginia Woolf's mandate: that they think, feel, and create through the mothers of invention, identifying with their hard-won examples. To help clarify this dynamic, I invited some students to research and present on Jessica Benjamin's notions of female identification as "overinclusive" (1995) and Nancy Kulish and Deanna Holtzman's theories of identification with female predecessors in order to offer our class a practical psychological framework within which to herald a model of creativity that allowed and accounted for the tributes to feminist legacy.

Perhaps in part because of the age of the students in this class and their only recent separation from parents, the young women in the class were very responsive to the tender depictions of Cheryl Strayed's pilgrimage of grief and mourning in her best-selling book *Wild* (2013) on the death of her mother (whose early death from cancer adds insult to the injury of her domestic abuse by her husband). The story, and the successful film *Wild* (Vallée, 2014), starring the young feminist actress Reese Witherspoon, charts the triumph of its valiant pilgrim, who hikes the Pacific Coast Trail in a quest for authentic selfhood, and channels both grief and sympathy in directions the students found encouraging. Likewise, despite considerable cultural differences, one of the texts which most moved the students and provoked some of the strongest sympathy and identification was *I Am Malala* (2013), Malala Yousafzai's personal memoir of resistance to political terrorism and personal agenda of activism on behalf of girls' education in Pakistan. Malala seemed to us all a latter-day Joan of Arc, being the youngest person ever to be awarded the Nobel Peace Prize (on October 10 2014) and who has confronted military and political leadership and won. Her triumph opened up the discussion of political possibilities for girls and women and the prospect of the election of a female president in our lifetime. Students were invariably struck by Malala's support by, and solidarity with, her father as the source of her courage. Her father's dedication to girls' and women's education consolidated the need for men to be feminists and brought many contributions to our Dropbox from Emma Watson's "He for She" speeches regarding her role as a spokesperson at the United Nations.[20] Some students took this introduction to the more strictly political aspects of feminist discourse as an opportunity to take up in discussions and presentation the dearth of female world leaders in general. The interesting, if challenging, cases of twentieth and twenty-first century figures such as Indira Gandhi, Benazir Bhutto, Golda Meir, Margaret Thatcher, Angela Merkel, and Hillary Clinton as world leaders led students to consider, perhaps for the first time, the ways that the political realities of the male dominated stage hamper women's aspiration to leadership, regardless of countries or ideologies. Here again, historical feminist legacy fueled possibilities for the future, particularly enacted in one young woman's decision to run for student government in this semester, and become involved in national political campaigns. Since part of the class assignment was to attend cultural, political, or other educational public lectures or events on campus that concerned feminism in some (widely defined) way, many students found themselves becoming interested in campus activities that had otherwise escaped their attention.

Exposure of the students to "heroines" of the literary and political scene, the new voices of women writers, artists, filmmakers, and activists created, not surprisingly, an avenue with which to introduce students to the wide reach of feminist thought, into poetic, artistic, and social expression. One such on-campus literary event highlighted the intersection of race, gender, and nation threaded through the luminous reading of Poet Laureate, Rita Dove. Poet-hero, Dove shared stories of her childhood and adolescence as an African American girl in the public schools of Akron, Ohio, her college years at Miami University, and her current stature as Professor at the University of Virginia and the voice of American poetry.

Wonder women

A large portion of the class was devoted to the emerging medium of comics, the female superhero and graphic memoirs of women because

I believe that this new form is one of the most promising and productive artistic expressions of popular feminism, today. The rise of comics in contemporary popular culture and the field of comics and graphic narratives written by women actively build upon a strong identification with, and elaboration on, the action and accomplishments of previous generations of women "heroines". The positive upsurge in comics today revisits the history of women in returning powerful women action heroines to the very comics' cartels that, in previous decades, demeaned and ignored them. The exemplary tale of Wonder Woman, for instance, who was created by William Moulton Marston in 1941, gave our class an opportunity to chart a recent history of American feminism: Gloria Steinem famously solidified Wonder Woman's universality as a feminist icon by extracting her from the increasingly sexist depiction of DC comics' and, in 1972 (the height of Second Wave feminism), placed her on the cover of *Ms. Magazine*, returning Wonder Woman to her 1941 empowered stature (Figure 2).

Figure 2.   Ms. Magazine's 1972 cover with Wonder Woman in her 1941 depiction.

From that vantage point, Wonder Woman was destined to endure as a feminist force.[21] The fortieth anniversary issue of *Ms. Magazine* made this endurance even more certain when its editors put Wonder Woman on the cover again in an updated re-drawing of her iconic stature (Figure 3). And now, Wonder Woman will have her own film in 2017 from Warner Bros, and her origins have been explored in a recent book by Jill Lepore entitled *The Secret History of Wonder Woman* (2014). So, since 1941, Wonder Woman has provided us with an archive of feminist history.

No less revered a news monitor than Katie Couric has recently presented a video news article on the skyrocketing popularity of the female superhero on *Yahoo! News* (2015). Her video seems virtually to be taken from our class discussion of the emergence of the superhero both in terms of the vexed history of Wonder Woman and the Renaissance of the female superhero with new origin stories and a new

Figure 3.   *Ms. Magazine*'s fortieth anniversay edition cover, with updated image of Wonder Woman (2012, reprinted by permission).

recognition of their "mothers" to the new generation of superheroes.[22] As Couric's news report also emphasizes, the new "Avengers" comic, *A-Force*, written by two women, Marguerite Bennett and G. Willow Wilson, will comprise a team entirely of female superheroes who, it is generally agreed, "rule."

Couric's video also stresses, however, that the current wave of female superheroes are also being invented with today's multi-cultural concerns, and today's heightened awareness of young women's hunger to be cast—even if in fantasy—in roles where they are active agents and not passive victims to be rescued. Our class agreed that the burgeoning field of comics constituted the most optimistic and innovative segments of the course curriculum. Another comic book character, based in history and currently springing brilliantly from the fountainhead of Marvel comics' conglomeration, is Ms. Marvel. A new character in the pantheon of Marvel's superheroes, Ms. Marvel demonstrates the impact of progressive, global feminism in popular culture through her identity as a teenage Muslim girl who "channels" the spirit of Captain Marvel (Figures 4 and 5), her female antecedent

Figure 4.   Cover of Captain Marvel, Vol. 7, Issue 1 (reprinted by permission).

Figure 5.   Cover of Ms. Marvel, Vol. 3, Issue 1 (reprinted by permission).

whose heroism had distinguished her as a fighter pilot in the army. This series is certainly one of the most interesting and innovative creations of the comics' industry as, under the signature writing of G. Willow Wilson, this comic takes on the topic of Muslim women in America. Ms. Marvel's devotion to female heroic predecessors, her adolescent resistance to parental constraints, and sexual coming of age for young women all come together to win a correspondingly new female audience. Ms. Marvel is indeed so popular among the new young women readers that the comic books literally cannot be stocked fast enough to keep up with sales.[23]

Such resonance with feminist history, identification with previous heroines, and the pressures of leadership and family is similarly explored in the characters of Catwoman, Batwoman, Captain Marvel, and other "new" and improved comic creations of female heroines. Each of these characters purposefully allude to their maternal antecedents (Catwoman writer Genevieve Valentine, for instance, literarily inscribes the letter of Queen Elizabeth I on the opening and closing pages of each issue of the comic series. Catwoman's thoughts are then encapsulated by the magisterial monarch, as she takes inspiration from her). Catwoman turns to other historical women, including Lucrezia

Borgia and Ching Shih, once again suggesting a historical as well as multi-cultural feminist impulse (Valentine et al., 2016). The entire field of comics, which is currently gaining critical and academic notice, as well as soaring popularity, has, correspondingly, only in the past few years fully grasped the power—economic, cultural, social, political, and psychological—of appealing to female readers and writers. They are far ahead of mainstream Hollywood producers. Ms. Marvel, along with her cartoon comrades, inhabit comic books that are literally flying off the shelves of comic stores. They outsell virtually every other brand of comic.

Graphic women

The graphic narrative is a form of memoir created in the medium of comics that emerged and diverged from the comic book in the late twentieth century, most notably through the Pulitzer Prize winning work by Art Speigelman about his parents and the Holocaust, entitled *Maus*. Since this ground-breaking work, the graphic narrative has taken off in recent decades, now reaching an artistic apex in the productions of women's memoirs such as Marjane Satrapi's *Persepolis*, Alison Bechdel's *Fun Home* (also adapted into a currently running Broadway musical) and *Are You My Mother?*, and Lynda Barry's graphic memoirs *One! Hundred! Demons!*, *What It Is*, and *Syllabus*. Even as I have alluded to Lorde's album title to focus my course on the feminism, so here I turn to a remarkable study by University of Chicago professor Hillary Chute entitled *Graphic Women: Life Narrative and Contemporary Comics* (2010) to refer to the turn by women around the globe to graphic narrative in today's culture in order to capture how, within our class, this same turn inspired many students to create graphic narrative of their own experiences as women. Chute considers how the emerging form of the graphic narrative as a mode of artistic production is especially suited to the depiction of trauma because of its peculiar rendering of time: as a form, it has fostered the testimonies of women from around the globe. Chute suggests that a comic

> lends itself to the autobiographical genre in which we see so many authors—and so many women authors in particular—materializing their lives and histories. It is a way to put the body on the page (which we see, then, both in terms of denotative content and in production). (2010, p. 10).

Each female graphic narrativist puts the "the body on the page" in their own way, along with the verbal narrative of their story. Traumatic memory, especially memories that are imaged from childhood and adolescence, join together with the adult narrator, pulling "every which way" on the page (Barry interviewed by Chute, 2008, p. 57). For Chute, these graphic narratives are preoccupied with traumatic experience but she says that the comics form allows them to "represent trauma productively and ethically" (2010, p. 3).

Our class closed with Lynda Barry, whose works explicitly inspire the reader to produce a narrative of her own. Thus, the last texts that we read for the class were Barry's graphic memoir of her childhood reminiscences, *One! Hundred! Demons!*, and *Syllabus* (2014), in which she outlines a university class on "how to" create a graphic memoir for "the Unthinkable Mind" (p. 1). Barry's high-spirited course description provided the ideal coda for members of a class that were, at times, overwhelmed by so many feminist calls to action, while suffering at the same time a subdued sense of mourning over indignities within a sexist culture. Barry sublimates her own complex past, yet her work inspires the creative imagination and capacities of her readers. Students thus found energy and even optimism in our final projects. I chose Chute's title for this subsection of my chapter to highlight the creative works members of my class produced as a kind of final integration of their embrace of feminism in the often painful context of their own lives and personal histories. My suggestion is that they became, in the final weeks of this course, "graphic women": women, that is, who were "drawn" to tell a story of themselves with agency, accuracy, and aesthetic discipline.

Barry's *One! Hundred! Demons!* bears witness to the traumatic origins of her childhood loneliness, abuse, longings, and losses; all the while, her graphics offer tribute art, literature, education, community, friendship, and love (Figure 6). The psychoanalytic theories of D. W. Winnicott, Marion Milner, and others provide a clear, well-lit path for her reader to follow toward self-knowledge. Her graphic narratives are monuments to hope and healing for the lives of young people, yet they are, remarkably, free from cant.

As she makes plain, in order to narrate and to diagram the true self one must accept that, as Virginia Woolf says, "lies will flow from my lips, but there may perhaps be some truth mixed up with them" (2005, p. 4): it means the making of something true and fantastic, and fright-

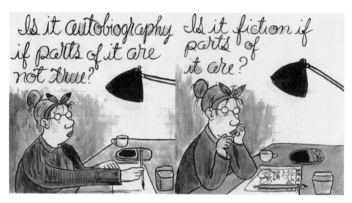

Figure 6.   Two panels from Barry's *One! Hundred! Demons!*
(reprinted by permission).

eningly familiar and new at the same time. This is why Barry gives her particular brand of memoir its own name: "autobifictionalography." Lynda Barry, among the cartoonists whose work epitomizes this process, is also, as I have suggested above, an artist who singularly reaches out to her readers in an active attempt to encourage them not only to enjoy the transformative journey through Barry's own narrative, but to return themselves to the place where they left off drawing, imagining, dreaming, and creating in their own childhoods. In this way, Barry became the ideal last stop on our sojourn through feminist history into our world today, for it was Barry's reach beyond the pages of her books into the potential creative space of her readers that offered students the instruction, modeling, and encouragement to tell their stories. As our class was soon to discover through student projects and pursuits during this assignment, the power of comics, graphic narratives, and graphic medicine is gaining recognition in many clinical and educational settings. In this way, my own commitment to the intersection of the clinic, the culture, and the classroom came together in the production of student creations. Thus, without purposefully imposing psychoanalytic theory or clinical applications within the classroom dedicated to popular culture and new feminism, I was able to witness the effect of artistic and narrative integration in the creative production of student work. Indeed, as I have analyzed elsewhere at length (Camden, 2016), the form of comics has intersected with psychoanalytic process in the graphic narratives of Alison Bechdel, demonstrating, perhaps, an inherent access to unconscious processes, embodiment of memory, and physical presence in drawing and the ways that comics uniquely can act "as a procedure . . . of embodiment, and the instantiation of handwriting as a gripping index of a material, subjective, situated body" (Chute, 2010, p. 193).

Lynda Barry ended up the last "pure heroine" of our course because she provided the students with evidence that art, too, is action. Not only did the students latch on to her capacious provision of creative transitional space through her own works, but they took her (and me) up on her invitation to create their own narratives. The search for the true self, in Winnicott's terms, is, in the end, a process that requires insight as well as creative expression within the world. Thus, while class members were able to take inspiration from the likes of Joan of Arc, Malala, Ms. Marvel, or, indeed, Emma Sulkowicz (whose traumas were far closer to the actual experience of these college women), it was in their personal narratives, as directed by the example of Lynda Barry's comic-encouragement, that they were able to draw literally from memory. They created remarkable and moving narratives illustrating their own lives and times. Their graphic narratives were produced under the pressure of the final weeks of the semester yet, nevertheless, provided a kind of *initiating* action that, with any luck, will lead to other outlets, avenues, adventures, and accomplishments.

My students were particularly emboldened by Lynda Barry's insistent interpretation, rendered at the end of *One! Hundred! Demons!*, and iterated in wonderfully entertaining, instructive, and liberating YouTube videos of her popular lectures about her work and the mission of cartooning, that all of us are capable of drawing expressive and lively versions of ourselves and our worlds, as the merest glimpse of children's art work will reveal. As Picasso famously said, it took him an entire lifetime to learn how to paint again like a child. Barry's point is that this native impulse is corollary to the capacity to speak and is inherently as amenable to therapeutic processes as any verbal formulations. Although she is no clinician and does not extend this observation beyond her own ambition to get students to draw out and from their lives as a means of self-discovery and the uncovering of D. W. Winnicott's "true self", it is one short step for us to recognize that in Barry's popular programs for student learners of all ages, unconscious processes are liberated and put to the uses of healing and personal development. Here again, I appeal to Freud's deep respect and recognition of the discoveries, devotions, and psychic achievements of creative artists and others who follow the paths of self-actualization that far exceed the narrow strictures of the rigid psychoanalytic standards and requirements of our crusty institutes that are somehow bolstered by the garrisoned conviction that psycho-analytic processes of unconscious discoveries are limited to clinical consulting rooms.

Only a handful of the students had had any artistic training: none was currently an "Art major", and certainly none had taken this course expecting to be drawing, coloring, and collaging alongside the antici-pated writing assignments of their final weeks of class. But among those who chose to create a graphic narrative, not one went away with-out seizing upon Lynda Barry's clarion call to cast off the shaming effect of childhood drawing regimes and rejections by harsh art teach-ers and to return to the muscle memory of the hand itself: Barry entreats her students to begin to draw from life and learn from the lineaments of time and memory. Barry stresses that when she invites adults to draw without self-censoring, they "pick up" where they left off as children. Such access to physical memory is evident in the students' creations—some more primitive seeming than others. Barry, though an accomplished artist, embraces a style that invokes child-like associations and spare "simplified" lines that end up amplifying emotional states.[24]

She asks us all—teachers and students alike—to try to remember childhood delight in drawing and the transcendent power of those transitional objects, which imbue our worlds with creative space and security to imagine ourselves thriving in the world. As the student works we will see here displayed reveal, however, it is often necessary to traverse trauma to get to the transitional place of creativity: further-more, it is not at all clear that each student can sustain the kind of promise Barry projects in the studied optimism that ultimately emer-ges from her own childhood misery. I do contend, however, that the rhetoric of popular feminism and the ubiquity of social media that relentlessly calls young women to witness to a "new feminism" can keep hope alive even within the spectrum of personal aspirations and identifications.

Emboldened by Lynda Barry's frank, poignant depiction of her childhood losses, humiliations, and traumas, coming as it did on the heels of a semester's worth of fearless and forthright heroines who

found ways to act in their world despite assault, silencing, or shaming, several students found the courage to tell their own stories: some
of these stories depict childhood and adolescent abuse, confusion, and
sexual initiation and rape; others portray intellectual and artistic
awakening coupled with first love; others show identities still locked
in body dysmorphia, eating disorders, stinging recollections of high
school degradations and helplessness of inevitable hierarchies; still
others simply depict the web of drug addiction, while yet others
assertively submerge all negative associations to their pasts to show
triumphant fantasies of superhero selves who take over the misogynistic worlds of video games and Hollywood films and promise a new
culture of gender equality. If Barry's *One! Hundred! Demons!* master-
fully narrates the impossibly complex origins of her anguish as a child
and the almost predestined artistry that was to emerge from the
complex contingencies of her ancestry and educational opportunities,
I would aver that my students attempted, and even accomplished, a
similar mastery over their own imagined and remembered worlds,
in each case infused with the prospect of a feminist future. If Barry's
One! Hundred! Demons! provided a narrative context and incentive
through the example of her own raw and yet remarkably sensitive
portrayal of childhood anguish and its traces in adult suffering,
conversely, her *Syllabus*, more of a "teaching" text, provided a pairing
with her personal testimony in its explicit record of her own (first)
class on creating personal graphic narratives at the University of
Wisconsin, entitled "What it is: writing and picture making class"; she
also called this class "Unthinkable minds". Her book, *Syllabus*, out-
lining the processes of the class contains explicit assignments and
examples of her students' work; it also contains, in its intensely
graphic notebook style, many of her own observations, feelings, and
appreciations of her students' work. In many ways, these volumes of
Barry's frank and unpretentious presentations of her life and her
creative, pedagogical, and artistic processes provided my class with
precisely the culminating mode of personal and creative expression
they needed to process the often disturbing, demanding, and paradigm shifting material of our feminist focus through the lens of the
intensely personal and freeing teachings Barry's texts (and YouTube
videos of her presentations readily available on the internet for class
and private viewing) provided. Barry's implicit weaving of psychoanalytic theories of Winnicott, particularly his emphasis on artistic

expression as a development of the true self and an expression of the transitional space and its objects that become the core of the child's— and ultimately the adult's—emergent sense of being and doing, facilitated our class discussion of how drawing and story telling taps into dormant aspects of our being.

Class comics

I have decided to present portions of three of the comics from the final course project, with little explicit discussion since I believe the works speak for themselves, by definition. I have chosen pages from these three narratives because of the power of the graphic rendering of personal experience, and evidence of what I would call, from a psychoanalytic perspective, an artistic and narrative effort at "working through" memory through insight. I reproduce these pages with the students' permission.[25] Choosing among the student productions was difficult and painful: the ones included represent many of the themes, trends, and traumas that were captured in the entire gathering of personal stories recounted by these young women. This final class contribution provided a strong testament to the need for a creative call to feminist consciousness: women's action, activism, and empowerment throughout history that now infuses contemporary popular culture and media can also mobilize creative change in student's voices, as I hope my representative examples will show. This small sampling of what young women on a Midwestern college campus are thinking and feeling about their own identities within the world serves to remind us that the status of women in America, as in the world, is urgent and inspiring, embattled and emboldened. In the narratives that I extract below, the new feminism that each student encountered in class fostered a perspective on her own experience that, as it were, allowed the narrative to emerge.

"Intrusive thoughts"

In this narrative, the student describes the origins and experience of her "intrusive thoughts." The vivid drawings and descriptive narrative show the progress of her understanding of her experience of her thoughts but also how these thoughts are felt in her body. This particular student took her graphic narrative to a conference on "Graphic medicine and narrative" and was approached by many at the conference, at which she was the only undergraduate, who would like to see her publish her work. She is now considering a career as a graphic narrativist and therapist.

In the first panel (Figure 7), the student describes her "origins" in terms very familiar to our superheroes' origin stories.

Figure 7.   First panel of "Intrusive thoughts."

She then describes the origin of her own thought disorder and how she has found ways to render her experience in image and word. The next three panels (Figures 8, 9, and 10) depict phases of her narrative in which she shows her own processes of working through reality and fantasy, the pressures of literally finding a place for thoughts and images that seem alien to her, and, ultimately, the ways that her experiences with mental health professionals themselves constitute expressive forces contained within her art.

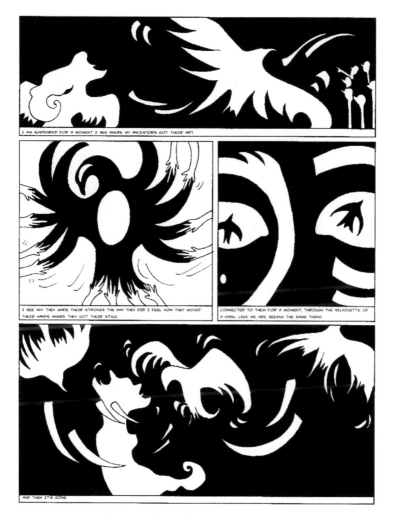

Figure 8.   From "Intrusive thoughts."

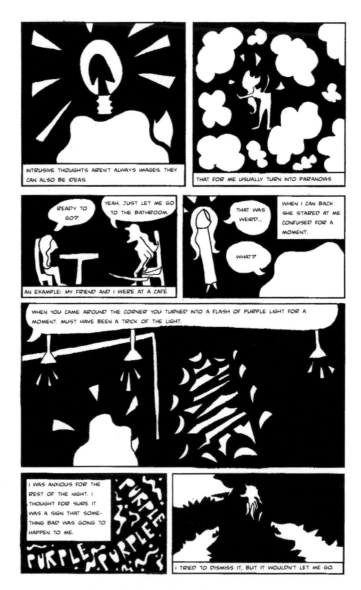

Figure 9.   From "Intrusive thoughts."

Figure 10. From "Intrusive thoughts."

"Everything counted"

This second narrative, "Everything counted", created by a student who is from a practicing Muslim family, depicts with wrenching honesty the conflict that she feels over the covering of her body and the teachings of her faith about feminine sexuality. Her collage of images, coupled with her narrative associations and her drawings propel the viewer into the tumult of her resistance to being "diagnosed" with mental illness and prescribed medication. She narratively and visually suggests the blood of her menstrual cycle and her loss of virginity (Figure 11).

Figure 11. From "Everything counted", suggesting menstruation and loss of virginity.

She depicts the shame for nameless deeds and suicidal impulses (Figure 12).

Figure 12. From "Everything counted", depicting shame.

In her reflection, the student writes, "I figured jail and torture, earthly punishments, would be better than Hell, so when I couldn't believe in Qur'anic teachings, I punished myself." Her narrative juxtaposes diagnostic categories with the rage she feels at being shamed for sexuality and her pull to religion as a place of rebellion and a refuge at the same time.

This narrative served to contain many of the frightened feelings that the course readings provoked in this student and allowed a creative contribution to share with the class (Figure 13).

This narrative was perhaps the one that was most powerful in terms of consolidating so many of the feminist conflicts and contradictions cross-culturally (Figures 14–15). Her title, "Everything counted", suggests the sense of the impossible pressure endured for this young woman whose very presence provokes long glances and prejudiced assumptions about identity, faith, and gender.

This Muslim narrative allowed our class and the student herself a way to testify, dramatize, and share in an increasingly enlightened group of fellow students. It is worth noting that this student is now thriving in her work as a performance artist: it might be that her capacity to find a place to put her own experience fostered a creative continuity. Here, reflections on the course that she included in the

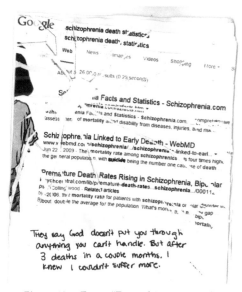

Figure 13.   From "Everything counted."

Figure 14.   From "Everything counted."

copy of her narrative collage highlight some of the processes that she identified from the context and content of the class:

> Our professors keep trying to stress that art reflects the times. That art has the power to move. I never really believed it, I thought activism without physical action is for suckers. Dada is minimalism trying to seem deep to be provocative. *Waiting for Godot* is absolute bullshit. What can a play, what can the lighting or paints do to change the world? Isn't it just for *fun*, something to keep the people quiet? Panem et circenses, and *all that jazz*. The class and this assignment provided evidence to the contrary.

Of her own processes of creating, reading, and reflecting she felt similarly affected: "The place was dark, yes, but after a week of sacrificing sleep to create a collage of my nightmares, I found a strange peace with the past. . . . I don't believe I need to suffer anymore".

Figure 15. From "Everything counts."

"Consequences"

This last student's narrative captures the ways that returning to drawing as an adult can bring the student back to a place that was left
behind in childhood. Here the drawings are lean and simplified,
amplifying, as Scott McCloud (1993) explains, the intensity of the
loss and the gravity of the events described in the narrative. The story
also speaks to the larger questions of the experience of sexuality
and the pressures felt by young women to conform to sexual expectations that are often not really consonant with their still uncertain selves. The stark description of this young woman's loss of
virginity in a manner that she forces upon herself to "stop being
different" (Figure 16) is premised upon conformity and peer pressure. The drawings, deceptively cartoonish (resembling the comic
strip of *Garfield*), mask a dissociation from self ("I was no longer
connected"), the coldness of the blue bed suggests the numbness from
her sexual body ("I pretended I was having fun"), and, finally, the
"Consequences" that she draws at the end muster an ambiguity as she

Figure 16.   "Feeling different", from "Consequences."

is alone in a doctor's office: is the bad news pregnancy and a probable abortion? Is it an STD? She effectively leaves this question unanswered, only to say that "I will never be the same." The final panel ends with a consoling message: We are not defined by our mistakes (Figures 17–21). And it does seem to me that the capacity, once again, to contextualize this traumatic teenage event in the light of feminist discourse, with some compassion for the pressures, social, sexual, and psychological, that young college women are under in our culture, allows this student a way to testify to her personal experience and understand it in terms that might well provide new ways of being a woman in the world.

Figure 17.   From "Consequences."

Figure 18.   From "Consequences."

Figure 19.   From "Consequences."

Figure 20.   From "Consequences."

Figure 21.   Last frame of "Consequences."

Conclusion: catching waves

In an issue of the psychoanalytic journal, *Studies in Gender and Sexuality* on "The fourth wave of feminism," editor Harriet Kimble Wrye (2009) proposes a "fourth wave" of feminism occurring today in which spirituality and community, and global awareness prevail even while incorporating the preceding movements and generations (p. 190). To this journal issue, the renowned actress, producer, and philanthropist, Jane Fonda, contributes an article "Gender and destiny," which disagrees with the very notion of "waves" of feminism. While acknowledging the evolution of the feminist movement, Fonda cautions against the formulation of "waves":

> I think it is more important to recognize that there's been an organic flow and consistency to the 20th Century women's movement. . . . global, and, yes, even spiritual. As early as the mid 1800s, Elizabeth Oakes Smith addressed a woman's conference, "My friends, do we realize for what purpose we are convened? Do we fully understand that we aim at nothing less than an entire subversion of the present order of society, dissolution of the whole existing social compact?" (Fonda, 2009, p. 190)

I conclude with Jane Fonda's article and also her example because I believe her point is worth taking up as we conclude this chapter in which I have heralded not a "fourth wave" of feminism that surpasses the previous and preceding waves that are familiarly periodized in the histories of feminism, but, rather, a "new feminism" that itself rides the waves of social media, culture, and the internet, and is espoused by popular and youth culture. I agree with Jane Fonda's insistence on continuity: her model does not surpass, or compete with, previous generations but relies—thinks through, as Woolf would say—the mothers of the feminist movement. She ties present day feminism to the past even as she welcomes the next generation and looks to the future.

Brilliantly, she generously illustrates what she means by describing her own personal psychoanalytic treatments. Her first analysis, conducted in the 1950s with a traditional Freudian analyst, she claims "didn't help" and made things worse; the other, more recent, conducted by a "relational" psychoanalyst and a woman, provided a space in which Fonda could find her voice, and, precisely, relate to her analyst and, ultimately, herself. Thus, by resisting the competitive model of the classically "oedipal" treatment of a Freudian analyst, Fonda eventually (sheer luck, she claims) ended up in the consulting room of a relational analyst who, precisely, helped her to *relate*. Fonda's association of a relational model with a more capacious, organic feminist history and contemporary practice is *apropos* to my claims in this chapter that contemporary popular feminism is communal and relates with previous pioneers of the feminist movement, embracing their example even as it integrates the powerful culture of contemporary media.

Acknowledgments

I would like to thank my graduate assistant, Valentino Zullo, for his editorial assistance and research expertise in the field of comics studies. I would also like to thank my doctoral student, Danielle French, for her active assistance with our "Pure heroines" class. Both emerging scholars give me great hope for the future of feminism. I dedicate this article to my students, the Pure Heroines and Heroes of Kent State University.

Notes

1. See Rudnytsky, who writes "[b]oth feminism and psychoanalysis rely on personal narratives as mode of knowledge and history-telling" (2000, p. 6). See also Bernheimer and Kahane (1990), and Rose (2005).

2. In the ashes of the "culture wars", we have witnessed what Littlefield and Johnson refer to as the "neuroscientific turn." In the place of culture, many disciplines now make a neuro-scientific turn, including " neuroeconomics, neurohistory, neuroanthropology, neuroaesthetics, neuromarketing, neurosociology, neuropolitics, neuroethics, neurotheology, and even the neurohumanities" (Littlefield & Johnson, 2012, p. 2).

3. See "Beyonce's fierce feminism" (Hobson, 2015). See also Taylor Swift,

> I think that when I used to say, "Oh, feminism's not really on my radar," it was because when I was just seen as a kid, I wasn't as threatening. I didn't see myself being held back until I was a woman. . . . Misogyny is ingrained in people from the time they are born. So to me, feminism is probably the most important movement that you could embrace, because it's just basically another word for equality. (Roy, 2015)

Other online blogs, news sources, and social media include *Jezebel*, *Huffington Post*, *Slate*, *Salon*, etc.

4. The scope of this article cannot begin to consider the debates over gender, which have spanned decades, including Lacan and colleagues' seminar on feminine sexuality (1985), Judith Butler's (1990, 1993) post-structuralist treatise on feminism, and the emergence of queer theory. See also, Tasker and Negra (2007) and Munford and Waters (2013, p. 10) on "hauntology" and the "postfeminist mystique". The model of "haunting" does not acknowledge feminist history but, rather, again conjures competition. Contrariwise, popular culture seeks action; see Baumgardner and Richard (2010) on technology and "fourth wave feminism."

5. In her lawsuit against Kleiner Perkins, Ellen Pao alleges gender discrimination. Pao lost this lawsuit, but "succeeded in prompting debate about women in technology and venture capital" (Streitfeld, 2015).

6. For we do not consider it at all desirable for psycho-analysis to be swallowed up by medicine and to find its last resting-place in a textbook of psychiatry under the heading 'Methods of Treatment', alongside of procedures such as hypnotic suggestion, autosuggestion, and persuasion, which, born from our ignorance, have to thank the laziness and cowardice of mankind for their short-lived effects. It deserves a better fate and, it may be hoped, will meet with one. As a "depth-psychology", a theory of the mental unconscious, it can

become indispensable to all the sciences which are concerned with the evolution of human civilization and its major institutions such as art, religion and the social order. . . . The use of analysis for the treatment of the neuroses is only one of its applications; the future will perhaps show that it is not the most important one. (Freud, 1926e, p. 248).

7. Miley Cyrus has previously been critiqued for twerking. In a satirical piece published in *The New York Times* entitled "Explaining twerking to your parents," Teddy Wayne explains that when speaking to your parents about the topic,

> [p]atiently respond that, for Ms. Cyrus, twerking is a brazenly cynical act of cultural appropriation being passed off as a rebellious reclamation of her sexuality after a childhood in the Disneyfied spotlight, but, in the end, who are we really to judge? (2015).

8. See the work of Patricia Hill Collins, Kimberlé Crenshaw, and Gloria Anzaldua, among others who consider the intersectionality of race, gender, class, and sexuality in feminist discourse.
9. In *Cultivating Humanity*, Martha Nussbaum remarks,

> Socrates saw himself as making a contribution to democracy . . . by getting people to sort out what they think they know, to test beliefs for consistency, inferences for validity . . . but at the same time they should ask themselves how well Socrates is arguing and whether his conclusions really do follow from his premises. This is the primary way in which Plato as a writer overcomes the danger of passivity inherent in the written word: by provoking the reader to logical analysis and criticism. (1997, p. 36)

Nussbaum threads a similar argument through most of her work, including *Not For Profit: Why Democracy Needs The Humanities* (2012). The model in the classroom was similar as we interrogated the many variant types of feminism that were emerging.

10. See Joyce Carol Oates' classic feminist short story, "Where are you going, where have you been?" (Showalter.)
11. Amal Kassir, PBS News Hour (2014) "Syrian-American activist Amal Kassir uses slam poetry to fuel her cause" by Mary Jo Brooks; "Sister Outsider Slam Poetry": Denice Frohman and Dominique Christina. "Standing at the intersection of art and activism, Sister Outsider uses poetry as a tool for social change, expanding conversations about identity, inclusion, race, gender and LGBTQ violence, and gender-based

violence. Inspired by the life and work of Audre Lorde, they connect deeply personal stories to a diverse range of social and political issues. They write their "otherness" into the center and encourage others, particularly those in marginalized communities, to do the same.

12. See Camden's review:

> Persephone's reconciliation to her marriage may provide a model for recovery and adjustment to traumatic history. It is not clear to me, however, that Kulish and Holtzman's use of this story captures the compelling model of female desire ascribed to it. For what does their Persephone complex really prescribe for the girl if not sexual initiation by force, unresolved dependence on a depressed and enraged mother's power and fertility, and resigned relinquishment to the father/uncle's bed as a concession to the "Name of the Father"? This constellation may indeed typify the lived experience of many girls and women seen in clinical practice, but it maps the terrain of trauma, not desire. (Camden, 2011, p. 147)

> See also Winnicott (1953).

13. In his essay "The concept of the false self", Winnicott (1986) outlines his theory of the false self, a private self divided from the "true." Winnicott suggests that divide is normal in daily life but can be the cause of a deep split or mental illness for the person.

14. I take the title of this section from the bestselling Young Adult novel by Suzanne Collins, *Catching Fire* (2009) the second installment in *The Hunger Games* series.

15. *The New York Times* published a piece in August 2015 on the research done by the Annenberg School for Communication and Journalism entitled "Report finds wide diversity gap among 2014's top grossing films." Manohla Dargis writes,

> The numbers are stunning: From 2007 through 2014, women made up only 30.2 percent of *all* speaking or named characters in the 100 top-grossing fictional films released in the United States. That's bad enough to repeat: For every 2.3 male characters who say "Dude," there is just one woman saying, "Hello?!"

Once again we witness the conspiratorial exclusion of women from Hollywood roles from actors to directors to producers to writers.

16. *The Hunger Games*, *Frozen*, and *Divergent* are regularly cited as the exceptions that prove the rule over the past few years. The only suggestion that these texts might make, considering that they are all

fictions geared toward adolescents and young adults, is that women do speak to one another before sexuality has entered or they have become entirely indoctrinated.

17. To quote Freud's famous act of reverence to the superior genius of the artist as compared to the analyst, "Before the problem of the creative artist analysis must, alas, lay down its arms" (1928b, p. 177).

18. The number of popular retellings of Elizabeth I are countless at this point. The same in recent years seems to be true of Joan of Arc, who, in recent years, has been the focus of several novels including *Joan of Arc: A Life Transfigured* by Kathryn Harrison (2014), a new biography, *Joan of Arc: A History* by Helen Castor (2014), a comic entitled *Messenger: The Legend of Joan of Arc* (Lee & Hart, 2015) and even Madonna's new album *Rebel Heart* features a song "Joan of Arc." As I write this, *Harper's Bazaar "Fall Fashion Issue"* features an image of Jessica Chastain as Joan of Arc in a series of photographs done by Carine Roitfeld and Jean-Paul Goude wherein they "transform today's icons into history's legends."

19. Previous theories of influence have identified struggles "even to the death" between authors and their predecessors, as Harold Bloom claims in *The Anxiety of Influence* (1973, p. 5). In response to Bloom, Gilbert and Gubar argue that females experience an "anxiety of authorship" (1980, p. 47). The name reflects Gilbert and Gubar's argument that the female writer is preoccupied with the fact that she can never be an authorial figure or a "precursor" (1980, p. 49). Gilbert and Gubar argue that the female writer cannot identify with her predecessors such as her male counterpart who represents history and law, or the female predecessor who is separated from literary history, thus making the female writer feel that "the act of writing will isolate or destroy her" (1980, p. 49).

20. See also heforshe.org, the website of Emma Watson's campaign where men come out in support of women's rights.

21. For the full story of Steinem's rescue of Wonder Woman in the 1970s, see the interview with her in "Wonder Women! The untold story of American superheroines", PBS 2/27/12 (Guevara-Flanagan, 2012). To commemorate Wonder Woman's 75th anniversary, a symposium to celebrate her endurance was held in September 2016 at the Cleveland Public Library in partnership with Kent State University and the Ohio Humanities Council. The website for this symposium is www.kent.edu/wonderwoman.

22. See also *Time Magazine*, "Behind Marvel's decision to create these controversial female superheroes" (Dockterman, 2015) http://time.com/4014894/marvel-female-superheroes-thor-ms-marvel/ on Sana

Amanat's influential decision to make Ms. Marvel into Kamala Khan, a Muslim teenager. Trina Robbins notes in *The Great Women Superheroes* (1996) that with the onset of the Second World War there was an emergence of powerful women superheroes in comics, including Wonder Woman, Miss Fury, and the Blonde Phantom. However, by 1955, all action heroines in comics, besides Wonder Woman (who would soon lose her powers anyway) were no longer featured in their own series.

23.   To put into perspective the popularity of this new heroine, the new *Ms. Marvel* series went into a sixth printing, which is almost unheard of in comics today. For example, just a little under a decade ago, the issue *Amazing Spider-Man* (#583), where Spider-Man saves President Obama, only went into a fifth printing. In an article entitled "It's a bird, it's a plane . . . it's Obama," (Last, 2009), *The Wall Street Journal* cited this as the best selling regular series comic book in a decade. In 2014, *Ms. Marvel's* comic went into more printings than Spider-Man and this does not include digital sales as well as graphic novels sales once the issues were collected. In 2014, the issue that premiered the new heroine Spider-Gwen, *Edge of Spider-Verse* #2, went into a fifth printing. These are only a few of the new female heroes that have appeared in the past year or two.

24.   In *Understanding Comics*, Scott McCloud suggests one of the powerful tools of the cartoonist is his or her ability to amplify through simplifying an image. He suggests that

> when we abstract an image through cartooning, we're not so much eliminating details as we are focusing on specific details. By stripping down an image to its essential "meaning" an artist can amplify that meaning in a way that realistic art can't. (1993, p. 30)

25.   I asked the students if they would permit me to reproduce or describe their work in this article, anonymously, and all agreed. I am grateful for their contribution and all that the entire class contributed to my own understanding of the new feminism.

Epilogue in action

Since writing this chapter in August 2015, the wave of "New Feminism" has continued to soar. Emma Watson, whose "HeforShe" campaign with the United Nations has since begun an online feminist book club with *Goodreads*. "I've been discovering so much that, at times, I've felt like my head was about to explode . . . I decided to start a Feminist book club, as I want to share what I'm learning and hear your thoughts too." Drawing inspiration and identification from the previous generation's activist icons, Watson chose Gloria Steinem's recent memoir, *My Life on the Road* and Alice Walker's *The Color Purple* as inaugural texts.

Hollywood likewise has hitched their wagon to the recent action heroine "stars", having released *Star Wars: the Force Awakens*, which has become the highest-grossing film of all time, with lead heroine, Rey, played by Daisy Ridley. This same drive can be seen in media: the February 2016 issue of *Teen Vogue* had a cover feature entitled "Power Girls: The New Faces of Feminism" featuring Amanda Stenberg from *Hunger Games* on the cover. And even the new *Pride and Prejudice and Zombies* movie, re-imagines Jane Austen's romantic heroines as action heroines fighting again the zombie hordes invading England.

This "active" revision of the heroine is perhaps most visible in the world of comics. The dedication to female characters, creators, and consumers underscores a cultural shift in the comics industry. Once again, this form once critiqued for its misogyny is now in the midst of a feminist renaissance. Over the past few months many of the major comics publishers have begun announcing or publishing new comics with women taking the lead, a development that is nothing less than astonishing to anyone who is familiar with the vexed history of the suppression of female comics' writers, readers and producers in the history of the genre in America. Having taken the lead, as we have already noted above, Marvel Comics continues admirably to set the pace with its new series, *Scarlet Witch*, *Patsy Walker, A.K.A. Hellcat!*, and soon a *Black Widow* series, and *Mockingbird*. Following on, DC Comics has begun the new *The Legend of Wonder Woman* series *Poison Ivy*, and an all female Justice League from the future: *Justice League 3001*. Lesser known publishers like Image comic have rushed to inaugurate the new series, *Monstress* and has seen continued success with *Bitch Planet*, which has a major online following on social media. Dynamite Entertainment, with the help of Gail Simone and Nicola Scott revamped and redesigned three of their major heroes: Red Sonja, Vampirella, and Dejah Thoris. Finally Valiant Entertainment has just begin publishing *Faith*, a series that features the first "plus-size" super-heroine, who is proudly triumphant and powerful. This series sold out before the first print even reached the comic shops. On television, the superheroine has similarly prevailed on with *Supergirl*, a new season of *Agent Carter*, and the success of the *Jessica Jones* on Netflix, which has already been renewed for a second season (Campbell, 2015). It is not just that Marvel, DC, Image, Dynamite, etc., are invested in the growing population of female readers, but they are offering valuable and powerful images of women in comics. It would appear that these extremely savvy, yet creative producers of popular culture have finally discovered that women, especially young women are half the population, and can rock the world as well as the cradle!

Gloria Steinem once said that she was rescued from the plight of passivity and victim-hood, where men could only rescue women by the appearance, in popular culture, of the most recognizable female action heroine, Wonder Woman: "I'm happy to say that I was rescued from this plight at about the age of seven or eight. Rescued (Great Hera!) by a woman" (Steinem, 2013, p. 204). Wonder Woman, whose figure, as we have seen in this chapter, exploded on to the first cover of *Ms.* magazine. It was Steinem who literally badgered DC comics to give Wonder Woman "back her powers" in 1972 so that she could foster the new generation of action heroines: that promise has surely come to fulfillment in our own contemporary moment as her heirs fill the pages, screens, and performances of popular culture.

Fighting supervillains is a cinch. Fighting misogyny is the real challenge.

References

Adichie, C. N. (2013). We should all be feminists. www.ted.com/talks.

Barry, L. (2002). *One! Hundred! Demons!*. Seattle, WA: Sasquatch Books.

Barry, L. (2014). *Syllabus: Notes From an Accidental Professor*. Montreal: Drawn and Quarterly.

Baumgardner, J., & Richards, A. (2010). *Manifesta: Young Women, Feminism, and the Future*. New York: Farrar, Straus and Giroux: Macmillan.

Bechdel, A. (2008). *The Essential Dykes To Watch Out For*. Boston, MA: Houghton Mifflin Harcourt.

Benjamin, J. (1995). Sameness and difference: toward an "overinclusive" model of gender development. *Psychoanalytic Inquiry*, 15(1): 125–142.

Bennetts, L. (2008). *The Feminine Mistake: Are We Giving Up Too Much?* New York: Hachette Books.

Bennetts, L. (2015). Sex lies and fifty shades. *Entertainment Weekly*, February 13, pp. 42–46.

Bernheimer, C., & Kahane, C. (1990). *In Dora's Case: Freud—Hysteria—Feminism*. New York: Columbia University Press.

Bloom, H. (1973). *The Anxiety of Influence*. New York: Oxford University Press.

Brooks, M. J. (2014). Syrian-American activist Amal Kassir uses slam poetry to fuel her cause [article]. Accessed at: www.pbs.org/newshour/poetry/art-blog-syrian-american-activist-amal-kassir-uses-slam-poetry-to-fuel-her-cause/

Butler, J. (1990). *Gender Trouble and the Subversion of Identity*. New York: Routledge.

Butler, J. (1993). *Bodies that Matter: On the Discourse Limits of "Sex"*. New York: Routledge.

Camden, V. J. (1992). *The Narrative of the Persecutions of Agnes Beaumont*. Ann Arbor, MI: Michigan University Press.

Camden, V. J. (2011). *A Story of Her Own: The Female Oedipus Complex Reexamined and Renamed* (review). *American Imago*, 68(1): 139–148.

Camden, V. J. (2016). Bechdel's mystic muse: a psychoanalytic allegory. In: *The Muse: Psychoanalytic Explorations of Creative Inspiration*. New York: Routledge. Print.

Campbell, J. (2015). "Erasing women: the importance of *Agent Carter* to comic culture" (January 13). Retrieved from http://www.comicbookresources.com/?page=article&id=58431

Castor, H. (2014). *Joan of Arc: A History*. London: Faber & Faber.

Chute, H. (2008). Interview with Lynda Barry. *The Believer*, 6(9): 46–58.

Chute, H. (2010). *Graphic Women: Life Narrative and Contemporary Comics.* New York: Columbia University Press.

Collins, S. (2009). *Catching Fire.* New York: Scholastic.

Couric, K. (narrator) (2015). Rise of the female superhero. *Yahoo! News.* Accessed at: www.yahoo.com/katiecouric/rise-of-the-female-super-hero-ever-since-superman-126459307033.html

Dargis, M. (2015). Report finds wide diversity gap among 2014's top grossing films. *The New York Times.* Accessed at: www.nytimes.com/2015/08/06/movies/report-finds-wide-diversity-gap-among-2014s-top-grossing-films.html

Dockterman, E. (2015). "Behind Marvel's decision to create these controversial females superheroes". *Time Magazine* (August 28). http://time.com/4014894/marvel-female-superheroes-thor-ms-marvel/

Eliot, T. S. (1975). Religion and literature. In: F. Kermode (Ed.), *Selected Prose of T. S. Eliot* (pp. 97–106). San Diego: Harcourt.

Fonda, J. (2009). Gender and destiny. *Studies in Gender and Sexuality, 10*(4), 190–194.

Freud, S. (1926e). The question of lay analysis. *S. E., 20*: 177–258. London: Hogarth.

Freud, S. (1928b). Dostoevsky and parricide. *S. E., 21*: 173–194. London: Hogarth.

Gilbert, S. M., & Gubar, S. (1980). *The Madwoman in the Attic: The Woman Writer and the Nineteenth-century Literary Imagination.* New Haven, CT: Yale University Press.

Guevara-Flanagan, K. (Director). (2012). *Wonder Women! The Untold Story of American Superheroines* [Documentary]. Canada: Phase 4 Films.

Harrison, K. (2014). *Joan of Arc: A Life Transfigured.* New York: Doubleday.

Hartman, A. (2015). *A War for the Soul of America: A History of the Culture Wars.* Chicago, IL: University of Chicago Press.

Hobson, J. (2015). Beyonce's fierce feminism [blog]. Accessed at: http://msmagazine.com/blog/2015/03/07/beyonces-fierce-feminism/

hooks, b. (2013). Dig deep: Beyond lean in [article]. Accessed at: www.thefeministwire.com/2013/10/17973/

James, E. L. (2012). *Fifty Shades of Grey.* New York: Random House.

Kapur, S. (Director). (1998). *Elizabeth* [Film]. Universal City, CA: Universal Studios.

Kapur, S. (Director). (2007). *Elizabeth: The Golden Age* [Film]. Universal City, CA: Universal Studios.

Kulish, N., & Holtzman, D. (2008). *A Story of Her Own: The Female Oedipus Complex Reexamined and Renamed.* Lanham, MD: Jason Aronson.

Lacan, J., Mitchell, J., & Rose, J. (1985). *Feminine Sexuality: Jacques Lacan and the École Freudienne*. New York: W. W. Norton.

Last, J. V. (2009). It's a bird, it's a plane . . . it's Obama. *The Wall Street Journal*. Accessed at: www.wsj.com/articles/SB124719493132621465

Lee, T., & Hart, S. (2015). *Messenger: The Legend of Joan of Arc*. Somerville, MA: Candlewick Press.

Lennox, A. (2014). 'You cannot go back': Annie Lennox on nostalgia. Interviewed in Tracy Wahl's (Producer) *Morning Edition*. Washington, DC: National Public Radio, October 21.

Lepore, J. (2014). *The Secret History of Wonder Woman*. New York: Knopf.

Littlefield, M. M., & Johnson, J. (2012). *The Neuroscientific Turn: Trans-disciplinarity in the Age of the Brain*. Ann Arbor, MI: University of Michigan Press.

Lorde (2013). Feminism is 'completely natural,' 'just part of being a girl'. Accessed at: www.huffingtonpost.com/2014/01/03/lorde-feminism-tavi-gevinson-rookie_n_4536018.html

McCloud, S. (1993). *Understanding Comics: The Invisible Art*. Northampton, MA: Kitchen Sink Press.

Munford, R., & Waters, M. (Eds.) (2013). *Feminism and Popular Culture: Investigating the Postfeminist Mystique*. New Brunswick, NJ: Rutgers University Press.

Nussbaum, M. C. (1997). *Cultivating Humanity*. Cambridge, MA: Harvard University Press.

Nussbaum, M. C. (2012). *Not for Profit: Why Democracy Needs the Humanities*. Princeton, NJ: Princeton University Press.

Oates, J. C. (1994). Where are you going, where have you been? In: E. Showalter (Ed.), *"Where Are You Going, Where Have You Been?"* (pp. 23–50). New Brunswick, NJ: Rutgers University Press.

Priya's Shakti (2014). http://www.priyashakti.com/portfolio/comic-book/

Rich, K. (2015). Miley Cyrus somehow gets *Grace and Frankie* renewed for Season 2 [article]. Accessed at: www.vanityfair.com/hollywood/2015/05/grace-and-frankie-renewed

Robbins, T. (1996). *The Great Women Superheroes*. Northampton, MA: Kitchen Sink Press.

Robbins, T. (2013). *Pretty in Ink: North American Women Cartoonists 1896–2013*. Seattle, WA: Fantagraphics.

Rose, J. (2005). *Sexuality in the Field of Vision*. New York: Verso.

Roy, J. (2015). Taylor Swift tops the 2015 maxim hot 100 [article]. Accessed at: www.maxim.com/entertainment/music/article/taylor-swift-tops-2015-maxim-hot-100

Rudnytsky, P. L. (2000). Introduction. In: P. L. Rudnytsky & A. M Gordon (Eds.), *Psychoanalyses/Feminisms* (pp. 1–10). Albany, NY: State University of New York Press.

Sister Outsider Poetry. Accessed at: www.sisteroutsiderpoetry.com

Steinem, G. (2013). "Wonder Woman". In: C. Hatfield, J. Heer, & K. Worcester (Eds.), *The Superhero Reader* (pp. 203–210). Jackson, MS: University Press of Mississippi.

Strayed, C. (2013). *Wild: From Lost to Found on the Pacific Crest Trail*. New York: Vintage.

Streitfeld, D. (2015). Ellen Pao loses Silicon Valley bias case against Kleiner Perkins [article]. Accessed at www.nytimes.com/2015/03/28/technology/ellen-pao-kleiner-perkins-case-decision.html

Tasker, Y., & Negra, D. (Eds.). (2007). *Interrogating Postfeminism: Gender and the Politics of Popular Culture*. Durham, NC: Duke University Press.

Taylor-Johnson, S. (Director) (2015). *Fifty Shades of Grey* [Film]. Universal City, CA: Universal Studios.

Tegnelia, A. (2015). *Grace and Frankie* highlights more than Jane Fonda's ageless beauty. *Huffington Post*. Accessed at: www.huffingtonpost.com/abby-tegnelia/grace-and-frankie-highlights-more-than-jane-fondas-ageless-beauty_b_7562068.html

Valentine, G., Brown, G., & Loughride, L. (2016). *Catwoman: Keeper of the Castle*. New York: DC Comics.

Vallée, J. (Director). (2014). *Wild* [Film]. Century City, CA: Fox.

Watson, E. (n.d.). Heforshe.org.

Wayne, T. (2015). Explaining twerking to your parents. Accessed at: ww.nytimes.com/2013/09/01/opinion/sunday/explaining-twerking-to-your-parents.html

Winnicott, D. W. (1953). Psychoses and child care. In: *From Pediatrics to Psychoanalysis*. New York: Routledge.

Winnicott, D. W. (1986) The concept of the false self. In: *Home is Where We Start From: Essays by a Psychoanalyst* (pp. 65–70). New York: W. W. Norton.

Woolf, V. (2005). *A Room of One's Own*. Boston, MA: Mariner Books.

Wrye, H. K. (2009). The fourth wave of feminism: psychoanalytic perspectives introductory remarks. *Studies in Gender and Sexuality*, *10*(4): 185–189.

Yousafzai, M. (2013). *I Am Malala: The Girl Who Stood Up for Education and Was Shot by the Taliban*. Boston, MA: Little, Brown.

CHAPTER FOUR

Pregnancy: a clinical and cultural experience of pregnancy in the Middle East and North America

Shabnam Shakibaie Smith

The sound of a baby's cry, what a relief! It might not seem sensible to feel relieved at hearing a baby cry, except when you are in the delivery room.

Pregnancy, although a very personal journey for a woman, is also a societal investment. Pregnancy, from the survival perspective, is by far the most important physiological phenomenon. It is a phenomenon that ensures the continuance of human race. Without successful pregnancies, the human race would be extinct. In order to maintain a thriving future for our civilization, we are invested in the health of the product of human pregnancy. Society, collectively, is dependent upon, and invested in, the result of this personal journey, the human pregnancy. And since society is invested, the approach to pregnancy is influenced by culture, politics, and, last, but not least, by science.

Advances in medicine, including genetics and obstetrics, have provided us with more ways to assess the baby's health; and also better understanding of the ways that baby's health can be compromised. There are more prenatal diagnostic tests to detect birth defects as early as possible. The majority of women are on board with these changes and even excited about them and would like to utilize these tests to their own and their unborn baby's advantage; however, as is usually the case, there is a subgroup who is unwilling or unable to utilize them, or possibly unaware of these advancements and, in one way or another, engages in a behavior that could jeopardize the unborn child's health and refuses to receive interventions. As it has become the norm for mothers to embrace these medical advancements and compliantly receive the treatments recommended to them, those who do not have the same views are pressured to follow suit and in this process the individuality of pregnant women can be forsaken. Pregnant women, as a group, are a small group relative to society at large, at any given time. Therefore, they are more likely to experience peer pressure. Also many women, in particular first time moms, do not know much about the pregnancy process and what it really entails. They are not aware that their bodies will change, seemingly with the speed of light, and they certainly are not aware of what it feels like to carry probably the most precious creation of their lives with them for the next nine months and then separate from him or her.

Pregnancy is a significant and defining moment in a woman's life. It changes her physiologically, physically, emotionally/psychologically, and socially. In psychoanalytic literature the desire to get pregnant has been viewed in different lights. Freud's view of it, that women's desire to get pregnant was the symbolic substitution of the child for the missing penis (Freud, 1940a), was rather primitive and revolved around his sexual theory of the psyche. It was postulated on insufficient studies and data on women and was based upon women's rights, status in society, and their style of behavior in society over a century ago. With growing material from analyses of women (Blos, 1980; Erikson, 1964), the original hypothesis for the women's wish to get pregnant was reformulated and modified and it was shifted to the theory of procreative urge in women, described as the essentially feminine quality of receptiveness (Deutsch, 1945). Some have hypothesized that pregnancy is a "maturational crisis" leading to "a new position not identical to that previously held" (Bibring et al., 1961). As a maturational crisis, such as what is seen during adolescence and menopause, pregnancy demonstrates an accelerated rate of change (regression, loosening of defenses, shifts in the organization of self-concept, new identifications, etc.), with the ultimate result of the physical separation from the baby. Others have highlighted the distinction between the psychic wish of becoming a mother and the wish of getting pregnant (Pines, 1982), an important concept in itself that can influence a woman's reaction to pregnancy and her behavior during that time.

Health professionals are invested in safe delivery and healthy pregnancy outcome while ensuring the health of the mother in this process. Health professional, as members of human race, have their own assembly of biases and attitudes toward pregnancy.

I remember the first time I witnessed the birth of a baby. I was a third year medical student with limited clinical experience, and my clinical responsibilities were confined to interviewing patients and to coming up with a list of possible diagnoses to be discussed, and each to be proved or disproved. That day was my first day on obstetrics–gynecology rotation and I was given permission to be present in the labor and delivery room while a woman was giving birth.

I was watching the birth process intensely from five feet away. It was a delivery that had started smoothly and had become very complicated and everyone was hard at work. They had called the senior person to be present in the room as the delivery was not going exactly the way they wanted it; it seemed that late in the process they had discovered the cord was in the wrong place and the pressure on the cord was interfering with baby's blood supply. Then, it was over, the baby was born. I watched, wide-eyed, the doctor pulling the baby out, holding him by his feet upside down. I was in awe, thinking "Wow, baby is born! But wait, why is he this color? He is supposed to be pink not blue! He is not breathing!" The silence was eerie.

There was quiet and stillness in the room for a few seconds, which seemed like an eternity. Baby was not crying! Then suddenly there was an orchestrated commotion, the doctor in charge was giving orders to the team members, everybody was doing something for the baby to breathe. The mother was lying quietly on the labor table and I think her eyes were closed: I really do not remember, I was not paying attention to her! All I was thinking about was the baby's survival. To this day I still remember the blue color on that baby's body. It is a hard image to forget. I was in a state of disbelief and desperation, thinking she carried the baby for nine months for this? And thinking, all the treating team's efforts are to end like this?

And when you realize it is not only the pregnant woman who is invested in the outcome of her pregnancy; her family, immediate community, and society at large is also invested in its outcome, as the survival of the human race depends upon it, the enormity of the moments like this strikes you and you understand why you would like to do anything in your power to prevent moments like this from happening.

The importance of pregnancy goes without saying. This journey affects the lives of women drastically and the impact on each woman varies. It is influenced by culture, socioeconomic status, and the laws and politics of where they live. The pregnancy process as a whole, its effect on women and the women's behavior in response to it, is also influenced by the unique psychological makeup of each woman (Benedek, 1959; Leifer, 1977). The behavior is usually bound within acceptable cultural and psychosocial parameters but its quality and style is mainly determined by the pregnant woman's psychological defenses before and during pregnancy, as well as past life experiences.

In some cultures, girls are deemed only good for procreation and other than reproducing and being a vessel for delivering a baby do not have any other sway in their community. In some cultures a woman is not valuable if she does not bear a son and it is only by giving her husband an heir that she can secure her status in the eyes of her husband, her family, and the larger community. In some cultures, a woman who is "barren", obediently allows her husband to marry another who could give him a child and, ideally, a son. If she cannot bear a child, she does not have a voice. Pregnancy can put a woman in power or it can bring a woman down, depending on the outcome, but one thing remains certain: that the potential to get pregnant puts women in a category of its own.

I have had the privilege of treating women in different parts of the world, from some of the most deprived to the most sophisticated and medically/technically advanced areas as part of my education in medical school, the first few years of my career as a general practitioner (GP) and now as a psychiatrist specialized in women's mental health. After graduation from medical school I decided to work in some of the most deprived areas to provide care to greatly underserved populations and refugees. I provided care to non-pregnant and pregnant women and supervised deliveries or delivered their babies myself. I have treated women who kept getting pregnant despite medical complications to prevent their husbands from marrying another woman. To them it was simple: if they are not able to get pregnant it means they are not "valuable" anymore and that would not be acceptable to their husbands and the families and, ultimately, themselves. It was extremely sad witnessing a human being putting her life in danger to maintain her status in her family and society. The thought is still bothersome, if not infuriating, that a woman thinks she loses her value once she is not able to get pregnant anymore; it seems such a narrow way of looking at a human being. I have seen women almost dying in the delivery room while having their fifteenth child in their early forties as their bodies could no longer tolerate the burden of physiological changes brought about by repeated pregnancies and deliveries back to back. It is unimaginable: the toll that it takes on the woman's body, and that they would do it willingly as it was their "duty", and the "only choice".

I have vivid memories of my conversations with women in a rural area in a Middle Eastern country. One conversation in particular, when I was painstakingly explaining to a woman with severe anemia what another pregnancy could do to her body and after having eight children maybe she would consider using contraceptives to prevent getting pregnant, at least for a while. She looked at me helpless, fear and tears present in her eyes, whispering, "Then he will marry another woman who could bring him more children". I remember the pain I felt at that time and later realized the anger. I felt rage and help-lessness, I guess as she did, that the laws of the country would allow her husband to marry another, if she were not to be suitable anymore. She would lose her place in her family and status in her society, and would have to take a step back and give the reins of the household to another woman, a younger one. She was willing to jeopardize her life as she saw no other alternative. Pregnancy was her only currency.

In the Western world, pregnancy could be empowering in a differ-ent way. There are teenagers who get pregnant before they are ready for motherhood because they will be emancipated and better able to receive federal and city assistance. Pregnancy could free them from an abusive environment, as society will step in to take care of them. Pregnancy is their currency for independence.

I have also seen many teenagers in inner cities who get pregnant before establishing their own identity in society because they have never experienced family life and hope that having children of their own would bring a sense of normalcy and completion they them-selves never experienced as a child. Pregnancy is their undoing.

On one occasion in a country in the Middle East, while I was deliv-ering the baby of a sixteen-year-old girl from an extremely impover-ished area (whose parents had married her off to a distant family member at least ten years her senior), just about when the baby's head became visible and was about to exit the birth canal, the young mother suddenly stood up, absolutely horrified, screaming, "I did not know baby came out of there! Stop it! Stop it! It hurts! I can't!" It sounds unimaginable even to me as I am writing it. No one had told her what the pregnancy entailed. No one had paid attention to her, what she knew of pregnancy, what she was feeling, or how it would feel to have a vaginal delivery, since everyone was invested in the result of her pregnancy except her. She was just a vessel to give birth. And I remember my reaction to it as if it was yesterday. I was absolutely horrified as well, for completely different reasons. All I was thinking at that time was "The baby is going to fall on the ground. Get her back on the delivery bed." I was mad at her for not letting me doing my job and for placing her baby's life in danger. There was no time to pay attention to her and understand her fear, every second counted. At that particular moment she, the mother, did not matter to me. All I cared about was to deliver her baby safely. I wanted to make sure the baby's cry would fill the room loudly.

I have seen patients who have delivered in some of the most well equipped hospitals by some of the best trained physicians and have felt that their voices were not heard and their needs were not met and only the safety and health of the baby was considered. They felt ignored and invisible. A mother who was taken to the operating room in the midst of childbirth for a Caesarean delivery instead of vaginal, as the life of her baby was in jeopardy, was very upset, despite delivering a healthy baby. She was appreciative for having a healthy baby but had felt extremely helpless and invisible throughout the process and had complex emotions about it afterwards. On the one hand, she was happy and appreciative that her child was healthy and, on the other hand, she felt very angry for reasons she could not quite understand. She recalled lying on the delivery bed, helpless, hearing the commotion caused by the fact that the baby's heartbeat was dropping dangerously and they would have to perform a Caesarean section to save the baby's life. Even though she was told about the steps that needed to be taken, after delivery she still felt very angry about what had happened. When we explored it further, she was able to recognize that, in fact, feeling helpless and powerless when her baby's life was in danger was extremely unsettling for her and she experienced her own presence as being ignored and invisible in those moments. And, at least in my experience, there are moments, however transient, that the safety of the baby overshadows everything else, even the mother.

The invisibility of the pregnant woman, the person making it all happen, occurs often. Many mothers talk about the attention their pregnancies receive and mention that they feel invisible and how the pregnancy takes over their being. Many complain that people feel free to touch their pregnant bellies and express their enthusiasm about their pregnancy, not considering that it is the body of another human being they are touching without their permission. For some months, the baby is the center of attention and the woman who is nurturing the baby and makes its life possible is forgotten as a person and is expected to take a back seat while simultaneously driving the vehicle of reproduction. Different women respond to the interpersonal changes differently, depending on their psychological makeup and past personal experiences. Sometimes, this invisibility takes an extreme form, when the woman's rights are compromised in favor of the baby. This happens in the cultural context as well as political and legal contexts.

In some cultures, women have no say in their prenatal care and they are expected to do as the doctor says. This is an example of the blurring of the boundaries between the mother and the baby's existence. It could be an indication of societal investment in the product of the pregnancy, or the societal and cultural views of women's capacity and capability. A woman who is consenting to bring a new life to this world is being treated like a fetus that has no voice yet and is in an extremely helpless and dependent state and unable to make decisions for itself. The status of the mother as an independent entity with her own rights and ability to make decisions is forgotten and blurred with that of her fetus. The "paternalistic" approach to pregnant women's medical treatment is acceptable and still practiced in many cultures. In some Western cultures, the issue of a paternalistic approach in medicine has been highlighted, discussed, and, to some degree, addressed for some time now. However, the paternalistic approach to pregnancy and pregnant women in Western cultures is mostly implied through the legal system and political maneuvers.

In some states in the USA, when a pregnant woman is jailed, or confined to a treatment facility against her will, because she is drinking alcohol excessively during pregnancy is another example of her as a human being becoming invisible, immaterial, and confused with her fetus. She, as a person, does not exist anymore and it is only the well-being of her fetus that is considered. Therefore, she can be jailed in order to protect the fetus. If it were not for her state of pregnancy, no one could have imprisoned her for drinking, as it would be unconstitutional and not the acceptable therapeutic approach. In cases like this, the law has stepped in and taken the side of the fetus against that of the mother. Consider, for example, the case of a woman who tried to kill herself while pregnant, but who lived to give birth to a daughter, named Angel, who died four days later. This woman was charged with murder and attempted "foeticide". She could spend the rest of her life in prison.

There are other situations in which the baby's wellbeing is considered more important than the mother's, when the law does not allow the mother to make decisions about her pregnancy, such as when abortion is not an option according to law.

During my medical training, I once took care of a woman who had to stay in hospital for the duration of her pregnancy as she had to take medication that could only be given in the hospital. She had three young children at home and her husband was the only breadwinner for their family, working in a full-time job. She wanted to terminate her pregnancy as she thought her family would fall apart as a result of her being in the hospital for months. It turned out that she was not allowed to do so. It was against the religious law and she was told if she terminated her pregnancy it would be considered murder and charges would be brought against her. I remember seeing her crying at nights, lying in her hospital bed alone. She was the ultimate example of being helpless, stripped of her rights to make medical decisions for herself, yet being fully competent and capable of making those decisions. And I recall how the treatment team felt sad, helpless, and frustrated by watching her suffering for months. A glaring example of when the baby's wellbeing collides with the pregnant woman's rights. I thought about her often and wondered how this situation could (or would) have an impact on her relationship with her baby—a baby who had, unwittingly, exposed this woman's life to such danger and had forced her to separate from her children and her husband.

I have also come across many mothers who are suffering through their pregnancy with a variety of psychiatric illnesses and are terribly conflicted about taking medication during their pregnancy. Many have severe symptoms due to rapid hormonal changes during pregnancy, yet are extremely reluctant to use medication to treat their symptoms. Despite rapid expansion of knowledge about psychiatric disorders in the past few decades, and growing awareness of neuro-biological processes contributing to the development of psychiatric disorders, mothers are apprehensive about taking medication during pregnancy to address their depression or anxiety because of the fear of harming the baby or due to experiencing shame about prioritizing their own needs over their babies. The medical decision-making process is always weighing the benefits *vs.* the potential harm. No one can guarantee that any medication is completely safe, but, then, what would be the alternative? Recent advances in science have also increased our understanding of the effects on babies of depression and anxiety during pregnancy. Many studies suggest that depression and anxiety of mothers during pregnancy can affect the baby negatively. Yet, it is a choice of the mother whether or not to take any medication.

Mothers do not usually think of themselves *vs.* the baby, as the law and politics often behave. Pregnancy is a time of ambiguity for a person; a time that the boundaries between a woman and her unborn child are blurred, both physiologically and psychologically. The fetus cannot survive without the mother for most of the pregnancy, and this vulnerable state for the fetus can be the reason for society stepping into the relationship between a mother and her fetus and, at times, exploiting it.

Women's rights in controlling their pregnancies have been fair game in politics. Laws are passed to limit the control of a woman over this process, such as preventing her from using her health insurance for the purposes of abortion or, in some countries, the woman does not have the right to have an abortion after a certain point in pregnancy, even though her life may be in danger, as it contradicts the religious law. It does make it seem that the woman is only a vessel during pregnancy, a vessel for safe delivery of the baby. Pregnancy is not viewed as a complicated and, at times, taxing psychological and physiological process during which a woman is considerably affected, body and soul.

It is well known that the body goes through drastic physiological changes during the miracle of pregnancy. There is a sudden surge and ongoing increase in female hormone levels, both estrogen and progesterone. In some women who are sensitive to hormones, these changes render them vulnerable to emotional dysregulation and, potentially, depression and, in severe cases, psychosis and mania. There have been cases of mothers who have hurt their babies in order to protect them, as they have lost their ability to recognize what is real and what is not. In response to their psychoses, they have taken unthinkable actions, believing they are saving their babies. Although these cases are extremely rare, they are examples of the degree of pregnancy's effect on a woman's physiological and psychological structure and how a vulnerable structure can succumb under this physiologically stressful time for the woman's body.

The care and attention a woman receives during pregnancy varies drastically and is influenced by culture, socioeconomic status, and societal norms (Faour, 1989; Farsoun et al., 1996; Gadalla et al., 1985; Vasey & Manderson, 2009). In terms of medical attention, as mentioned before, due to increased knowledge of the science of pregnancy and the availability of a multitude of prenatal diagnostic tests and of medical treatments to prevent birth complications or defects, women are poked and prodded. Some are shamed if they do not take advantage of these medical advances and some do not have access to any of these preventative measures. Some women are urged to do Yoga and take vitamins and go to spas, and some continue to work on the farms until they give birth. Once, a woman came to the hospital really late in labor; by the time she got to the hospital the baby was about to exit the birth canal and we had to deliver the baby in the emergency room rather than the labor and delivery room. I asked her, "Why did you come this late?" in a not very friendly tone. She responded, looking embarrassed, that she did not have money to get a car and had to walk a long distance to get to the hospital. In some communities, the pregnant woman does not do anything, as it could hurt the baby, especially if it is the first pregnancy. The pregnant woman is treated gently, as gently as a newborn needs to be treated. Many pregnant women talk about the kindness of strangers and pleasant smiles on the streets or subways. This is another example of societal investment.

Also, society at large feels invested in the pregnancy and care of a pregnant woman. There are many stories of pregnant women being approached by strangers asking about their habits while pregnant: a stranger commenting that they are not to smoke, or have alcoholic beverages, or run, or drink coffee, for that matter. I have witnessed horror in the eyes of many when realizing a pregnant woman is using drugs or alcohol, which, I may add, is not an unusual occurrence. What happens when a pregnant woman might jeopardize the health of her unborn child? There have been cases of the legal system taking action and trying to incarcerate a woman who would not stop drinking while pregnant. The suggestion of incarcerating a non-pregnant woman who drinks heavily would be unacceptable, but when it happens during pregnancy and it is in service of protecting the fetus, is acceptable by some.

Pregnancy, a personal journey and an exciting endeavour, has different meanings for different people in different parts of the world. It is a miraculous physiological phenomenon that ensures the continuity of our civilization and the human race. It is a societal investment while being also extremely personal. It is a state in which some approaches to it can impinge on a human's rights in order to protect a voiceless being and, since it is such a complicated and necessary process for society, can easily be exploited.

In many years of my work as a physician in different capacities, I have never experienced such intensity of relief as I have with a successful delivery, witnessing the miracle of birth.

References

Benedek, T. (1959). Parenthood as a developmental phase. *Journal of the American Psychoanalytic Association, 7*: 389–417.

Bibring, G., Grete, L., Dwyer, T. F., Huntington, D. S., & Valenstein, A. F. (1961). A study of the psychological process in pregnancy and of the earliest mother–child relationship. *Psychoanalytic Study of the Child, 16*: 9–44.

Blos, P. (1980). Modifications in the traditional psychoanalytic theory of female adolescent development. *Adolescent Psychiatry, 8*: 8–24.

Deutsch, H. (1945). *Psychology of Women, Vol. II*. New York: Grune and Stratton.

Erikson, E. H. (1964). Inner and outer space: reflection on womanhood. *Daedalus, 93*: 582–608.

Faour, M. (1989). Fertility policy and family planning in the Arab countries. *Studies in Family Planning, 20*: 254–263.

Farsoun, M., Khoury, N., & Underwood, C. (1996). *In Their Own Words: A Qualitative Study of Family Planning in Jordan*. Baltimore, MD: Johns Hopkins for Communication Programs.

Freud, S. (1940a). *An Outline of Psychoanalysis. S. E., 23*: 141–207. London: Hogarth.

Gadalla, S., McCarthy, J., & Campbell, O. (1985). How the number of living sons influence contraceptive use in Menoufia governorate. *Studies in Family Planning*, *16*(3): 164–169.

Leifer, M. (1977). Psychological changes accompanying pregnancy and motherhood. *Genetic Psychological Monographs*, *95*: 55–96.

Pines, D. (1982). The relevance of early psychic development to pregnancy and abortion. *International Journal of Psychoanalysis*, *63*: 311–319.

Vasey, K., & Manderson, L. (2009). *Cultural Dimensions of Pregnancy, Birth and Post-natal Care*. Queensland Health, Victoria Team, Social Science and Health Research Unit, School of Psychology, Psychiatry and Psychological Medicine.

CHAPTER FIVE

Women and migration: "children on the move"

Alexander D. Kalogerakis

Mass global phenomena, such as migration, are often tragic for the individual child. However, they are most often studied from the vantage point of large systems. These phenomena should also be considered from the psychoanalytic perspective. An informed developmental viewpoint can complement other ways of understanding the phenomena; conversely, psychoanalysis and allied fields can benefit from the study of children in these difficult, but not rare, conditions.

Roughly thirty-five million children are migrating or internally displaced in the world today. Increasingly, many travel unaccompanied by adults. For some, migration might lead to a better life as immigrants. For many, it is associated with one or more traumata, including separation from parents or siblings, cultural challenges, refugee status, neglect, abuse, sexual and labor slavery, with adverse impacts on education and physical and mental health. For those who remain at home while family members migrate, other challenges ensue. Girls are particularly vulnerable to some of these experiences. In this chapter, I consider:

1.   Psychoanalytic views on the impact of these external events on the internal world of a child's psychological development,

including ego development, identifications, attachment, trauma and resilience, and mourning.

2. Psychosocial data on the experience of migration, including the impact on children left behind.
3. Biological correlates of trauma and resilience.
4. Psychoanalytic ideas about interventions, including prevention.

In psychoanalysis, we often find the concept of average expectable environment (Hartmann, 1939) and its progeny to accompany descriptions of child development and pathology. Theories of child development tend to rely on the premise that basic needs of children are met and that deviations cause, or contribute to, pathology. Similarly, in adult clinical work, analysts often assume that we are working with a person whose mind/brain is reasonably intact, and this allows for the analyst–analysand pair to observe the individual variations of mind that typify the person who seeks our help, his symptoms, strengths, personal narrative, and so on. In this chapter, I will focus on some of the instances in which children have experiences that can in no way be considered average and expected, and how these experiences influence their development. Migration is such a circumstance, and overlaps with other experiences such as culture shock, immigration, trauma, refugee life, and trafficking. I shall consider these related topics from several points of view: psychoanalytic developmental theory, psychiatry, social sciences, and interventions.

We will see that these realities of twenty-first century life are not frequently engaged by psychiatry or psychoanalysis, for many reasons, including that mentioned above. Within medicine, epidemiology, trauma medicine, and pediatrics may more regularly encounter or study children of migration. In the humanities and social sciences, social work, children's rights groups, lawyers, educators, economists, sociologists, and religious groups may be more involved than psychological organizations. At the level of governments, there can be a broad—or narrow—array of relevant agencies. In the USA, the State Department, the Department of Homeland Security, the Department of Education, the Department of Justice, and others, are responsible for various pieces of the puzzle. At the United Nations, similarly, there are many overlapping entities that are interested in children on the move: the High Commissioner on Refugees, UNICEF, the United Nations Office on Drugs and Crime, the World Health Organization, to name a few.

In 1989, the United Nations produced what has become the most ratified treaty on human rights in the world, the Convention on the Rights of the Child (CRC). This treaty set out to codify a basic set of rights to be recognized and protected universally. Its articles span issues like infant mortality, education, and children and the justice system. It has very few references to mental health and child development, but they are as follows, (paraphrased from treaty legalese):
Children have the right to:

- life and to a maximum extent the right to survival and development;
- a name, national identity, and to know and be cared for by one's parents;
- not be separated from parents unless it is in the best interests of the child;
- express their views on all matters related to the child;
- freedom of thought, conscience, and religion;
- a standard of living adequate for the child's physical, mental, spiritual, moral, and social development;
- an education that should include: equality of sexes; development of the child's personality, mental and physical abilities, and talents to the maximum potential;
- rest, leisure, play, and recreation.

Other provisions require that states protect children from abuse, torture, underage employment, trafficking, recruitment as soldiers (below age fifteen), and discrimination based on migrant or refugee status, or disabilities. In addition, the CRC requires states to promote the psychological and physical recovery of child victims of any of the above situations.

Concerns about a child's individual psychology are mainly addressed in three ways in the CRC. First, it identifies the bare bones conditions that are the minimum for a child to thrive. Second, it states the goal of allowing the maximum possible positive development. Third, it recognizes that major disturbances in a child's life lead to psychological damage. These are very broad categories. How can we, as psychoanalysts, fill in the picture?

We know a good deal about normal development, and, especially, a good deal about how it can go awry. But let's begin with some ideas about what analysts and other developmentalists say about children's psychological needs.

Anna Freud, in a 1968 paper on child analysis, referred to some of the things children require from their parents to develop well. These included the parents' stable presence for the child; an undisturbed attachment to the mother, especially in infancy; the mother's tending to the infant's need to be touched and cuddled; the mother's availability as an auxiliary ego; the child's need for sufficient mental stimulation; the parents' tolerance for drive activity, that is, sexual and aggressive behaviors; parental help and modeling for impulse control. She also noted that each child needs the opposite sex parent's pride and interest in their masculine or feminine bodies and traits.

This partial list of Anna Freud's has been updated and expanded by subsequent analysts and developmentalists. Fathers' roles in child development have been described more fully (Cath, 1986; Diamond, 1998; Liebman & Abell, 2000). Mahler's separation–individuation stages have led to many elaborations of pre-oedipal development, including the importance of parental self-regulation in the rapprochement subphase for the child's development of affect tolerance and an integrated sense of self (Gilmore & Meersand, 2014). Attachment research over several decades has differentiated among several forms of early attachment, and found correlates with later behavior (Fonagy, 2001). Affect "marking" in infancy has been described as a particular interaction of key value to the developing child, contributing to the development of the child's capacity for theory of mind and mentalization (Gergely & Watson, 1996). Mother–baby interactions have been detailed at the microsecond level, detailing patterns of attunement (Beebe, 2000). Adult theorists like Brenner (1982), working from the viewpoint of structural theory, have grouped key childhood concerns into the "calamities of childhood": the loss of the object, the loss of love, castration anxiety, and superego anxiety. While these were conceived of as present in all children to varying degrees, it is readily apparent that each can be heightened given particularly adverse circumstances. How is fear of the loss of the object experienced when the object—one's parent—might actually be deported at any time? Or when a child is left behind when a parent or siblings emigrate? How are castration and bodily anxieties managed when physical abuse or hardship is a given?

This brief review of developmental needs of children, when paired with an awareness of the situations that children on the move encounter, immediately suggests the likelihood of psychological trouble. When we consider the scope of the problem, we understand that we are not speaking of rarities or medical zebras. In 2013, the UN estimated that there were 232 million people living as migrants in the world, with almost thirty-five million of them under twenty years of age. In the USA, the corresponding figures are almost forty-six million migrants, with about four million children. About 50% of migrants overall are women. Another estimated 1.2 million are trafficked yearly (UNICEF, 2012), and 300,000 child soldiers are thought to exist. Based on more recent data, reflecting the intensifying wars in the Middle East, the total number of forcibly displaced people is increasing each year (UNHCR, 2015). What cumulative psychological burden will these millions bear? What impact will this have on societies throughout the world? We can start to answer these questions by thinking about what forms the individual experiences take.

A psychoanalytic understanding of migration

When we consider the phenomenon of migration, as analysts we are most likely to think of the experience of a given individual. We know from routine clinical work that individual meaning is critical: that similar external circumstances can lead to very different internal outcomes for individuals. At the same time, it is essential to have a full picture of the external world of a patient so that we may help the patient best understand his inner experience. With children in analysis, this is recognized most readily in the practice of meeting with parents as an important adjunct to the individual work with the child. In considering migration, it is also true that there are many versions of this process, in today's world and in times past. Like the phenomenon of parents' retrospective brightening of their child's early life history, we may idealize the lives of prior generations of immigrants, while feeling that migration now is more problematic. In the USA, a nation of immigrants, immigration has increased substantially in recent decades and the topic is a matter of national debate.

Migration, for most people, in most places, and at most times, is a response to life problems in the home country. These may be economic, social, political, related to environmental disasters or warfare, or for other reasons. For most, then, there is the impression that things are not well at home and that they will not improve, and the hope that things will be better elsewhere. From the point of view of children in a family that migrates, the home situation forms the first part of their experience. Is there hunger? Are the parents able to provide adequately, and if not, how does this affect other aspects of parenting? Is the family living in a dangerous place? The idea of "pre-migration trauma" (Perez Foster, 2001) describes this phase of the experience. While Perez Foster highlights the most severe traumas, such as rape, physical violence, imprisonment, and torture, we can understand that even the less dramatic situation of poverty without hope can lead to family trauma. Depending on the age of a child in the pre-migration situation, what might be experienced? For the youngest, we would be most concerned with the functioning of the mother–child pair. When a mother is caught in difficult circumstances, can she maintain her own psyche well enough to nurture and care for her infant or toddler child? In many families, this challenge is complicated by loss of the father, either due to previous emigration or abandonment; sometimes there is also emigration of older children. If a mother has already seen her teenage child go, and their separation is complicated by unauthorized status or other factors, how might this affect the bond with the young child at home? It is not hard to imagine that unresolved mourning of an older child will burden the attachment with a younger child. Maternal emotional wellbeing, emotional control, and modulation of anxiety are always crucial to the young child still primarily engaged in dyadic, pre-oedipal relationships. When the father has gone, or is intermittently available (often the case with migrant workers), this not only encumbers the mother's efforts, but leads to the insufficient realization of key roles that fathers play as modulators of aggression, as the "second object", as the representative of the larger world outside the dyad, and as critical to gender identity development (Liebman & Abell, 2000). For an oedipal child, the role of each parent in the migration, and the frequent situation of a father leaving to find work, has particular significance. Either gender may become prematurely parentified; boys might struggle as oedipal victors, girls might have greater difficulty loosening the dyadic tie with the mother. For an older child, other challenges present themselves. Should they stay or go? Who will they be with if they stay or go? Is there a pressure on them to prematurely assume adult responsibilities? (Some of these scenarios are illustrated in the 2009 documentary, *The Other Side of Immigration*.) If a nuclear family is migrating together, how are the different wishes and needs of each child recognized and incorporated? This is seen in families in the commonplace situation of moving to a new neighborhood or city. Friends, schools, and extended family may be left behind. With migration, there might not be time to process any of the anticipated changes prior to leaving. This, in turn, can complicate mourning and other psychological tasks that lie ahead.

Increasingly, more children, including pre-adolescents, are migrating alone, especially from impoverished Central American countries to the USA (UNHCR, 2014; US Customs and Border Protection, 2014). Often, these children have endured abuse in the home or rampant violence in their community, and are particularly desperate. Here, the child might feel abandoned by the abusive or insufficiently protective parent, or conflicted and guilty, as is often true in abused children. For some, grandiose fantasies of revenge, or, alternatively, saving one's family as the adventurous hero, quickly meet the harsh conditions and long odds of migrant life. Girls are particularly vulnerable in these situations—to sexual assault, forced labor, and other manipulations and abuse. The peer group, a developmentally appropriate focus when supported by family and community, cannot sustain and protect the individual child, as peers are suffering from the same unmet needs, and lack the same skills.

Indeed, life on the move is likely to add to any trauma that precedes the migration.

Since much immigration in the USA and around the world is illegal or unauthorized, how people travel can itself be dangerous. En route to the USA by land from the south, migrants might cross desert landscapes with little or no basic resources. From Cuba, overloaded boats confront storms and other dangers; this is increasingly true in the Mediterranean North Africa to Europe route as well. Migration is even more dangerous in active war zones, such as in Syria and neighboring countries. In "south–south" migration, that is, from one developing nation to another, resources are scarce and armed violence is common. In many places, profiteers prey on the desperation of those on the move. For children with a parent, they might experience the parent as helpless in the face of physical or geographic obstacles, or a victim of those adults who are ostensibly helping the family get to their destination. This directly undercuts the parental functions of providing safety and protection. If a parent is compromised along the way, this leaves children even more vulnerable. For the child migrating alone, the challenge of who to trust can become a constant worry; the child must depend on the paid strangers—often called "coyotes"—to get across the border safely. The potential for trauma does not end across the border. There is a wide range of experience for those apprehended by border patrols, depending on the approach and resources of the host country. Children, with or without their parents, may be held in detention facilities that do not meet their basic physical needs, much less their psychological needs. Interviews and other border procedures may themselves be traumatizing. For those who remain in the new country, a new host of challenges begin, challenges that can span generations.

Akhtar (1995) described a number of the variables that will affect the psychological experience of the immigrant. These include the degree of choice in one's leaving; the expectation of temporary or permanent status; the ability to visit the old country or not; the degree of cultural change from the old to the new; the sense of either moving away from trouble or moving toward possibilities; the welcoming—or not—attitude of the new country: all these play important roles. The last mentioned is particularly important in the undocumented immigrants, where the individuals exist in a legal no-man's-land. This has a major impact on every aspect of life.

Most often, children do not make the decision to migrate, and a child's understanding of why the migration occurred is often limited or distorted. This, in turn, can affect the adaptation and mourning processes.

> John was five when his family left their home city. The parents' main motivation was economic. The migration itself was relatively painless, and the family was able to enter the new culture with some degree of adaptive success. However, John believed that they had left their old home because of an infestation in the home—something that held a kernel of truth but was irrelevant to their departure. He thought this meant they could never return to the home country, and was anxious that something similar would force them to leave their new home.

The complexity of the family situation of many immigrants is worth highlighting. Children often end up with some members of the nuclear or extended family and not others.

Maria was ten when she immigrated to the USA, sent to stay with an older cousin and her husband, while her parents remained in the home country. When she was twelve, her cousin's husband seduced her, beginning a sexual relationship that lasted several years. Her parents remained unaware and the cousin did not protect her. She sought analysis years later to address chronic difficulties with intimate relationships. As an adult, Maria struggled to reconcile her rage at being abused with her childlike feelings of specialness and protection that she experienced as part of the abusive relationship in the unfamiliar environment.

These two vignettes demonstrate some of the range of post-migration experiences. In the first, the boy's efforts to manage the transition expresses itself in a fantasy that does not fully solve his difficulty even as the outward appearance of the family's move and adaptation were non-traumatic. The traumatic trigger to the fantasy is located in the old home, tied to feelings of loss and an inability to return; the symptoms occur in the new home.

For Maria, a trauma related to the post-migration phase is initially overlooked and hidden but remains as a potent shaper of her object relationships decades later. This example also illustrates several related vulnerabilities for girls. First, there is the risk of seduction or forced sexual activity. Second, there is the ego vulnerability typical of many adolescent girls, with reduced self-esteem and increased sensitivity to the perception of others, often related to expectations of femininity (Brown & Gilligan, 1992; Keefer & Reene, 2002). Finally, there is the intensification of superego pressure in the face of puberty and the resurgence of oedipal desires, often leading to unmanageable and persistent guilt.

One of the classic analytic papers on immigration is Garza-Guerrero's (1974) description of culture shock. The author noted that he was drawing upon migration situations that were mainly voluntary and not crisis-driven; usually, the home being left *did* provide an average expectable environment. Despite this, his model considers the encounter with a new culture to be a violent shock that severely threatens the psychic organization and the identity of the immigrant. He conceptualized mourning and identity processes as central to the culture shock experience. His use of "shock" and similar affectively charged words is notable. I think the idea of shock can encompass several aspects of the process: the sense of surprise at the reality of the new culture, as distinct from prior available·information and fantasies that might have developed; the sense of disturbance that the immigrant feels, which may be proportional to the degree of differences from the home culture, but also an analogue to a physical jolt to the body; and the high intensity of these factors. For Garza-Guerrero, the most pertinent analogy is to the death or loss of a loved one, and, hence, the focus on mourning. This initiation of mourning is an internal response with a range of manifestations, including idealization of the old culture, a heightened sense of loyalty or identification with aspects of the old culture, a resistance and criticism of the new culture, or, alternatively, a rapid but skin-deep immersion in the new culture with denigration of the old. These early reactions then may play out over time in varied ways. As in other forms of mourning, a psychic reorganization is set in motion. The quality of internalized object relations and ego identity is key to the achievement of successful mourning. If the immigrant can successfully revive past good internalized object ties to maintain aspects of identifications with the old culture and, at the same time, develop a more realistic view of both cultures, then new identifications—with new objects and the new culture—can occur in a way that fosters individual growth. In less favorable circumstances, pathological mourning and difficult acculturation prevail. Here, the existing psychic structure cannot cope with the new challenges so that temporary coping states noted above may persist, without successful integration, adaptation, and new identifications. In Bowlby's (1960) terms, rather than grief, protest, and detachment leading to new attachments, the person remains stuck in some part of the mourning sequence.

Grinberg and Grinberg (1984) also explored the vicissitudes of the adult immigrant experience from an analytic viewpoint. They likened certain aspects of normal development to other "migrations", for example, the move from dyadic to triadic oedipal relationships, the move in latency to school and peer relationships, and the move away from parents typical of adolescence. Following this metaphor, they consider the immigrant experience to proceed in stages, beginning with the reason for leaving. They distinguish voluntary from forced migration, paralleled by attitudes of hoping for something new and desirable *vs.* escaping something painful. They note the pain of leaving the familiar objects and depressive anxiety that can ensue; the sense that lost people and places cannot be recovered or managed without, as in separation anxiety, guilt about leaving, and, sometimes, the response of manic idealization of the new at the expense of the old. In the new home, confusion and persecutory anxiety might develop. Regression in the face of anxiety can take various forms, including a reluctance to participate in the new culture, staying as close as possible to people, food, language, and customs of the old. They note that the "nonhuman environment" of the old home can take on major emotional significance and symbolic meaning, while often expressed in concrete ways—the need for keepsakes and other belongings of the former life. This also reflects a special component of mourning in immigrants—mourning lost parts of the self. They describe three ego strengths as most important to successful adaptation to the new environment: the capacity to tolerate change and loss, the capacity to be alone, and the capacity to be patient. In children, these functions begin as shared ego capacities with parents, and through processes of identification and cognitive development, gradually become more internalized. Without an adult to successfully model and share their ego functions in this way, the child is less likely to master the challenges that are part of acculturation.

Ainslie and colleagues (2013) extended some of these ideas, particularly recognizing the impact of the sensory characteristics of the old world; how these sights, smells, tastes, and rhythms shape the self; that the feeling of dislocation is inevitable; that these losses represent a "cultural mourning". From a self-psychology perspective, this is described as a disruption of the continuity of the self-experience. A special instance of this has to do with language. If the immigrant must learn a new language, this is often experienced as another loss—the loss of facility and depth of expression. Here, children have a significant advantage over adults—the younger the child, the more adept they will be in the new language. Regarding modern technologies, these contemporary authors noted that with the tremendous increase in internet communication such as Skype, it is often possible to remain more connected to the old country than in prior times.

Bonovitz (2004) is one of the few psychoanalytic writers to address child development in the immigrant setting. She presented a handful of clinical vignettes of young children at different developmental stages. In each instance, her focus is on the availability of the parents to the child to help negotiate a particular developmental challenge, especially separation–individuation and the oedipal dilemma. The parents' abilities to do so, in turn, are affected not only by their own

psychological makeup, but also by the circumstances of their migration and post-migration setting. Variables such as cultural differences
in the expectations of communal *vs.* independent living, availability of
help from the extended family, depression in a parent, parents' new
work responsibilities, and ease of school and social integration all
affect the children's success. These observations, in a clinical sample
of mainly middle-class immigrants, are similar to much of the larger-
scale survey data reviewed below, which often involve children from
much more impoverished backgrounds. This closer clinical focus,
however, does allow for more refined considerations, such as the
particular need of a child in the rapprochement subphase for help
with management of aggression.

Mann (2004), a child analyst, examined the specific situation of
adolescents who immigrated with their parents at a young age or
were born in the USA shortly after their parents arrived. She suggested that immigrant parents, because of their own struggles with
identity, are less available to assist their adolescent children with
impulse control and other facets of ego development, including the
development of the adolescents' own identity. Comparing the adolescent second individuation to a migration away from the parents,
her clinical material shows how this is complicated by the parents'
ambivalence about their own cultural identity. From the parents' point
of view, the adolescent's move away from them and their culture may
be doubly threatening. Depending on how this is handled, the adolescent might have less support in navigating this process of separating
while also continuing to identify with aspects of the parents. One
specific example of this would be if the immigrant parents limit their
adolescent's ability to affiliate with their peers because of concerns
about negative aspects of the new culture. While this tension is typical of all adolescent–parent relationships, it can become more rigid
and intense when it evokes parental anxiety about their own losses of
culture, home, etc. From the adolescent's side, if the old culture
becomes too closely associated with the parents and entangled in the
"object removal" (Katan, 1951) task of adolescent development, it
makes selective positive identifications with the old culture less available for the developing identity of the adolescent.

Anagnostopoulos and colleages (2006) presented two adolescent
cases that illustrate the difficulty of identity formation in adolescence
for immigrant teenagers. Both cases are of young male ethnic Greeks

who had been forced to leave neighboring countries to repatriate to Greece. Thus, they were ethnic minorities in the old country, but in Greece were part of the dominant culture. Despite this, they were seen as immigrants and marginalized in a variety of ways. The psychological effects of this were multiple. The new home, Greece, became a place of disillusionment; the would-be welcoming motherland was not. The old home was idealized, and yearned for, but, due to political realities, could not be returned to. The parents, struggling in the new country, were seen as ineffectual or worse. For adolescents to individuate optimally, parents must be experienced as able to withstand the attacks of the next generation; parental fragility creates what can be intolerable anxiety for the teenager. In one of the cases, the boy experienced the new home as the castrating father revived from the oedipal phase; his defensive responses included acting out and projection, leading the therapist to feel helpless. The other young man blamed his parents for their forced expulsion (which probably saved all their lives) and his solution was to be as depressed and incompetent as he imagined they were. In both instances, psychoanalytic therapy with attention to development, ego function, and object relations, as well as the specific life circumstances, allowed the adolescents to resume healthy development, in particular, identity consolidation.

One of the ways we can try to understand the psychology of migration is through the lens of trauma and resilience. While the migration experience of children and families varies, it often includes a range of traumatic exposures, whether acute or chronic. Levy and Lemma (2004) have proposed a psychoanalytic view of trauma that emphasizes attachment, mourning, and related changes in ego functioning and identifications. They consider trauma to be an attack on attachment. It causes a breakdown in the capacity to mourn, and often is characterized by identifications with the person or thing that caused the trauma. Narrative meaning is interfered with and the use of symbolic language and thinking compromised. The ability to distinguish signal anxiety from actual danger is weakened, and the capacity to mentalize suffers. Rather than the resolution of feelings about the lost object in normal mourning, the ambivalently held object is clung to, associated with powerful affects such as hatred and guilt. Sometimes, identifications with the trauma-inducing object, like Anna Freud's identification with the aggressor, becomes a dominant and rigid part of the personality.

Resilience may be defined as the capacity of a person or a system to withstand or recover from situations that threaten its function. In a classic study, Anthony (1987) considered the relation between risk, vulnerability, and resilience. Anthony noted a number of ego functions that typify resilient individuals. These include activity rather than passivity, humor, readiness to take risks, developmental competence, and confidence and optimism. He described a particular nine-year-old girl who, despite tragic home circumstances, was able to muster enough tolerance to focus on a better future of her own making; in her words (p. 46) "good things can come out of bad things". He suggested that one among many factors that can facilitate this resilience is a strong early bond with the mother. Another finding relates to the experience of adversity; in some individuals, adversity facilitates adaptation and growth. This might explain the effect, found in some studies described in the following section, of a "protective" mental health benefit for immigrants.

Fonagy and colleagues (1994), in their study of resilience, noted a number of characteristics of resilient children: higher SES, younger age at the time of trauma, absence of early separation or losses, easy temperament. Finding these already established correlations not practically useful, they set out to find more specific and measurable psychological factors at work. They used instruments of attachment research—the strange situation and the Adult Attachment Interview—to see if the expectant parents' type of attachment would predict their infants' style of attachment after birth. It did: adults who were dismissive of close relationships or unhappily entangled with their own early objects were more likely to have children who, at twelve and eighteen months, had poorer attachments. They theorized that this transgenerational transmission was mediated by self-reflective functioning and the ability to know and distinguish another's mind: "Thus we see the parent's reflective-self function as having the potential to prevent negative experiences from her past influencing her relationship with the child" (p. 250). This kind of work offers some understanding of psychological mechanisms underlying the crucial early bond with the mother that Anthony and others highlighted. While Fonagy and collaborators studied attachment style and history in the parents, we can also expect that poor self-reflective function would also limit a parent's ability to protect a child from current life stressors that might be overwhelming, such as those encountered in many migrating families.

Mourning in children

Joshua, age eight, lost his father at age three. In school and in community activities, he seemed unable to control his anger and aggression,
particularly when engaged in sports. While his memory of his father was
hazy, he had made a partial identification with something he knew about
his father: his intense interest in certain sports. Lacking his father's presence, he had limited success in modulating aggression through his toddler
and early latency years. He had not yet internalized a fully integrated male
role model.

We have seen that the process of mourning is highlighted by many
psychoanalytically informed studies of migration. I would like briefly
to consider specific aspects of mourning in children, starting with a
question that has been discussed in the literature for decades: can children mourn? In order to answer that it is necessary to define the term.
Most analysts refer to Freud's classic paper, "Mourning and melancholia" (1917e), in which he defines mourning as a withdrawal of
all libidinal energy from a lost object. This work of mourning is done
piecemeal over some time; at its conclusion, the ego is free to reinvest
its libidinal energy. This classic statement has been revised and
expanded subsequently (e.g., Hagman, 1995; Pollock, 1961). Particularly suspect are the absolute qualities of Freud's description: that *all*
cathexis is withdrawn, that the ego becomes "free and uninhibited".
In line with early analytic theory, many child analysts felt that children could not mourn (see Menes, 1971), not until the normal decathexis of parents occurs in adolescence. This view can be supported by
various observations in children not often seen in adults: for example,
some children might not believe the lost parent is gone forever, or
could create an imaginary companion from the lost object. However,
if we follow the developmental model of ego functioning in general,
that is, that ego functions develop over time with progressive movement toward full adult function, we might allow for gradations of
mourning processes as well. Garber (2008) presented case material
that illustrates this viewpoint; a young woman, seen from early
adolescence intermittently over twelve years, explored her reaction to
the sudden death of her father when she was eight. The early years of
this work include typical reactions of children to such loss: denial,
isolation of affect, idealization, and introjection. It was only over time,

with the growth of her ego capacities, that she came to a more realistic appraisal of her father, and also of her mother, who, for her own reasons, had supported the patient's idealizing defense. The author argues that mourning can occur at all ages, but only to the extent that is developmentally possible. In a sense, he takes Freud's idea of "piecemeal" decathexis and extends it over a much longer time frame to accommodate the capacities of children. For our purposes, it is fair to say that all psychoanalytic considerations of mourning in children recognize that processes *related to mourning* occur at all ages and that the outcome of these processes has considerable developmental significance.

Psychosocial studies

Suarez-Oroszco and collaborators (2011) brought together much data about child immigrants in the USA in recent years. They noted that while about one million children themselves are unauthorized, another 4.5 million are citizens by virtue of being born in the USA, but their parents and older siblings are unauthorized. This mixed status contributes to the sense of impermanence, with the possibility of deportation, or limited access to standard markers of community life—school enrollment, health care, drivers' licenses, social security numbers, etc. They described the situation of "interminable liminality"—no longer belonging in the old country, but not fully belonging in the new. With children's rights in mind, we could say that this state reflects an imperfect realization of the CRC goal that each child deserves a national identity. Psychologically, it is associated with anxiety, ambivalence, fear, loyalty conflicts, difficulties with identity development, and separation.

Much of the psychosocial research on young immigrants does not distinguish by gender. However, a handful of investigators have tried to parse girls' distinct experiences. Khanlou and Crawford (2006) studied adolescent girls who immigrated to Canada. They emphasized the importance of self-esteem to overall resilience and health. As noted earlier (p. 99), female teens in general report lower self-esteem than boys. The researchers used group discussions, interviews, and various written instruments to assess self-esteem in newcomer female immigrants, most of whom were non-Caucasians; some were refugees.

Newcomer females felt they were more restricted by their families than immigrant boys were, and more likely expected to be involved in housework or child care of siblings. These expectations also brought them into some conflict with their native Canadian female peers who were also seen as less restricted. Immigrant boys were seen as more confident. Girls' efforts to adapt to the new culture included Anglicizing first names and adapting to local fashions; impediments included race and, especially, the language barrier.

Goodenow and Espin (1993) interviewed a number of immigrant adolescent females to explore gender-specific issues with identity formation and immigration. The teenage girls, all from Latin America, but varied countries and situations, had some similar experiences. These included some degree of rejection by their new American peers, a perception that friendships were shallower than in their home countries, and a view that American girls tended to be insincere and not respectable in their relationships with boys. The immigrant girls also saw themselves as closer to their mothers than their native born peers, though their life goals were more closely aligned with American young women than with their peers in their country of origin. To varying degrees, a state of tension existed between the girls' move to acculturate and integrate a new identity with the pull to maintain the identity of the family's origins. This was particularly so in relation to the nature of sex roles for girls in the two cultures.

Altinyelken (2009) studied girls who had migrated internally in Turkey, with a focus on self-esteem. These teenagers and young women faced ethnic, cultural, and language changes when they moved from rural eastern Turkey to the suburban west. The study found that their self-esteem was lower than both their local peers and their peers who stayed in the original areas. A number of girls voiced a longer-term psychological effect: that what began as feeling looked down upon by their new peers eventually was internalized as low self-regard. This untoward outcome seemed likelier when the girls' parents suffered from low self-esteem.

While we consider the impact on individual psychology and development, it is also important to understand broader data related to risk and psychiatric illness. Cantor-Graae and Pedersen (2013) examined psychopathology rates among immigrants in Denmark. Using the remarkable Danish Civil Registration System, they were able to look at large numbers of first- and second-generation immigrants, native Danes, and expatriate Danes. They found that there were increased risks for schizophrenia or other psychiatric disorders in all immigrant groups except people born abroad to Danish expatriates. Interestingly, there was an inter-group difference between those individuals with two foreign-born parents and those with one foreign-born parent. In the former, schizophrenic spectrum risk was increased but all other psychiatric risk rates were decreased. In the group with one foreign-born parent and one native Dane, all psychiatric disorders were increased. The authors are not certain how to explain this finding. Given the significance of identity conflict in the immigrant experience, I would wonder if the dual cultural background in those families complicated the children's acculturation and contributed to increased psychiatric vulnerability.

Patino and colleagues (2005) found a link between the development of psychotic symptoms in immigrant children and family dysfunction. In their study of thousands of children aged six and older in the Netherlands, they found that most of the increased risk of psychotic disorders was attributable to situations which also included family stressors. These were defined as:

> poor relationship between adults in the household; lack of warmth between parents and child; overt disturbance of father–child relationship; overt disturbance of mother–child relationship; overt disturbance of sibling–child relationship; parental overprotection; and child abuse. (p. 442)

While these seem to reflect commonsense factors related to normal or neurotic development, the correlation with psychotic states is notable.

The phenomenon of children migrating without parents is not limited to the USA. Vervliet and collaborators (2014) undertook a study of unaccompanied minors arriving in Belgium. They interviewed youth in the first or second week in the country and then again at six and eighteen months. They found high scores on anxiety, depressive, and PTSD symptoms that correlated with the degree of traumatic experiences as well as ongoing daily stressors. Girls reported more intrusive PTSD symptoms than boys. The level of symptoms did not decrease over the eighteen-month period, suggesting persistence of initial reactions as well as ongoing difficulties in the new country contributing to symptoms.

As noted earlier, migration can also lead to growth and success. Some studies (Grant et al., 2004; Salas-Wright et al., 2014) have found protective effects of immigrant status, particularly with mood and personality disorders. Salas-Wright and colleagues (2014), examining immigrants from all global regions to the USA, found that first generation immigrants had a more robust protective effect than second generation immigrants, and that these lower rates of psychopathology were stronger in ethnic/racial minority immigrants than in non-minority immigrants.

Perez Foster (2005) highlighted some of the problems in assessing post-migration mental health in general. Immigrants with uncertain legal status strive for invisibility, due to the fear of mistreatment or deportation. This makes them less likely to seek health care except in emergency situations. Practitioners, in turn, may be ill equipped to handle the socio-cultural aspects of immigrant families' lives, and even larger facilities might struggle with providing services in the migrants' native language. I would add that, as psychoanalysts or other clinicians whose main concern is the welfare of the individual patient, we might be less prone to think about important social contexts and how these have an impact on the individual.

Children left behind

When a parent migrates and a child is left behind, much may change for that child. In this section, I review the psychosocial data on this phenomenon. Some of the important considerations include: is one or both parents migrating? Is the migration seasonal or more prolonged? Who remains to care for the child? How invested in the child are the new caretakers? How many other children remain, and of what ages?

There is little in the way of psychoanalytically informed writing on this subject. Home countries are often lacking in basic services, including mental health infrastructure. Much of the data is more in the nature of survey studies. However, Perez Foster (2005) presented case vignettes that include children left behind. The situation that a child remains in may vary from adequate to traumatizing. One boy, left with a grandmother in Haiti, lived for years in terror of battles between insurgents and police, and beatings and disappearances of local citizens. When he joined his mother in the USA, he became symptomatic and came to treatment. An important part of the work was helping the mother to understand her son's traumatic experiences that occurred while they were separated. In another case, a teenage girl immigrant struggled with sequelae of traumas that preceded her migration—being sexually "given" to an older man in return for his help to her family. As in the first case, the retelling of the prior traumas became a starting point for further psychodynamic work to allow for healthy growth and a more integrated acculturation.

An often-overlooked type of migration is internal displacement: it occurs within different regions, and usually subcultures, of one country. Su and colleagues (2013) studied children left behind when parents move within China to urban areas for work. Their study found that children whose parents (one or both) left to work were more lonely than controls, and that those who had both parents leave had lower life satisfaction scores. Children who had more frequent communication with parents who were away were happier than those who had less. This finding suggests a quantification of Ainslie and collaborators' observation that new technology can mitigate some of the disruption and separation due to migration.

Marchetti-Mercer (2012) studied those left behind by emigrating family or friends in South Africa, using semi-structured interviews. She noted that some authors have theorized that the task of mourning in those who leave can also occur in those who remain behind. In her findings, those adults across the age range who had friends who emigrated experienced a range of emotions, including anger, abandonment, and loss, with some describing it like a death.

Kandel and Kao (2000) found that family members' migration to the USA increased children's desire to study in the USA, thus having a generally positive effect on their aspirations.

Rossi (2008, 2009) took a broad psychosocial look at the impact of migration on children, particularly those left behind. One of the practical aspects that is considered in this type of assessment is the impact of money sent home, known as remittances. This is important, as the additional funds can often facilitate a child's general health, nutrition, and education. However, there are complex factors that can have an impact on this, and the effect of remittances is not always an overall benefit to children. In Mexico, there is some evidence that girls benefit more than boys, as measured by years of schooling completed. There is also data suggesting that when mothers remain as head of the household with the children, they are more likely to use these funds to directly benefit their children; fathers tend to spend additional monies on other priorities like farming equipment or other work-related expenses.

Antman (2012) discussed another variable related to children left behind. Some studies show that children who have a migrant parent develop higher aspirations for themselves, including educational achievement. For example, Kandel and Kao (2000) found that family members' migration to the USA increased children's desire to emigrate so that they could study in the USA. However, as with the impact of remittances, this effect is not robust and depends on many more detailed and individual factors.

Psychobiology of trauma and resilience

As we have seen, the range of childhood adverse experiences related to migration is substantial. Often, they are frankly traumatic. While detailed psychological study of migrant children is in the early stages, the study of traumatized children is more fully developed. In this section, I review some of the neurobiology of trauma and resilience in children, as well as selected psychological studies.

There are a number of ways that the brain is affected by psychological trauma. Young brains are especially susceptible to insult, and plasticity decreases over time. Stress and trauma can predispose to development of anxiety, mood disorders, dissociation, conduct disorder, and executive function problems, similar to attention deficit hyperactivity disorder; and PTSD (Glaser, 2014; Weber & Reynolds, 2004). The two major types of early disturbance that have been studied are neglect and trauma. In the former, a child does not receive sufficient stimulation for optimal growth; in the latter, there is over-stimulation of a noxious type that overwhelms the child and produces severe or prolonged stress responses. Either may occur in the migration experience; both have specific brain consequences. Several comprehensive reviews (Nemeroff, 2004; Perry, 2008; Teicher et al., 2002; Weber & Reynolds, 2004) inform the following summary.

As the young mind grows, the young brain matures. The major elements of early brain development postnatally include neuronal migration and differentiation, dendritic arborization, synaptic growth, and sculpting. All of these are active in the first year of life, some continuing well beyond. Myelination also begins in the first year, but has an important phase of rapid growth in adolescence and is not completed until young adulthood. The healthy unfolding of neural networks becomes increasingly dependent on the experience of the person. For instance, early maternal separation, loss, or neglect has biological effects in animal models and humans. These effects, in turn, can have impacts on language, attachment, and social development. Athough less well defined than in animal models, there appear to be sensitive or critical periods in these areas, so that if proper stimulation is not available (or adverse experience occurs) at a particular time, prolonged deficits may ensue. The clearest example of this in humans is prenatal alcohol exposure, which has deleterious permanent effects on the brain, but the model is the same throughout maturation. Adults abused as children might show changes in the size or morphology of the hippocampus and amygdala. Teicher and colleagues (2004) found corpus callosum size reduced in boys and girls who had been abused or neglected. Young children raised in substandard orphanages later show IQs below average—and the longer the time spent institutional-ized, the greater the deficit. This latter finding illustrates a key issue: that often the persistence of stressful conditions is a determinant of future pathology. If the "dose" of stress is low, the neurobiology might not be derailed; however, sustained trauma is more likely to turn fear, for example, into chronic anxiety.

The impact of stress on the developing brain occurs in multiple brain systems, notably the cortisol system, including the HPA axis, the sympathetic nervous system, and the vasopressin–oxytocin system. Environmental stress creates a cascade of neurobiological changes. Early activation of the stress response system can affect the growth and organization of the brain; these effects include changes at the molecular level, myelination, and synaptic connections. Differ-ent brain regions may be affected depending on underlying genetics, gender, and timing. Types of measurable outcomes include morpho-logical—such as decreased left hemisphere development, electrical (EEG), for example, changes in limbic circuits, and hormonal—for example, sustained changes in the functioning of the cortisol sys-tem. The latter has been particularly well studied with alterations in corticotrophin releasing hormone (CRH) and corticotrophin releasing factor (CRF) related to postnatal stress and early adverse experiences. These changes translate to affects, symptoms, and behavioral states.

An exciting, recently emerging field of study related to human behavior is epigenetics. In biology, this refers to molecular factors affecting gene expression rather than effects due to gene sequence. Genes are turned on and off, and there is increasing data about how these epigenetic phenomena are related to life experience (National Scientific Council on the Developing Child, 2010). Much of the examination of these gene-experience interactions uses animal models. Some key areas of investigation at the cellular level are the methylation of DNA and fluctuation of nuclear histones, both of which modulate transcription of DNA and, therefore, expression of the genetic code. One study in humans (Oberlander et al., 2008) looked at the effect of maternal depression during pregnancy on methylation of a gene related to the HPA axis in the infants. Their data showed that maternal depression led to increased methylation at birth. They then measured salivary cortisol stress responses at three months of age—and found an increase in these infants. This suggests that the pregnant mother's mood state has a quantifiable effect, seen at a molecular level, on an infant's capacity to respond to stress months later. Another study (McGowan et al., 2009) looked at post mortem brains of adult suicide completers who had been abused as children and found evidence of epigenetic modulation of the same HPA cortisol system. While this kind of research in children is in its infancy, the potential for understanding some of the biological mechanisms of observable clinical and developmental phenomena is promising.

At the intersection of trauma research and migration lie the phenomena of refugees and child soldiers. Drury and Williams (2012) reviewed a range of studies of children and youth affected by mass conflict, including refugees and victims of violence, as well as child soldiers. The severity of violence and traumatic events correlates with a range of psychological symptoms, including PTSD and depression. Both maternal loss and paternal loss are predictors for increased distress in children. Poor parental mental health also increases risk for children. Unaccompanied girl refugees fare more poorly than boys. For all refugee children, protective factors include stable settlement, parental support, peer support, and successful school placement. Child soldiers suffer in additional ways. These youngsters—mostly ten and older, mostly male—have often suffered major losses before becoming child soldiers, for example, loss of home or family members. Their time as soldiers can be thought of as a period of captivity. They are often both witnesses *and* perpetrators of intense brutality and violence. In a range of studies, it appears that both victim/witness experiences and perpetrator experiences predict later psychopathology, though the latter has a stronger association. Also important to these children's long-term adaptation was the nature of their community reintegration after their time as a soldier. In many instances, hostility and stigma complicated their return to society; this seemed even more so for girl soldiers. These authors caution that the tendency to focus on PTSD as a syndrome in these children is problematic; many children report symptoms but do not meet diagnostic criteria, or have other psychological symptoms. They note that factors associated with resilience include a range of what we would call ego functions: problem-solving, emotional regulation, avoidance, and cognitive restructuring. They note that many of the findings reported with children in war situations are similar to those who are victims of natural disasters.

The neurobiologists have also been studying resilience. Most of this work is in animal models, and centers on some of the properties discussed above: brain plasticity, epigenetics, neural networks' growth and change, and feedback loops like the HPA system which modulate stress response. There is some promising data: for instance, in rats, disruption to cortical structures related to vision in early life was reversible later under certain conditions (Karatsoreos & McEwen, 2013). The notion that one can demonstrate that brain circuits that have gone awry can be reshaped much later is, in one sense, breathtaking science; in another, given our understanding of the capacity for character change, or reworking of long-standing internalized object relations, not surprising at all.

Interventions

Miguel, a foreign student, came for a consultation due to conflicts about where to live after his studies were completed, his ambivalent attachment to a local young woman, and his guilt about his distance from his parents, who remained in his country of origin in increasingly dangerous circumstances. Miguel had selected me among several analysts because he thought that my (Greek) cultural background, though different from his, would permit me to "know" what he had left behind, and that I would share his criticism of American culture. This fantasy was a subset of a larger set of fantasies that involved idealization of the time and place of his childhood and a parallel denigration of American society.

This vignette alerts us to the complexities that exist when treating children and families on the move. Even under relatively favorable, non-traumatic circumstances, powerful affects and fantasies about the old and new cultures may influence the individual's capacity for the formation of a therapeutic alliance and the nature of the transference.

Although the difficulties and needs of children who migrate are attracting greater investigation and concern, in the area of interventions, much remains unexplored. Even in the broader area of trauma not necessarily associated with migration, we know less than we would wish. In this section, I discuss interventions informed by psychoanalytic and related ideas.

Markese (2011) reviewed the impact of trauma in early childhood, from the point of view of developmental and, especially, attachment theory and research, and with an eye toward intervention. She noted the tendency of parents to underestimate the impact of shared family trauma on young children. Children who have suffered a traumatic loss are likely to feel depressed, have sleep and conduct problems, and have greater difficulty with separation. These responses have been conceptualized in two different neurobiological patterns: hyper-arousal and dissociation (see also Perry, 2008). The former is reflected in oppositional or defiant behavior, the latter in emotional withdrawal or lack of feeling. Each may be misconstrued and the relation to the trauma overlooked. Another brain model of infant trauma involves right brain effects. These are thought to influence affect modulation, regulation of interpersonal states, and development of self-concept, with the potential to change developmental trajectories and increased risk for psychopathology.

In the case of parental loss, the impact on the surviving parent has a major effect on the child. Often, there is a decrease in the parent's emotional availability. The parent's own reactions, ranging from inhibition of affect to significant mood symptoms, can inhibit or distort the child's ability to adjust. Preverbal trauma can also be recalled in nonverbal ways and have an impact on attachment. Markese summarized that trauma can yield "unresolved," "preoccupied," or "dismissive" attachment representations. In favorable circumstances, healthy parental interactions are "critically important positive mediating factors in a child's recovery following trauma and loss." From this consideration of the importance of early trauma, she proposed that more use of dyadic treatment for mothers and infants is warranted.

Reviewing a wide range of literature related to mass trauma and children—including instances of forced migration—Masten and Narayan (2012) noted that evidence about intervention strategies is weak, and that two of the best known crisis interventions, stress debriefing and grief counseling, have not shown positive benefits and might actually be harmful. Their review suggests that all large-scale manualized interventions may be limited by the intricacies of developmental timing, specific cultural or situational factors, and individual variation.

One psychoanalytically informed systems effort was detailed by Osofsky (2003). This program aimed to prevent trauma and treat children traumatized in the community by working with police, providing a hotline, and offering free psychoanalytic psychotherapy. Some of the preventive effect had to do with educating the police, as the first responders, to the needs of children in traumatic circumstances; also, encouraging clinical consultation sooner rather than later had a significant impact on outcomes. Another important part of this work was the attention to countertransference and burnout in therapists working with traumatized children.

Marans, in a series of publications (e.g., 1996, 2014), has described a sophisticated and long-running collaborative program between psychoanalysts and other mental professionals and local police in New Haven, Connecticut. Clinicians and officers attend seminars on development, and clinicians ride with police as they respond to calls, all in the service of optimizing the protection of children in traumatic circumstances related to household violence, crime, poverty, etc. Seminar topics covered include developmental needs of children at different stages, typical defenses of children and adults, preconceived ideas (i.e., fantasies) about police and authority figures, and the impact of racial, socioeconomic, and cultural differences. These all contribute to sensitize police to the situations they face, help clinicians understand the demands made on the police, as well as help attune clinicians to issues faced by those children they see clinically. As noted by Osofsky, the simple effect of bringing needy youngsters and family to clinical attention sooner can be a major positive outcome of this work.

In working with another form of trauma in children, Frenkel (2004) reported on treatment at a burn unit in South Africa. As in other situations where the tragedy of the patients can be overwhelming, an important part of the effort has been to identify the stressors on the caregivers. In the unit described, the nurses and hospital had developed ways of working that, in a sense, protected the nurses from fully experiencing the horror of the individual child's situation. Nurses rotated whom they cared for, organizing their efforts by tasks rather than patients. At the same time, what was evident to the psychodynamically informed researcher was that, from the child's point of view, the most crucial need was to develop a personal bond with an individual staff member. This could be seen even in very young toddlers: for example, one who would play with the bracelets of a particular nurse. This yearning for contact was all-important, and these observations dovetail with much of what others have found regarding children in diverse difficult circumstances. In the same volume (*The Perversion of Loss*), in a study of adults who had all been abused in a specific foster group home, the authors (Hume & Kleeberg, 2004) found that the adults who had the presence of a good object even briefly in their childhood fared much better that those who did not. Another retrospective finding was that those adults who, as children, had a particular talent or skill also were more likely to adapt better as adults, and were able to make better use of psychoanalytic therapy. These recent findings echo the observations made by Anna Freud and Dorothy Burlingham (1944), who studied children in foster care after the Second World War, and noted multiple developmental problems related to the lack of a dependable mothering figure.

Concluding thoughts

We have considered the available data that bear on the experience of children who migrate. As a phenomenon, we have seen that, while widespread and increasing in many parts of the world, our understanding of the psychological effects of this process and needs of the population is incomplete. Clearly, we can say that this is a population at risk. What are the potential deleterious effects of migration on children? We can summarize the developmental, psychodynamic, and neuropsychiatric data in this way:

- disrupted attachment;
- altered neurobiological development;
- difficulty with tasks of normal ego development and object relations at multiple stages;
- pathological mourning;
- interference with healthy identifications;
- increased risk for anxiety, mood, and other psychiatric disorders;
- difficulties in identity formation;
- difficulties in acculturation.

Since none of the above is an inevitable outcome, and we know that migration can also lead to successful immigration and healthy development, how can we, as clinicians and as a society, minimize risk and promote health? What can we add to the Convention on the Rights of the Child specific to children on the move? I suggest that the data point to the following range of actions:

- Normal protective and auxiliary ego functions of parents must be supported.
- Children must have access to mental health services.
- Liminality as a social and legal reality must be minimized insofar as is possible, as it serves to interfere with optimal processes of mourning and adaptation.
- Basic needs such as food and shelter must be secure. Educational access and integration is required.
- Cultural barriers to use of mental health and social services must be minimized.
- Physicians, psychiatrists, and other mental health workers should have training (e.g., Ferrell et al., 2014) that includes awareness of clinical issues related to migration and related trauma.
- Girls are known to experience added risks, and therapeutic and societal efforts must reflect this.
- Other specific factors that affect migration experiences, such as age and language barriers, need to be recognized and studied further.

- Psychoanalytically informed interdisciplinary programs similar to that described by Marans may be developed to target areas of high immigrant density and need.
- Keeping families together, barring intrafamilial abuse or neglect, must be a priority.
- Technology should be harnessed to mitigate aspects of loss and disruption.
- Efforts to minimize especially vulnerable sub-groups—unaccompanied minors, trafficked children, child soldiers, refugees—are crucial.
- The desperate conditions in countries that produce many vulnerable emigrants must be ameliorated.

Hagman (1996) addressed the role of the "other" in the mourning process. He sought to expand on the intrapsychic processes that had been well articulated to focus on the role of important objects in facilitating healthy mourning. These tasks of the "other" include recognition of the reality of loss, putting feelings into words, facilitating and modulating the expression of affect, and provision of narcissistic and libidinal supplies. His case report is of a late adolescent whose mother dies; the father and the rest of the family do not provide the necessary supports to the patient's mourning process, which becomes pathological. This draws our clinical attention to the importance of the interpersonal context in which any individual must deal with separation, loss, and change.

I would say we are all the "other". Of course, the most significant others are those closest to the youngster—typically parents and siblings. Extended family and peer groups often play critical roles. But it may be useful to also think of how different entities can become important intrapsychic "others". The internalized version of the community and culture being left, and the new one being joined, each function as dynamic players in the mind of the child. If we imagine, based on the data presented, a sophisticated program in a receiving country that aims to foster health in the immigrant, we would say this would assist in the adaptation to reality, facilitate expression of feelings, provide emotional support, and so on. In psychoanalytic terms, welcoming and psychologically informed interactions in the new culture should provide a temporary ego support to child and family alike, maximizing the possibility that they can then use their own internal resources to face the challenges we have outlined. In this way, stakeholders from the international level to federal and local governments, to charitable organizations and communities, all can contribute to this important social goal, which is also the aim of any child analysis: the promotion and resumption of optimal development in children.

References

Ainslie, R. C., Harlem, A., Tummala-Narra, P., Barbanel, L., & Ruth, R. (2013). Contemporary psychoanalytic views on the experience of immigration. *Psychoanalytic Psychology, 30*: 663–679.

Akhtar, S. (1995). A third individuation: immigration, identity, and the psychoanalytic process. *Journal of the American Psychoanalytic Association, 43*: 1051–1084.

Altinyelken, H. K. (2009). Migration and self-esteem: a qualitative study among internal migrant girls in Turkey. *Adolescence, 44*: 149–163.

Anagnostopoulos, D. C., Vlassopoulos, M., & Lazaratou, H. (2006). Forced migration, adolescence, and identity formation. *American Journal of Psychoanalysis, 66*: 226–238.

Anthony, E. J. (1987). Risk, vulnerability, and resilience: an overview. In: E. J. Anthony & B. J. Cohler (Eds.), *The Invulnerable Child* (pp. 3–48). New York: Guilford Press.

Antman, F. M. (2012). The impact of migration on family left behind. Accessed at: www.iza.org/MigrationHandbook/16_Antman_The%20 Impact%20of%20Migration%20on%20Family%20Left%20Behind.pdf in August 2014.

Beebe, B. (2000). Co-constructing mother–infant distress: the microsynchrony of maternal impingement and infant avoidance in the face-to-face encounter. *Psychoanalytic Inquiry, 20*: 421–440.

Bonovitz, J. M. (2004). The child immigrant. *American Journal of Psychoanalysis, 64*: 129–141.

Bowlby, J. (1960). Grief and mourning in infancy and early childhood. *Psychoanalytic Study of the Child, 15*: 9–52.

Brenner, C. (1982). *The Mind in Conflict*. New York: International Universities Press.

Brown, L., & Gilligan, C. (1992). *Meeting at the Crossroads: Women's Psychology and Girls' Development*. Cambridge, MA: Harvard University Press.

Cantor-Graae, E., & Pedersen, C. B. (2013). Full spectrum of psychiatric disorders related to foreign migration: a Danish population-based cohort study. *Journal of the American Medical Association Psychiatry, 70*: 427–435.

Cath, S. (1986). Fathering from infancy to old age: a selective overview of recent psychoanalytic contributions. *Psychoanalytic Review, 73D*: 65–75.

Diamond, M. J. (1998). Fathers with sons: psychoanalytic perspectives on good enough fathering throughout the life cycle. *Gender and Psychoanalysis, 3*: 243–299.

Drury, J., & Williams, R. (2012). Children and young people who are refugees, internally displaced persons or survivors or perpetrators of war, mass violence and terrorism. *Current Opinion in Psychiatry, 25*: 277–284.

Ferrell, N. J., Melton, B., Banu, S., Coverdale, J., & Valdez, M. R. (2014). The development and evaluation of a trauma curriculum for psychiatry residents. *Academic Psychiatry, 38*: 611–614.

Fonagy, P. (2001). *Attachment Theory and Psychoanalysis.* New York: Other Press.

Fonagy, P., Steele, M., Steele, H., Higgitt, A., & Target, M. (1994). The Emanuel Miller Memorial Lecture 1992: The theory and practice of resilience. *Journal of Child Psychology and Psychiatry, 35*(2): 231–257.

Frenkel, L. (2004). "I smile at her and she smiles back at me": between repair and re-enactment: the relationship between nurses and child patients in a South African Paediatric Burns Unit. In: S. Levy & A. Lemma (Eds.), *The Perversion of Loss: Psychoanalytic Perspectives on Trauma* (pp. 145–162). New York: Brunner-Routledge.

Freud, A. (1968). Indications and contraindications for child analysis. *Psychoanalytic Study of the Child, 23*: 37–46.

Freud, A., & Burlingham, D. T. (1944). *Infants Without Families.* New York: International Universities Press.

Freud, S. (1917e). Mourning and melancholia. *S. E., 14*: 237–258. London: Hogarth.

Garber, B. (2008). Mourning in children: a theoretical synthesis and clinical application. *Annual of Psychoanalysis, 36*: 174–188.

Garza-Guerrero, A. C. (1974). Culture shock: its mourning and the vicissitudes of identity. *Journal of the American Psychoanalytic Association, 22*: 408–429.

Gergely, G., & Watson, J. S. (1996). The social biofeedback theory of parental affect-mirroring: the development of emotional self-awareness and self-control in infancy. *International Journal of Psychoanalysis, 77*: 1181–1212.

Gilmore, K., & Meersand, P. (2014). *Normal Child and Adolescent Development: A Psychodynamic Primer.* Washington, DC: American Psychiatric Publishing.

Glaser, D. (2014). The effects of child maltreatment on the developing brain. *Medico-Legal Journal, 82*: 97–111.

Goodenow, C., & Espin, O. M. (1993). Identity choices in immigrant adolescent females. *Adolescence, 28*: 173–184.

Grant, B. F., Stinson, F. S., Hasin, D. S., Dawson, D. A., Chou, S. P., & Anderson, K. (2004). Immigration and lifetime prevalence of DSM-IV psychiatric disorders among Mexican Americans and non-Hispanic whites in the United States: results from the National Epidemiologic Survey on Alcohol and Related Conditions. *Archives of General Psychiatry, 61*: 1226–1233.

Grinberg, L., & Grinberg, R. (1984). A psychoanalytic study of migration: its normal and pathological aspects. *Journal of the American Psychoanalytic Association, 32*: 13–38.

Hagman, G. (1995). Mourning: a review and reconsideration. *International Journal of Psychoanalysis, 76*: 909–925.

Hagman, G. (1996). The role of the other in mourning. *Psychoanalytic Quarterly, 65*: 327–352.

Hartmann, H. (1939). *Ego Psychology and the Problem of Adaptation.* New York: International Universities Press, 1958.

Hume, F., & Kleeberg, B. (2004). Playing a poor hand well: succumbing to or triumphing over developmental adversity: a study of adults sexually abused in care. In: S. Levy & A. Lemma (Eds.), *The Perversion of Loss: Psychoanalytic Perspectives on Trauma* (pp. 71–86). New York: Brunner-Routledge.

Kandel, W., & Kao, G. (2000). Shifting orientations: how U.S. labor migration affects children's aspirations in Mexican migrant communities. *Social Science Quarterly, 81*: 6–32.

Karatsoreos, I. N., & McEwen, B. S. (2013). Annual Research Review: The neurobiology and physiology of resilience and adaptation across the life course. *Journal of Child Psychology and Psychiatry, 54*: 337–347.

Katan, A. (1951). The role of "displacement" in agoraphobia. *International Journal of Psychoanalysis, 32*: 41–50.

Keefer, B. P., & Reene, K. J. (2002). Female adolescence. *Annual of Psychoanalysis, 30*: 245–252.

Khanlou, N., & Crawford, C. (2006). Post-migratory experiences of newcomer female youth: self-esteem and identity development. *Journal of Immigrant and Minority Health, 8*: 45–56.

Levy, S., & Lemma, A. (2004). *The Perversion of Loss: Psychoanalytic Perspectives on Trauma*. New York: Brunner-Routledge.

Liebman, S. J., & Abell, S. C. (2000). The forgotten parent no more: a psychoanalytic reconsideration of fatherhood. *Psychoanalytic Psychology*, 17: 88–105.

Mann, M. A. (2004). Immigrant parents and their emigrant adolescents: the tension of inner and outer worlds. *American Journal of Psychoanalysis*, 64(2): 143–153.

Marans, S. (1996). Psychoanalysis on the beat: children, police, and urban trauma. *Psychoanalytic Study of the Child*, 51: 522–541.

Marans, S. (2014). Intervening with children and families exposed to violence (Part I). *Journal of Infant, Child and Adolescent Psychotherapy*, 13: 350–357.

Marchetti-Mercer, M. C. (2012). Those easily forgotten: the impact of emigration on those left behind. *Family Process*, 51: 376–390.

Markese, S. (2011). Dyadic trauma in infancy and early childhood: review of the literature. *Journal of Infant, Child and Adolescent Psychotherapy*, 10: 341–378.

Masten, A. S., & Narayan, A. J. (2012). Child development in the context of disaster, war, and terrorism: pathways of risk and resilience. *Annual Review of Psychology*, 63: 227–257.

McGowan, P. O., Sasaki, A., D'Alessio, A. C., Dymov, S., Labonte, B., Szyf, M., Turecki, G., & Meaney, M. J. (2009). Epigenetic regulation of the glucocorticoid receptor in human brain associates with childhood abuse. *Nature Neuroscience*, 12: 342–348.

Menes, J. B. (1971). Children's reactions to the death of a parent: a review of the psychoanalytic literature. *Journal of the American Psychoanalytic Association*, 19: 697–719.

National Scientific Council on the Developing Child (2010). Early experiences can alter gene expression and affect long-term development: working paper No. 10. Accessed at: http://developingchild.harvard.edu/resources/reports_and_working_papers/working_papers/wp10 in August 2015.

Nemeroff, C. B. (2004). Neurobiological consequences of childhood trauma. *Journal of Clinical Psychiatry*, 65(Suppl 1): 18–28.

Oberlander, T. F., Weinberg, J., Papsdorf, M., Grunau, R., Misri, S., & Devlin, A. M. (2008). Prenatal exposure to maternal depression, neonatal methylation of human glucocorticoid receptor gene (NR3C1) and infant cortisol stress responses. *Epigenetics*, 3: 97–106.

Osofsky, J. D. (2003). Psychoanalytically based treatment for traumatized children and families. *Psychoanalytic Inquiry*, 23: 530–543.

Patino, L. R., Selten, J., Van Engeland, H., Duyx, J. H. M., Kahn, R. S., & Burger, H. (2005). Migration, family dysfunction and psychotic symptoms in children and adolescents. *British Journal of Psychiatry, 186*: 442–443.

Perez Foster, R. (2001). When immigration is trauma: a review for the individual and family clinician. *American Journal of Orthopsychiatry, 72*: 153–170.

Perez Foster, R. (2005). The new faces of childhood perimigration trauma in the United States. *Journal of Infant, Child, and Adolescent Psychotherapy, 4*: 21–41.

Perry, B. D. (2008). Child maltreatment: a neurodevelopmental perspective on the role of trauma and neglect in psychopathology. In: T. Beauchaine & S. Hinshaw (Eds.), *Child and Adolescent Psychopathology* (pp. 93–129). Hoboken, NJ: John Wiley.

Pollock, G. (1961). Mourning and adaptation. *International Journal of Psychoanalysis, 42*: 341–361.

Rossi, A. (2008). The impact of migration on children in developing countries. Accessed at: globalnetwork.princeton.edu/bellagio/Rossi.pdf in August 2015.

Rossi, A. (2009). The impact of migration on children left behind in developing countries: outcomes analysis and data requirements (March 2, 2009). Accessed at: http://papers.ssrn.com/sol3/papers.cfm?abstract_id=2490380 in August 2015.

Salas-Wright, C. P., Kagotho, N., & Vaughn, M. G. (2014). Mood, anxiety, and personality disorders among first and second-generation immigrants to the United States. *Psychiatry Research, 220*: 1028–1036.

Su, S., Li, X., Lin, D., Xu, X., & Zhu, M. (2013). Psychological adjustment among left-behind children in rural China: the role of parental migration and parent–child communication. *Child: Care, Health and Development, 39*: 162–170.

Suarez-Orozco, C., Yoshikawa, H., Teranishi, R. T., & Suarez-Orozco, M. M. (2011). Growing up in the shadows: the developmental implications of unauthorized status. *Harvard Educational Review, 81*: 438–473.

Teicher, M. H., Andersen, S. L., Polcari, A., Anderson, C. M., & Navalta, C. P. (2002). Developmental neurobiology of childhood stress and trauma. *Psychiatric Clinics of North America, 25*: 397–426.

Teicher, M. H., Dumont, N. L., Ito, Y., Vaituzis, C., Giedd, J. N., & Andersen, S. L. (2004). Childhood neglect is associated with reduced corpus callosum area. *Biological Psychiatry, 56*: 80–85.

United Nations Children's Fund (UNICEF) (2012). *Child Trafficking*. Accessed at: www.unicef.org/protection/57929_58005.html in February 2015.

United Nations High Commissioner on Refugees (UNHCR) (2014). *Children on the Run: Unaccompanied Children Leaving Central America and Mexico and the Need for International Protection*. Accessed at: www.unhcrwashington.org/sites/default/files/1_UAC_Children%20on%20the%20Run_Full%20Report.pd in February 2015.

United Nations High Commissioner on Refugees (UNHCR) (2015). *Global Trends: Forced Displacement in 2014*. Accessed at: http://unhcr.org/556725e69.html#_ga=1.225701913.2095888809.1417795315 in August 2015.

US Customs and Border Protection, Department of Homeland Security (2014). *Southwest Border Unaccompanied Alien Children (FY2014)*. Accessed at: www.cbp.gov/newsroom/stats/southwest-border-unaccompanied-children-2014 in February 2015.

Vervliet, M., Lammertyn, J., Broekaert, E., & Derluyn, I. (2014). Longitudinal follow-up of the mental health of unaccompanied refugee minors. *European Child and Adolescent Psychiatry*, 23: 337–346.

Weber, D. A., & Reynolds, C. R. (2004). Clinical perspectives on neurobiological effects of psychological trauma. *Neuropsychology Review, 14*: 115–129.

CHAPTER SIX

Women and power:
a developmental perspective

Ruth Fischer

In 1941, Wonder Woman, the comic book superhero, broke free of her shackles and burst on to the comic book scene, heralding the birth of feminism (Lepore, 2014a, p. 59; Lepore, 2014b, p. 20). She hailed from ancient Greece where men kept women in chains. The new woman, freed from her chains, developed great physical and mental powers. She left Paradise Island to fight fascism with feminism, democracy, and equal rights for women. Wonder Woman is pictured bound and gagged with a metal collar, double bands on her wrists, and Amazon bracelets. The chains and ropes relate to the history of the bondage of women and the fight for women's rights. The bursting of her shackles represented the powerful influence of the suffrage, feminism, and birth control movements, each of which used chains as central to their iconography. Wonder Woman chronicled a new movement, the release of women's power.

A very different picture of female power is portrayed in the current popular film, *Frozen*, in which Princess Elsa acquires an amazing magic power. Whatever she touches turns to ice. She enjoys this for a short period of time, but then begins to fear the consequences. She withdraws from the world to avoid any harm that might result were she to inadvertently touch something or someone, or even if her power is revealed.

Why is this such a compelling story for today's young girls? It is such a contrast with the Wonder Woman story of the mid twentieth century. Elsa must contain her power as she fears its destructiveness. Wonder Woman's power is released from its constraints, the ropes and chains applied by the male population in her country of origin. What is this about, these contrasting views of women's power, the super-powerful Wonder Woman and frightened Elsa?

There is a cultural tendency to minimize girl (and woman) power that conveys our concern. It is as if we fear it to be dangerous. How is it, then, that Wonder Woman broke free and we celebrated her physical and psychological strength in 1941? Now, in 2015, Elsa returns us to earlier myths and fantasies of femaleness. There are intrapsychic, developmental, and environmental influences at play here that lie behind the need to contain women and their ability to assert themselves (Applegarth, 1976; Lerner, 1980). Fables, fairy tales and comic books serve as a gateway to important psychological truths.

"Sugar and spice and everything nice, that's what little girls are made of." This is the environmental social expectation into which girls are born and in which they grow and develop. Any of us who have been little girls or have had contact with little girls knows that this is not the whole story. Girls are not always sugar and spice and all things nice, but that is the *zeitgeist*.

In fairy tales, the boy goes out into the world and proves himself by facing and overcoming dangerous enemies and forces. He uses his mighty power. The girl, in contrast, falls asleep and is awakened by her Prince. In no way does she assert herself. She waits passively to be awakened by her hero. Why is this the female story and why do we continue to retell it? I suggest three overarching reasons: (1) we are expressing a concern, (2) we are reassuring ourselves, and (3) we are warning girls that their power might be dangerous.

The story of *Frozen* is so compelling because it draws on this prominent belief of the excitement and danger of female power. We discourage girls from acquiring agency to avoid the possibility of their acquiring power. If, by some fluke, they do, they certainly should not use it. Whom are we protecting and from what danger? Why is it so important that girl power be minimized, if not eradicated? How does the Wonder Woman phenomenon fit into all of this?

The recent release of the biographies (Hale, 2014, p. 52) of three powerful reigning women, Hatshepsut of ancient Egypt, Isabella, the

Castilian monarch (1400s), and Queen Victoria of Britain, confronts us with the issue of female power, its conflicted nature and a not uncommon resolution. It is suggested that the simultaneous publication of these three books indicates a surge of interest in the lives of authoritative women and represents a widespread feminist trend. This is countered with the common cultural idea that powerful women are witches or are placed in some similar frightening category. By way of resolution of these conflicting ideas, it is postulated that these three women, each on her own, but in similar fashion, aligned herself with a powerful man. I suggest that this served to reassure those who were frightened by the prospect of female power. It is not easy for a woman to attain power. Over the years, alignment with a powerful man has been one way in which the problem has been solved for the woman herself as well as for others in the surroundings.

Interviews with current women leaders (Bryant, 2014, p. 6) emphasize that women are both underestimated by others and underestimate themselves. They play down their successes and diminish their accomplishments. Most striking and consistently noted is the woman's reluctance to take a stand for fear of some negative consequence. Women prefer to fit in while men more comfortably enjoy being the stars and crowing about it. The assertive woman is frequently accused of being a bitch, castrating, at best, unlikeable, epithets of little concern for successful men. The bottom-line advice given from these women leaders is, if you want to attain leadership status, discover your own voice, speak up, do not diminish your accomplishments, do not hide yourself, and do not run from conflict. Not so easy for the girl/woman who has grown up under powerful influences telling her to contain her power.

One way out of this conflict of the desire for power and the fear of attaining it is to find someone with whom to share it and thereby experience it vicariously. This is the royal road to attaining power through alignment with a powerful man noted in the biographies of Hatshepsut, Isabella, and Queen Victoria.

A report of the reunion of the University of Stanford class of 1994 (Kantor, 2014, p. 1) is interesting in this respect. This class was the first at Stanford to be exposed to the diversity curriculum, the goal of which was to empower women and minorities. Their entrance into the workforce coincided with the onset of the internet revolution. Many members of this class became great innovators, more men than women, but there were also several outstanding women with revolutionary ideas. However, few of the women remained in the forefront. They took on more supportive roles. They married and worked with some of the outstanding male innovators. However, few of them played more than a limited role in building the enterprises that power the World Wide Web today. Gina Bianchini, a member of this class, had been on the cover of Fortune magazine for her creativity and fortune building. However, it was largely the men who were the true creators, founding companies, making fortunes, and funding new projects. Many of the women dropped out or remained in safe jobs. Even the most successful women did not match their male classmates' achievements.

Clearly, there are external obstacles with which women must contend. Possibly, it is when these are diminished, as they were during the Second World War, that we find a Wonder Woman phenomenon. This was a time when female power was needed, as male power was in short supply. External, environmental, sociocultural forces are powerful deterrents. Perhaps, however, the most powerful obstacle is the internal one, the discomfort with power that leads women to downplay their accomplishments and undermine themselves. External forces reinforce internal inclinations. Is this not what Elsa expresses in the story *Frozen*? It is dangerous to use her magic power for, if she does, she will frighten herself and endanger her kingdom.

But, we say, things are different today. Women are liberated. They are no longer confined to the home. They vote, they own property, they are CEOs, Supreme Court Justices, Congresspersons, Senators, candidates for high office, technology innovators, mathematicians, engineers, and scientists. We have come a long way. Political, social, and cultural influences have been both causative and contributory. The experience of the graduates of the class of 1994 at the Stanford University reunion reminds us that major vestiges remain.

The cultural context in which this is being played out needs to be appreciated: the American ideal, the Man of the Wild West, the strong, independent frontiersman. Interdependence, caring for others is less valued. At times, it is scorned, seen as weak and consigned to the world of women. Independence is not only culturally sanctioned but promoted, encouraged, even demanded for status and self-esteem. For women, however, there is a mixed message. Independence is impeded by the same socio-cultural forces which demand it. All of this, the pros and the cons, remain embedded in the female psyche. We need to consider these competing ethics, that of independence and that of interdependence.

In order to understand the internal factors that both promote and inhibit these ways of being, I turn to female psychological development while appreciating the importance of the environment and the ebb and flow of Wonder Woman and Princess Elsa.

Common gender differences are noted. Boys play with action figures with superpowers that they use in overcoming powerful enemies in direct conflict. Girls play in the doll house and enact aspects of Cinderella and Snow White. These are stories of a girl abandoned or victimized by a mother's envious rage over which she ultimately triumphs via the intercession of a prized male smitten with her overwhelming beauty. The boys aggression is expressed directly, the girl's much more circuitously. They are both in conflict with a powerful same sex parent, but the manner in which this is played out is drastically different. Of course, this is culturally influenced, but there is reason to believe that it is also intrinsically or intrapsychically determined. In an effort to counteract the sociocultural influence, mothers have tried to give girls guns and boys dolls. Interestingly, the girls used their guns as dolls and the boys used the dolls as guns. There is something more than environmental influence going on here.

Freud (1931b) explored the different ways in which boys and girls asserted themselves and expressed their aggression. He noted that little girls were active, assertive human beings until they reached the point in their lives (3–6 years) when they recognized the anatomical difference between the sexes. This, he believed, led to the girl's relinquishing her masculine activity and sexuality and turning to passive femininity (Hoffman, 1996). Is this the story of Elsa in *Frozen*, withdrawing from the world, abandoning her sense of self, her use of her power, her aggression and sexuality as she becomes aware of, and frightened by, the strength of her magic power, her burgeoning sexuality and fecundity? How much of this has to do with physical maturity and the impact of hormones and powerful genital sensations? No doubt these all play a role. Perhaps there is even more to the story.

This Freudian understanding of female development was promulgated a long time ago (Freud, 1905d) and we have come a distance since then. We now appreciate that girls have their own line of development, the result of the impact of their genes, hormones, and body sensations in interaction with important others in their lives as well as the influence of the culture into which they are born. How much to attribute to nature? How much to nurture? With this we continue to debate and to struggle. We are agreed, however, that although there is some overlap, the girl faces different forces operating on her body and, consequently, on her psyche than does the boy. There are differences in biology, in body sensations, and in cultural pressures. These lead to differences in, and expansion of, the arenas of connectedness with others and exploration of the environment. As a result, we see a greater development of self-assertion in boys and of relatedness in girls. It is on this particular difference that I shall now focus.

I begin with hormonal differences (Korner, 1973, p. 27). In fetal life, the child, male and female alike, is bathed in maternal estrogen. For the boy, as testosterone is released, aspects of fetal development are influenced that determine genital anatomy, body musculature, and brain development in a more male direction. There are early after birth influences as well, due to another burst of testosterone in the early postnatal period. Fetal and early postnatal testosterone surges are highly determinative in setting these male–female differences in place.

Sex of assignment at birth (Stoller, 1976, p. 63) or, more recently, at the time of the ultrasound, is the next important influence on infant development, determining indices of connection and self-assertion. The sex of the infant alerts parental hopes and expectations with consequent pressure on the child to comply. The pressure may be quite subtle or it may be profound. Parental expectations are conveyed to the child in blanket color, the manner in which the child is held, caressed, responded to, fed, diapered, talked with, and put to sleep. There are notable male–female differences in the manner in which infants are handled that promote and hinder connection and self-expression. There are gender determined parental preferences for interaction on a verbal or visual basis. This is determined by parental proclivities, but also by the multiple environmental influences that come into play with consideration of what a girl or boy should be like in this particular environment (Korner, 1973, p. 19). No doubt, there is also something innate, on a more biological level, in the parental response to a male or female infant.

There is an understanding underlying all of this that every child is born with a specific constitution and temperament that interacts with parental inclinations and comfort zones (Mahler et al., 1975). An example of this is seen in a parent who is comfortable only with a quiet child, or another who interacts better with a child who is very active and outgoing. The same comes into play when there is a preference or comfort level with a boy or a girl.

One major gender difference with great relevance for our investigation of female–male difference in connection and autonomy is the regulation of bodily rhythms (Olesker, 1990, p. 339), the alternating sleep and awake states. Regulation diminishes internal chaos, freeing the infant to focus outward, concentrate, and interact.

Infant girls regulate earlier than their male cohorts, due to an earlier maturation of the right occipital cortex. This allows for an earlier focus on the caretaker's face, with the resulting intense mutual gaze between mother[1] and child. The mother's emotionally expressive face is the most potent visual stimulus from the infant's environment. (Feldman et al., 1999, p. 223) The child's interest in the mother's face gives the infant high levels of cognitive and social information while promoting attachment, the mother–infant bond that occurs in the first year of life. The high level of affect synchrony (Papousek & Papousek, 1995) between infant and mother increases the engagement. The baby's brain is affected by these transactions (Trevarthen, 1990, p. 357) and the brain requires this for growth (Emde, 1988, p. 32). The attachment relationship shapes the maturation of the infant's right brain during the first year of life (Bowlby, 1969, p. 344), thereby laying the groundwork for the attachment experience, the development of empathy, the growth of affect states and affect tolerance, burgeoning socialization, and much more.

The earlier awareness of, and attachment to, mother as the important other in the infant's life carries with it a dawning awareness potential vulnerability, a need for mother's presence for safety and security and an awareness that she might not always be present. Connection is fostered and autonomy hampered as the sense of vulnerability and need to please mother escalates. The girl is more aware of the connection, of her need for it, and the potential of losing it. She becomes wary of mother's reactions to her independent forays and the possibility of maternal displeasure. She behaves and stays close to home. Autonomy is hampered and connection promoted.

Connection with mother is also heightened by the sense of sameness, the body familiarity, that mother and daughter share. For the boy, gender difference promotes and demands separateness and self-definition. This is further reinforced with the boy's identification with his father (Greenson, 1968, p. 372). Generally, fathers and maleness foster boundary formation. The girl's identification with her mother reinforces sameness, closeness, connection of self and other. Of course, we are speaking of a nuclear family with one mother and one father in today's Western cultural context. The few studies we do have of other family settings tend to confirm that the pattern set in the early child–parent interaction is that required of the culture to which they belong. So, at the moment, we would say that in this culture, the different emphasis on connection *vs.* exploration is biologically determined and socially reinforced.

It is not just the girl who is dealing with these issues. Mothers react to their child's increasing self-assertion and forays out into the world (Olesker, 1990, p. 334). There is a different response to the son's assertion than to that of the daughter. Seeing herself in her daughter, the familiarity, promotes a more sticky connection for the mother. The sense of the boy's difference allows for an easier push for, and acceptance of, his moving out and away. Mothers are more comfortable with their son's aggression, often encouraging it, at other times, not even appearing to notice. For the daughter, the mother's response is more cautious, expressing more concern. She encourages her son's moving out and her daughter's close contact (Hoffman, 2003). It is not clear which comes first. Is this a response to the child's wariness or is the child's wariness a response to that of her mother?

Comfort level in states of separateness and autonomy underlie the differences in the sense of connection and intimacy in girls and women and of agency and advocacy in boys and men. It also relates to the idea that women are more open to intimacy and connectedness while men are often avoidant of emotional closeness. Here, we see the basis of the ideas conveyed in the book, *Men Are from Mars, Women Are from Venus* (Gray, 2009).

Separateness and autonomy become problematic in female development as so many factors work against it. Herein lies the source of the problem with self-assertion, with knowing her mind, expressing a contrary opinion, standing out, confronting others, excelling, being successful, or even having an original idea. It is going against the golden rule of never asserting yourself, never using your power. The template is that to insure that connection is maintained there is a need to dumb down, hide exceptional talents or any original ideas and connect with a powerful man. This was the solution for Hatshepsut of ancient Egypt, Isabella of fifteenth-century Spain, and Queen Victoria of Britain, as well as the 1994 graduates of the University of Stanford.

What is it about self-assertion that challenges connection? Asserting a divergent opinion might lead to disagreement, a sense of threat, or possibly anger. It might result in loss of love, rejection, or even abandonment. It might also lead to self-enhancement that, in and of itself, might become problematic as it challenges the *status quo*, might threaten the other, and, thereby, threaten the girl's sense of safety. Any self-expression has the potential to become problematic in this scenario. Anger stands in stark opposition. It proclaims separateness, as does any interesting new thought, good idea, or creative solution. So, best to avoid it, try to find a way around it, inhibit oneself, or outsource the credit—all solutions frequently utilized by girls and women.

This has everything to do with being in a leadership position. Asserting oneself, taking a stand, establishing rules, drawing a line, saying this is me without regard for where the other stands is proclaiming one's authority. This is exactly what women leaders are telling their younger colleagues that they need to do (Bryant, 2014, p. 6). This does not come easily for the girl. It is problematic as it goes against both cultural forces that promote an ethos of maintaining connection and internal prohibitions that reinforce the social expectation as well as the external prohibition. It challenges the awareness of vulnerability, the need for mother, the need to please mother, as well as the need not to compete with her, in order not to jeopardize the position of either the girl or her mother.

One way out of this dilemma is not to recognize the self-assertion, the independent voice, to deny it or displace it onto another. Triumph, then, is accomplished by way of a proxy, a fairy godmother, an adoring prince, or a powerful man. In this way, the girl relinquishes responsibility, denies autonomy or competition with the all-powerful other, who remains the most beautiful in the land, the fairest of all. The self-assertion was not a willful act; it just happened to her. Elsa did not search out her magic power. It was visited upon her, as was her physical maturity and taking on the role of Queen. She could not help it. She takes neither credit nor responsibility, thereby avoiding any consequences. And what are the consequences from which she is so desperately running? The change in the nature of the tie with the all-powerful mother, the fear of being abandoned, the terrible sense of existential loneliness, the realization that one is alone in the world and must rely only on oneself. As long as there is a Prince, a fairy godmother, or an accompanying male, the girl is home free.

At this point we must turn to a consideration of body sensations. Genital sensations make their presence known somewhere in the third year of life (18–36 months) and are quite different for boys and girls. For boys, they push outward into the environment. This is expressed in interests in objects that are propelled into space: balls, cars, planes, trains, missiles, bodies pushing into each other (Galenson & Roiphe, 1980). Girls' genital sensations (Mayer, 1991; Schiller, 2012) radiate inward and are expressed in dancing, turning, spinning. The boy's body sensations pull him out of himself. The girl's circle back internally. These powerful internal sensations reinforce the direction already laid down by brain maturation, hormones, gender determination, the sense of sameness or difference with mother, as well as environmental expectations, comfort with intimate connection, and independent functioning. Or, possibly, body sensations are the source of it all: body sensations as powerful organizing factors. The problem, however, is not with the body sensations themselves but with how they are experienced by the young woman herself, along with the social response (Horney, 1933). With the onset of genital sensations, the girl is awakened as a sexually mature woman with desires of her own. Awareness of desire establishes a sense of self that inevitably leads to self-assertion to satisfy this desire. Unless, of course, opposing forces, internal and external, overwhelm the young girl's strivings.

This is noted in the many forms of symptomatic behavior that arise with the onset of puberty. Eating disorders are most common, but there are multiple ways in which girls work at avoiding their burgeoning sexuality, growing up, and leaving mother behind. This is expressed as not feeling ready to move on to the next developmental step, fear for self and fear for mother, who may be devastated by this new chapter. Primarily, the adolescent girl is dealing with her budding sexual body. To acknowledge sexuality is to acknowledge desire, her special magic and power that will lead to the excitement and danger of separateness and independence. This is a big step for someone bathed for so long in connectedness and disowning power.

Freud (1931b) struggled with the issue of femininity and aggression. For him, the impact of the girl's body on her psychic evolution was determinative. An assertive woman was, by definition, a woman who has not matured into her femininity. She is, in some way, awash on the island of penis envy, unable to make the final voyage to submissive femininity. Identity as a mature woman is consolidated as she recognizes her genital inferiority, turns away from mother in anger and disappointment, and turns to father with the hope of obtaining the prized genital from him, later substituted for a wish for a baby from him. In so doing, she accepts her castrated state, turns activity into passivity, gives up her masculine sexuality and aggression, and submerges her power as she turns to father as her strength and savior. A very different and largely outdated explanation and consideration of normal femininity! It is also determined by an observation of genital anatomy, not on body sensations, on which the entirety of Freud's opus rests.

As the girl matures, she and her mother move on to the need to adjust to the perturbations of puberty and adolescence. Scholars of female psychology have taken the Persephone myth to be the female equivalent of the oedipal myth (Kulish & Holtzman, 1998), the conflict that the boy has with his father. Here, we see the vicissitudes of the conflict the adolescent girl and her mother experience with the advent of cognitive, psychological, and physical maturity. The cognitive change is noted in the now more complex development of the capacity to think in terms of three persons, one with whom you are relating and another who is excluded. At this point, intimacy and sexuality are added to the mix, further complicating matters. Physical maturity brings with it the potential for pregnancy and all that that evokes. The psychological change involves being in the middle of the experience of loving and hating each parent separately and needing to resolve these conflicting feelings. This is the traditional oedipal situation revived in adolescence.

In the Persephone myth, Kore, the daughter of Zeus and Demeter, is walking in the field, looking at flowers when she is abducted by Hades, who carries her off to the underworld, where she is introduced to sexuality. In this way, the girl avoids taking either credit or responsibility for what has occurred. Her mother, mourning the loss of her daughter, finds a way to have her return to Earth for a portion of each year. It is winter on Earth when the daughter is with Hades. Spring approaches as she returns to be with her mother. Life is split between time spent with Hades and time spent with mother. In this way, the need to make a definitive break is avoided, resulting in a less separate and independent girl who is more connected and interdependent than her male sibling. She is both blessed and limited. She is less the subject of her own desires and is more comfortable in relatedness.

As the myth goes, she has been abducted by Hades. None of this is of her own free will or desire. To be abducted, taken hostage away from her idyll with her mother, to have an accompanying prince or fairy godmother, is to be free of guilt or evil intent. It is not always as smooth flowing as in the myth or in fairy tales. As frustration builds, the result of the inability to express herself, resentment and anger often intensify with consequent increasing fear of retaliation and increasing conflict experienced in relationships. There is an underlying fantasy of being Wonder Woman, breaking free, being physically and psychologically strong and performing heroic acts. It is interesting to speculate on the emergence of this fantasy with such clarity in the 1940s and its subsequent submergence. Has there not always been a backlash, both internally and externally, as women's power has expressed itself?

Fairy tales and myths point to a road out of the woman's dilemma. The assertion, the power, the responsibility is displaced onto another. Triumph is accomplished by way of a proxy, a fairy godmother or an adoring prince. It just happened without the girl seeking it or even willing it. In this way, she relinquishes responsibility, denies autonomy or competition. The father is not challenged and the mother remains the most beautiful in the land, the fairest of all. The girl's self-assertion then is not a willful act. She could not help it. This is the story of Persephone, of Queen Elsa, of Cinderella, and of Snow White.

So, there are hormonal issues, brain maturation differences, timing of onset of bodily regulation determining awareness of mother, a sense of vulnerability resulting in a need to maintain connection at the price of autonomy, body sensations that push outward or circle inward, social pressures, and family expectations. To this list, we must add the hopes, fears, feelings, and fantasies invested in the important adults of our childhood that we carry forward into our present day relationships. The reaction to the powerful woman carries with it the ambivalence we experienced toward the first powerful woman, the mother of our childhood, who both satisfied and denied us, responded to us and ignored us, who supported us and punished us. She was a mighty force with which to contend, a force to be feared and respected. The father, another powerful person in childhood, was experienced as able to counter the mother's power. This is the substrate for our tendency to idealize the powerful man and fantasize that attaching our fates to his will make us safer, wiser, and more powerful. Again, I reference Hatshepsut, Isabella, and Queen Victoria, as well as Cinderella, Snow White, Princess Elsa, and the graduates of the class of 1994 from Stanford University.

The conflict over self-assertion, the taking on of one's power, is present for men and women alike, but men do not traditionally take on a submissive stance. Men who fight for what they believe are considered heroes. Aggressive women make others uncomfortable. This, no doubt, relates to the power attributed to the omnipotent mother of infancy who both gratifies and punishes, who has the power of giving birth and, therefore, has the power of taking life attributed to her. I am assuming a family constellation in which the mother or some substitute female figure is in this role. At this point, this is the only family constellation about which we have any data. This is the mother upon whom the child is dependent and from whom the child strives for autonomy.

Why does the girl not identify with this powerful mother, her earliest female role model? Why only consider herself at the mercy of this powerful person? The answer might lie in the fantasy of the evil stepmother, who so often turns up in fairy tales. This is the vengeful, angry, all possessive, all powerful bad mother who restricts the child's independence, inadequately satisfies dependency needs, and brooks no competition. This is the stepmother in the story of Cinderella, the mother of Hansel and Gretel, and of Snow White. Here, we can identify the problem that hinders the girl's identification with the active, powerful mother. In order to do this, she must be able to integrate aspects of the evil stepmother with the all-good fairy godmother. One readily available resolution seems to be the presentation as a weak victim in an effort to avoid the destructiveness of this fantasied early mother figure.

Then we must wonder what it is that allows a few women the freedom to more comfortably take on their power and set the rules? What allowed for the bursting forth of Wonder Woman on the scene in the 1940s, the appearance of the suffragettes, the rise of feminism? And what suppressed all of this? One answer lies in the reaction to female assertion, the cultural response, the external response as well as the internal response within the individual woman and within the other in the interaction. The girl, identified with this powerful mother of infancy, fears her power, her destructive anger, the revengeful retribution, and the danger of standing alone. Her own growth and autonomy may be sacrificed to avoid such an outcome. As connection has been fostered, agency has been hampered. Self-assertion, autonomy, competition is feared. She fears floating out in space with no connecting umbilical cord if she disturbs the connection. Anger is inhibited as well as any autonomous self-expression, be it creative, intellectual, or emotional.

What will it take to overcome the infantile fear of the omnipotent mother that resides in all of us? I believe that our daughters and granddaughters will continue to identify with Cinderella, Snow White, and Princess Elsa. Our sons and grandsons will continue to limit the intensity of their connections and express contempt for girls. But this need not be the end point of their development. It will be one step in their efforts in dealing with the all-powerful mother and their innate push for independence. Both boys and girls will continue to revise and reintegrate the mother–child relationship.

What will aid this project? Sports have offered girls an opportunity to learn the rules, to fight in a socially accepted manner, in a socially accepted arena. Learning how to fight, how to assert herself, how to deal with self-expression, has been an uphill battle for girls without a socially sanctioned arena in which to play this out. Sports have become just such a socially sanctioned arena.

Experience with women who assert themselves comfortably and effectively will also promote this goal. Giving weak women positions of power or promoting the appearance of power is not the answer. Girls need an opportunity to play with asserting themselves, to act independently, experience the exhilaration and the danger that results. Only then will women be free to make their own unique contribution, not to rule as men, but to set the rules as women. The world is in desperate need of this.

At a time of such violence and trauma in our midst, women have much to offer. They need to be freer to use their authority and leadership skills in a society in which competition rules and cooperation takes a back seat. When women take on positions of leadership, they often bring forward a different perspective, different values and priorities that reshape the agenda. They are often better communicators, better listeners, and better consensus and alliance builders. Women are frequently more collaborative (Bryant, 2014, p. 8).

We need the focus on caring and interdependence to counter the relentless drive for autonomy, self-reliance and personal striving. It is important to understand the forces that are in play in and on the woman and her psyche in order to free her from the constraints on her self-development and to free her to use her power and contribute to society. It is important for women. It is important for men. It is important for all of us.

Note

1.   I use mother as she represents the most common early caretaker situation in our present environment, although changes are certainly in process. Change might well take place when the primary caretaker is male. This will need to be taken into consideration but cannot be included in this chapter.

References

Applegarth, A. (1976). Some observations on work inhibitions in women. *Journal of the American Psychoanalytic Association, 24S*: 251–268.

Bowlby, J. (1969). *Attachment and Loss, Vol. I: Attachment.* New York: Basic Books.

Bryant, A. (2014). Finding, and owning, their voice. *New York Times,* November 16, pp. D 6–8.

Emde, R. N. (1988). Development terminable and interminable. I. Innate and motivational factors from infancy. *International Journal of Psychoanalysis, 69*: 23–42.

Feldman, R., Greenbaum, C. W., & Yirmiya, N. (1999). Mother–infant affect synchrony as an antecedent of the emergence of self control. *Developmental Psychology, 35*: 223–231.

Freud, S. (1905d). *Three Essays on the Theory of Sexuality. S. E., 7*: 173–243. London: Hogarth.

Freud, S. (1931b). Female sexuality. *S. E., 21*: 223–245. London: Hogarth.

Galenson, E., & Roiphe, K. (1980). The pre-oedipal development of the boy. *Journal of the American Psychoanalytic Association, 28*: 805–827.

Gray, J. (2009). *Men Are from Mars, Women Are from Venus. Practical Guide for Improving Communication.* New York: HarperCollins.

Greenson, R. (1968). Disidentifying from mother. *International Journal of Psychoanalysis, 49*: 370–374.

Hale, K. (2014). The three queens. A triad of royal biographies invokes woman power. *Time Magazine,* October 27, pp. 52–53.

Hoffman, L. (1996). Freud and feminine subjectivity. *Journal of the American Psychoanalytic Association, 44S*: 23–44.

Hoffman, L. (2003). Mothers' ambivalence with their babies and toddlers: manifestations of conflicts with aggression. *Journal of the American Psychoanalytic Association, 51*: 1219–1240.

Horney, K. (1933). The denial of the vagina. A contribution to the problem of genital anxieties specific to women. *International Journal of Psychoanalysis, 14*: 57–70.

Kantor, J. (2014). The reunion of the University of Stanford class of 1994. *New York Times,* December 23, A1, A18–19.

Korner, A. (1973). Sex difference in newborns. *Journal of Child Psychoanalytic Psychiatry, 14*: 19–29.

Kulish, N., & Holtzman, D. (1998). Persephone, the loss of virginity and the female Oedipus complex. *International Journal of Psychoanalysis, 79*: 57–71.

Lepore, J. (2014a). The origin story of Wonder Woman. *Smithsonian,* 59–65.

Lepore, J. (2014b). *Courageous Womanhood. The Secret History of Wonder Woman.* Alfred A. Knopf. *New York Times,* December 14, Book review section: p. 20.

Lerner, H. (1980). Internal prohibitions against female anger. *American Journal of Psychoanalysis, 40*(2): 137–148.

Mahler, M., Pine, F., & Bergman, A. (1975). *The Psychological Birth of the Human Infant.* New York: Basic Books.

Mayer, E. (1991). Towers and enclosed spaces: a preliminary report on gender differences in children's reactions to block structure. *Psychoanalytic Inquiry, 11*: 480–510.

Olesker, W. (1990). Sex differences during early separation–individuation process: implication for gender identity formation. *Journal of the American Psychoanalytic Association, 38*: 325–346.

Schiller, B.-M. (2012). Representing female desire within a labial framework of sexuality. *Journal of the American Psychoanalytic Association, 60*: 1161–1197.

Stoller, R. J. (1976). Primary femininity. *Journal of the American Psychoanalytic Association*, *24S*: 59–78.

Trevarthen, C. (1990). Growth and education of the hemispheres. In: *Brain Circuits and Functions of the Mind.* Cambridge: Cambridge University Press.

CHAPTER SEVEN

Maternal genealogy: narcissistic identification in three generations of women

Johanna Mendoza Talledo

It was only a few decades ago that the psychoanalytical community began to take more interest in the experience of motherhood and to try to understand it in greater depth. It required a change of theoretical and ideological perspective for the subject of the motherhood experience to come to the fore in all its complexity.

Today, we have access to original theoretical and clinical proposals and psychoanalytical publications that include a variety of articles and serve as a reference on the subject. They agree in affirming that motherhood is an experience lived in body and in mind, a conscious experience shot through with unconscious desires, anxieties, and personal, family, and cultural expectations. It has its roots in very early infancy, in the first exchanges with the primal mother, that will have to be interwoven with oedipal vicissitudes and that will encourage or hinder maternal desires. While the mother carries out the constant work of meeting the baby's specific needs, holding its attempts to process reality so that the world makes sense to him or her, she experiences a range of feelings, especially a state of fragility and vulnerability produced by the manifestation of primary "wild" aspects (Raphael-Leff, 1994), which are generally little understood and held by the environment (Zelaya & Mendoza y Soto, 2006). The purpose of this chapter is to explore one of the fundamental dimensions of the experience of motherhood: the transgenerational aspects of unconscious narcissistic identification that inevitably link the mother with her mother and her mother's mother.

The newborn's condition of helplessness (*Hilflosigkeit*) determines that parental narcissism is inserted into the infant's psyche through a type of alienating identification with which his or her vital experiences will be woven. The experience of motherhood, hence, includes dealing with a history that corresponds to the other who is never absent: the mother (Chasseguet-Smirgel, 1976; Faimberg, 2005, Raphael-Leff, 1993, 1994; Marrioti, 2012; Mendoza, 2014). This process of primary identification condenses the history of a lineage that is traversed by unconscious forces whose existence precedes that of one's own (Faimberg, 2005). To process this alienating subjection and for "the past to be truly past" (Faimberg, 2005, p. 35), the mother will have to resignify her early narcissistic identifications. We could consider that all repetition is an unconscious narcissistic affront. If the woman follows the path of de-identifying with that which alienates her, she will be in a better position to experience motherhood and the link with her child as something that is enriching and open to what is new.

Motherhood and its vicissitudes today

Paola Mariotti (2012) states that there are three interrelated aspects that are particularly relevant for addressing the issue of motherhood: (1) the meaning of being and the desire to be a mother begin to become structured in the first affective and bodily exchanges of the daughter with her mother; (2) the psychic manifestations of maternality (the quality or condition of being a mother) are organized around the identification with the mother image, in which there are major transgenerational aspects that link a girl to her mother and to her mother's mother, and which will link her to her own daughter and her daughter's daughter; (3) maternality is also the profound expression of multiple layers of desires structured within the framework of the oedipal configuration. This chapter takes into consideration these axial themes to explore the transgenerational aspects of the mother's unconscious narcissistic identifications.

Bodily feeling

From the start, the body is part of an intersubjective community and from those primordial times comes up against the presence of the other. While birth produces the bodily separation between the baby and its mother, physical exchanges continue and favour a level of differentiation that is the source of the first representations that will give them meaning. This psychosomatic space between the mother and her child that corresponds to the primary process and precedes the entry of the subject in the symbolic order has been called *"jorá semiotics"* by Julia Kristeva (1980), because of its preverbal organisation ruled by forces, rhythms, sounds, and caresses, which leads to the unfolding of meanings. Alizade (1992) conceives a primal, experiential body that records the first pleasant and unpleasant visceral–sensitive and erogenous sensations, which will subsequently link up with the representational world. *El sentir del cuerpo* (Alizade, 1999), this world of sensations, may be linked to both the phenomenological experience developed through the senses, perception, and affective experience, and the representational level. This experience might be the basis of the sense of self described by Donald Winnicott (1960).

This sensorial–affective matrix, the anchor of the incipient bodily ego, requires the other to unfold.

> The first representation that the psyche forms of itself . . . will take place through the relationship established between the effects that originate in its double encounter with the body and the productions of the maternal psyche. (Aulagnier, 2001, p. 31, translated for this edition)

This nearness of the baby to the body of the mother and the productions of the maternal psyche are central to the exploration of the role that narcissistic identifications with the mother and their transgenerational aspects have in the experience of motherhood.

The first exchanges between the baby and its mother occur through a series of contacts involving the whole body, especially the skin, gaze, and voice. Didier Anzieu suggests that skin contact is a fundamental aspect of the mother and child relationship, as this is the place and main means of communicating with others, "a surface where the marks left by others are inscribed" (Anzieu, 2007, p. 40, translated for this edition). Besides having the quality of being an erogenous zone throughout life, skin acts as an interface between the baby and its mother, and thrills to sensation, emotions, mental images, and the vital rhythms of both.

If all goes well, these exchanges between the mother and the infant produce mutual pleasure. The oral pleasure the baby obtains from feeding corresponds to that of the mother, not only because her identification with the satisfaction of the baby gives her narcissistic gratification, but also because nursing her child gives her the erotic enjoyment of her own orality and of her breast, which produces the milk. In this way, maternality has an intrinsic erotic quality rarely spoken of.

The body *is* the scenario in which the mother communicates to her daughter the first messages about maternality through the first physical contacts. The communication of the pleasure of the mother and the response of her daughter revive the mother's memory of the same experience with her own mother, which, thus, becomes more present than one might imagine. Anxiety and fear are part of this interaction that, on being gradually joined by other affections, strengthens the bonds between mother and daughter (Raphael-Leff, 1993). These early bodily communications are mostly unconscious.

Moving on to the second aspect found in the origin of the child's psychic apparatus, the productions of the mother's psyche, the ideas of Jean Laplanche (1997) regarding the theory of seduction are particularly enlightening. According to this author, from the beginning the mother sends out unconscious communications about sexuality that captivate the newborn and guide its sensations and proto-sexuality. Encrypted in the manifest content, these enigmatic messages allude directly or indirectly to parental sexuality, to which it must be the object of desire, to which it must be perceived as a threat of transgression and other elemental issues about sex, gender, etc. The unconscious is at the centre of the infant's psychic apparatus: an internal foreignness sustained by an external foreignness (the *other*, the mother), sustained in turn by the enigmatic relationship of that *other* with her own internal foreignness (Laplanche, 1997).

This is the royal road of entry for transgenerational experience.

The vicissitudes of identification

In *Group Psychology and the Analysis of the Ego* (1921c), Freud describes identification as the first emotional tie with an object. Several decades later and almost at the same time, Jessica Benjamin (1991) and Haydeé Faimberg (2005) proposed that besides being an internal process, identification is a type of relationship. Faimberg goes further in her contention that identification is a link that occurs between generations. This transmission between generations is one of the "invisible" objects of psychoanalysis, as infant sexuality was in its time. Although this can be discerned, particularly in the clinical setting, it does not usually give rise to theoretical reflection, less still with regard to its importance in the experience of motherhood.

The helplessness of the newborn child determines that its survival depends on the other. Hence, otherness is the *sine qua non* condition of the process of subjectivation. So, through necessarily alienating identifications, parental narcissism comes into play in the formation of the infant's psyche. The objects that the subject identifies (the mother and the father) "includes in their structure fundamental elements of their own history" (Faimberg, 2005, p. 30). Hence, the whole process of identification always distills one history which, at least partly, precedes the existence of the subject and goes back to previous generations. Faimberg calls this process "alienating unconscious identification". From her point of view, the infant's psyche is made up of the interweaving of the alienating unconscious narcissistic identifications of three generations.

If motherhood updates the primary bonds, then the mother has to deal with *that* history, which corresponds to her parents, more specifically her own mother, and whose transmission is driven by unconscious forces that carry with them her family genealogy.

As the weeks go by, a dynamic develops in the mother and child dyad that oscillates between symbiosis and the intersubjective relationship that begins gradually and becomes particularly important in the separation–individuation stage (Benjamin, 1991). A good symbiotic bond, which implies the development of intimacy, is the foundation of what will be an adequate, gradual process of individuation that makes it possible to tolerate separation. If the mother has considerable difficulty in facilitating her child's individuation process, these failures will hamper the process and will often be expressed as the idealization of the mother. In other words, a poor primary symbiosis can open the way for a new idealization of the mother which will be the corollary of the first and which will probably be translated into a secondary compensatory symbiosis.

While the daughter is in the process of achieving her autonomy through identification and separation experiences, the mother also reviews her own in the light of her relationship with her daughter and with her own mother. This is a negotiation process between symbiosis and the intersubjective relationship that includes transgenerational aspects (Faimberg, 2005; Mariotti, 2012; Mendoza, 2014).

The image of the all-powerful mother has its roots in the early experience of dependence, but the fact that the mother is in a position of omnipotence does not mean that she is omnipotent. She, in turn, will have to use her imagination creatively to fill the gap between her own unconscious fantasy of omnipotence and a more realistic image of herself. The transitional phenomena described by Winnicott (1969) allow a process of decantation aimed at delineating the "real mother". Raphael-Leff (1994) has stated that dealing with the idealised mother figure is a life-long process and one that is relived every time she evokes intense feelings of love or hate. Depending on how she has been able to deal with it, the mother will be able to balance it with a narcissistically satisfactory mental state, and appropriately flexible limits (Mariotti, 2012). One of the failures of this process that has an eloquent result is that of postpartum depression (Zelaya & Mendoza y Soto, 2006).

The internalisation of an unattainable ideal mother can mean that, in later years, the woman feels she is a prisoner of a tyrannical mother figure that provokes in her feelings of inadequacy and of little confidence in her contact with her baby. On becoming a mother, she might try to impose a similar pattern on her child, especially, but not only, if she has a daughter, which opens up the possibility of the process being repeated over generations in the same family (Faimberg, 2005; Welldon, 1988).

Identifications do not occur via the mother alone. In a different but equally important manner, they also develop via the father.

The indispensable third party

The discovery of the existence of the *other* as different from oneself is a process that presupposes a growing awareness of otherness that goes through critical periods of reorganization in which the skills for establishing object relations qualitatively different from pre-existing ones are developed (Benjamin, 1991; Ogden, 1987; Winnicott, 1951, 1969).

In the process that goes from the protective illusion of the subjective object (from four to six months) to the capacity to perceive objects as independent from oneself (from eight to twelve months), according to Winnicott (1969), or from the separation phase to the rapprochement phase (in the view of Mahler and taken up by Benjamin (1991)), the gender and genital difference that begins to be registered between the father and the mother takes over the symbolic direction of the psyche. The father, present until then fundamentally through the mother's mind, now represents a different kind of object.

Towards the second year of life, both for girls and boys, the father is an important figure as he represents the possibility of moving from the dyadic relationship and entering the shared world. With the advent of symbolic representations begins the process of identification with masculine and feminine traits on the basis of identifications with both parents, but these are still developed as aspects of the child's own self. At this stage, the presence of a third person is particularly important, for whom the child develops a kind of identificatory love and who becomes a second vector of the future triangle that the infant will construct in the oedipal scenario. Benjamin (1991) maintains that at this point the role the father plays of being *the other* for the girl or boy is more important than his function as the mother's partner. The father is seen as the desiring subject *par excellence*, and the identificatory love for him reveals the child's desire to be like him. In the case of the girl, her identification with the father would not be a reaction to castration, as indicated by classical psychoanalysis, but, rather, the result of admiration and love for the father and what he represents.

Ogden has said that before the change in the object that has to occur in order for the oedipal development to take place, the girl is in love with "father in the mother". Initially, the feminine Oedipus complex does not revolve around the relationship with the father, but "with the mother's unconscious identification with her own father" (Ogden, 1987, p. 101). The primary period of the development of the feminine Oedipus complex supposes a triangulation of the object relations achieved in the context described above: that of a relationship between two people, more specifically, between two women. Before the little girl is able to establish a relationship with the *other*, mother and daughter engage in a "dress rehearsal", conducted in the safe intimacy of the dyad. In this situation, the mother will let herself be used as a conduit towards a relationship with the other, as a transitional oedipal relationship (Ogden, 1987).

The oedipal father performs an essential role. He will offer the small girl the chance for both of them to identify with the mother and also to differentiate from her. The recognition and acceptance of her daughter's sexual identity will confirm that it is not an anatomical destiny, but a matter of gender and cross-identification (Benjamin, 1991). At the same time, in his relationship with his daughter and his partner, the father must have clearly established a distinction between the sexuality of the girl and that of an adult, that is, he must have internalised an oedipal structure. If any kind of problem arises regarding the space of the third party, this will produce in the daughter feelings of rivalry with the mother and also with the father figure.

If it is difficult for a mother to encourage the transitional oedipal relationship, this produces in the fantasy of the girl the prohibition of approaching the father, suffocates the development of her interest in him, and rather confirms the belief that "the feelings she does have are bad: too disloyal, too dirty, intense, too greedy, directed at the wrong person, etc." (Ogden, 1987, p. 103). At this point in development, the mother's inability to serve as a transitional oedipal object—because she was unable to identify herself with her own father—is interpreted as a lack of will to help the girl move into the phase of object oedipal relations. Both Ogden (1987) and Faimberg (2005) underline the importance of the way the relationship with the primal mother, the primal parents, the Oedipus complex, etc., are registered in the psyche through identification with the parents and, through them, with the parents' parents; in other words, generational transmission.

Unconscious narcissistic identification in three generations of women: clinical notes

What follows is a series of extracts of the register of weekly observations made in an infant observation seminar using the Esther Bick method. Although the purpose of this experience was the observation of the bond between Gabriela and Ana Paula, mother and baby, respectively, to discuss early identifications and transgenerational aspects, I focus on the relationship between Gabriela and Alicia—

Gabriela's mother—and between Alicia and her mother, whom I call "great-grandmother": that is, on three generations of women.

Gabriela was twenty-three when I met her. She was short, slender, soft-spoken, with long, wavy hair, and she dressed like any young person of her age. She was the second of three siblings, had studied Hotel Administration and Cuisine and specialised in desserts and confectionery. Her parents had separated when she was seven. Alicia, her mother, also worked in preparing food and confectionery and was self-employed. Victor, Gabriela's husband, was the head chef of a restaurant in a large city. They met at the institute where they studied and decided to live together when she became pregnant with Ana Paula, who was a first child for both of them. The fact that Gabriela's family constellation revolved around food is of special importance because she had suffered from anorexia and bulimia until a year before becoming pregnant, and her mother was overweight.

When Gabriela's daughter was born, her feminine family network (mother, elder sister, and great-grandmother) took care of her, and provided her with support and company, but as the months went by this situation gradually moved towards a polar opposite of demands, control, and narcissism. For a number of reasons, the masculine figures in the family—her husband Victor, Gabriela's father, and her older brother—were essentially absent. Alicia said that Gabriela's father: ". . . loves his children, but doesn't give us any money. If we had put our hopes in him, we would never have managed." About Victor, her son-in-law, she said, ". . . he is a nice boy, but from a poor family; I don't think he will provide a future for my daughter."

First six months

The first few months were a time for the mother and child to bond. Gabriela's mother and elder sister looked in every day to keep them company. Alicia taught her to put the baby's nappies on, cut her nails, and give her a quick bath if necessary. She always brought something for the two of them: fruit, for example, or pretty hairpins. The sister dressed Ana Paula like a little girl, played music, and taught her to dance. Nearing the second six months, there were changes in the relationship between Gabriela and her daughter, at the same time that the relationship between Gabriela and her mother began to show a more complex side. Gabriela, who breast-fed her daughter whenever Ana

Paula wanted, began to move beyond a prolonged period of primary maternal concern coinciding with the development of the infant, which moves from the protective illusion of the subjective object (from four to six months) to the capacity to experience objects as independent of oneself (eight to twelve months), and permits greater bodily separation from the mother (Winnicott, 1969). During this time. I witnessed the repetition of difficulties in the separation–autonomy process and observed the manifestations of some kind of unconscious identification conveyed over three generations.

Seven months

I arrived at the flat when Victor and Gabriela were going out for a work dinner of his. I saw Gabriela with make-up on for the first time; she looked very feminine. This was the second time I had seen Victor, which confirmed my perception of him as a manly man. At that time, I saw a couple making some space for themselves, not like parents raising their little baby. I went in and greeted Alicia, Ana Paula's grandmother, who began to complain indirectly: "Poor little Ana Paula, she's had a bad cold, she's been chesty, and had a runny nose all day. Poor little thing. Gabriela has given her drops and medicines, but I think she has a temperature. It's very damp in this neighbourhood!" Then she added, "I am really scared, I hope she doesn't cry because otherwise I'd have to take a taxi and go and get them. It's happened twice already." At the end of the hour's observation, when I was about to leave, she said: "Ana Paula can only sleep when she is nursing, I hope she doesn't cry, because I won't know what to do!"

Seven months and three weeks

> A: Gabriela, doesn't this onesie do up any more?
> G: No, mum, I forgot to button it up.
> A: And what about this one, dear?
> G: It got dirty at lunch time.
> A: (in a little girl's voice) But Mummy, you should have changed me, my botty's an ickle bit dirty". . . . I think she has a temperature (Gabriela didn't answer) . . . let's see, look . . . (Gabriela, under pressure, took Ana Paula and gave her a kiss) . . . Now stop kissing her so much and check if she's got a temperature.

G: No, mum. (She started breast-feeding Ana Paula. Meanwhile, the grandmother took some clean clothes and started to change the baby while she was nursing). Oh, mum, you're so annoying . . . (and, visibly angry, she said to me), Look, Johanna . . . the other day we left Ana Paula at my mother's house because we wanted to go to see the Expovino at the Wong supermarket. We left her at 7: 30 p.m.

A: At 7:00 p.m.

G: And at 9:30 p.m. she called us, but Victor only saw the call ten minutes later.

A: It was later, around 9:50 p.m., almost 10 p.m.

G: No it wasn't, Mum, but it doesn't matter. What with all the traffic, we got back to my mother's house at nearly 11.30 p.m . . .

A: She was restless, she started crying, it was horrible.

G: Both of them were crying!

A: I can't stand it when she cries. The point is, Gabriela wants her to have a bottle because she wants to work part-time. Isn't it too soon? What do you think?

Observer: That she wants to wean her bit by bit.

G: I only want to give her a bottle at night so that she gets used to being more independent. You cry because you're very nervous, and she cries because she can feel that.

A: How can you leave her to cry, if she is unhappy?

G: Mum, she is not unhappy, just crying.

A: I never had trouble with my daughters. My eldest slept from 7:30 p.m. till the morning. I realised she did her "poo" in the morning, so I would sit her on a special potty when she was eight months old and play her some music and play with her. By the time she was nine months old she never pooed in her nappy. (I saw that Alicia had a childish expression, she was making a face, practically pouting. It was then that I realised the true scope of what was happening. I was observing a discussion that showed interference in the relationship between Gabriela and Alicia that corresponded to an old, shared world. I understood that both felt the need to confide in someone else who could listen to them and help them out of the *impasse*.

A: (with a look of genuine concern) It's all so difficult, I don't know what to do!

G: Now I know why I've always been so anxious. Even when I was older I could never go to do my homework at my friends' houses because I was scared stiff. I didn't know what would happen, what I had to do, it must have been because you were anxious too . . . that's why.

Ana Paula had gone to sleep. Gabriela tried to put her to bed and she woke up again. She lifted her hand signing "stop" to Alicia, who wanted to approach, and said, "I can do it".

Nine months

I was with Alicia, the mother of Alicia (i.e., Ana Paula's great-grand-mother), and Victor, who was changing the baby's nappies. Gabriela was not there.

> B: (with a big smile) How are you, Johannita?
> Observer: Fine, thanks.
> B: Have you come to visit Ana Paula? (She took my hand). Come, she's here.
> A: Where would you like to sit, Johanna?
> Observer: Wherever Ana Paula is.

Victor had finished changing Ana Paula's nappy and she was laughing with him. He was carrying her, Ana Paula smiled at him and he kissed her, and she went on laughing happily. She was over the moon with her father. Victor then said goodbye and went to work.

> A: Did you see that? She is standing up now.
> B: She is standing up now, did you see?
> A: Sometimes she wants to walk a bit.
> B: She already wants to walk. Children today! I think they are brighter than they used to be. My son started to walk when he was a year and two months.
> A: (speaking to me) Look!
>   Ana Paula was standing, holding on to the index finger of each of her grandmother's hands.
> B: (touching my leg so that I would look at her) Isn't she lovely? Do you believe it is good for children to walk early? People used to think it wasn't good, until they were a year old. How things have changed! Do you remember the nappies we used to have? I used to wash the nappies in the mornings and hang them out on the roof. At five in the afternoon I would go and bring them in. Even though we had three maids, because the house was big, I did that myself. There were three nappies, do you remember? Johannita, is it good for children to use baby-walkers? My husband didn't want our son to use a walker and I would rather Ana Paula didn't use one because she might fall over. Alfredo fell over and got a very nasty knock.

A: Mum, that was ages ago! Alfredito is sixty-two now. Anyway, that is up to Gabriela and Victor. Mind your own business.

B: Well, and what about you, Johannita, do you think Ana Paula will crawl? It would be better if she crawled, wouldn't it?

A: Mum, she doesn't want to crawl, we've tried it several times and four days ago she wanted to stand by herself. (She sat Ana Paula on the swing which had a canopy with lights and sounds.)

B: You shouldn't put her in the swing, she'll fall out. The things they do nowadays!

A: Don't meddle, Mum. (She brought me a dessert). Here, Johanna, Gabriela left this mousse, it is a new recipe she has tried out, but I put it in the freezer and I think it is rock-hard, isn't it?

Observer: Yes, the spoon won't cut it! (We both laughed. Ana Paula turned round, laughed with us and blinked both her eyes at us. The great-grandmother looked as if she was going to say something.)

A: Mum, please. It's Ana Paula she's come to see, not you.

For further thought

I have described some of the characteristics of the relationship between three generations of women, Gabriela, her mother, and the "great-grandmother", that show the presence of early alienating identifications in the mother–daughter relationship in the stage when the latter in turn becomes a mother. It was around the time of Ana Paula's development stage of bodily separation from the mother (from seven to nine months) that pending psychic processes were stirred in three generations of their female lineage: those that come into play in the dynamic that occurs in the move from the phase of symbiosis to that of separation and individuation.

When little Ana Paula was achieving greater autonomy through identification and separation experiences, Gabriela, under pressure from her daughter's evolutionary demands, reviewed her own processes of separation from Ana Paula and from Alicia. A similar review occurred at the same time in the relationship between Alicia and her mother. It is clear in this example that the process of negotiation between symbiosis and the individual intersubjective relationship is also a transgenerational process (Mariotti, 2012; Mendoza, 2014).

Alicia's difficulties with separation–individuation from her daughter and her mother might have hampered Gabriela in leaving her stronghold of power and control. The separation anxiety arising from Gabriela's fusional relationship with her mother was probably felt to be catastrophic at times. Pines (1982) said that when the mother–daughter relationship has these characteristics, the daughter can use her pregnancy to prove that she is separate from her mother. As Welldon has said (2011), she can also use it to reaffirm that there is something good in her body. The prolonged use of breast-feeding on demand (which went on for over fourteen months) could be understood as a consequence of Gabriela's need to confirm that she was able to produce good milk, but also as an attempt to avoid the separation–individuation process that would lead Ana Paula to place her in the position of the mother from whom she would have to separate. How could she facilitate this process if she herself has remained trapped in the separation–individuation dynamic with her own mother and her mother's with her mother? Gabriela had probably tried to modulate these difficulties by extending the weaning period, in contrast with the haste and coercion of her mother in sphincter control training (with her older sister, for example), and the great-grandmother's demands, disguised as concern, who insisted that things should be done "as they were in her day".

A daughter's motherhood is not always experienced as a happy event. A mother might feel particularly unfortunate in her circumstances when her daughter seems to have a life full of opportunities ahead of her. This would seem to be case with Alicia. The envy that Melanie Klein (1987) has described as frequently felt by the infant towards its mother, who can give life, could be revived in the opposite direction, which would make the mother feel, more or less consciously, an intense envy towards her daughter. I witnessed how Alicia felt jealousy and envy at a vital time in the life of Gabriela, a young woman in the fullness of her sexuality and fertility, when she tried to interfere in the couple's private time. I also observed her attempt to erase the image of the devoted and self-sacrificing mother which she has constructed of herself in the past, which also led her to face up to her own mother to support Gabriela's decisions and independence and affirm her own individuality.

When the mother's unconscious oedipal structure has had a pathological development, this pathology will color the evolution of the daughter's oedipal structure. Alicia's overweight and Gabriela's food disorders could be an example of this. What emptiness was Alicia trying to fill by eating too much food? What message did she wish to convey by changing Ana Paula's nappies so capably? Ogden (1987) says that if the mother has the unconscious belief that she is a defective woman, or feels ashamed of some deficiency, the daughter can be expected not only to identify with the mother's feeling of internal imperfection and concomitant shame, but she also feels narcissistically wounded by her mother. The narcissistic wound is manifested in a fantasy of a bodily wound, loss, or defect. In this sense, Gabriela's anorexic body prior to her pregnancy and the birth of Ana Paula, a body emptied of anatomical sexual differences, might have been the expression of a narcissistic wound that harks back to that time of the evolutionary process.

The importance of the father, the indispensable third party in the development of a healthy maternality and of the condition of being a subject, can be glimpsed in the vignettes of the observations. The presence of Victor seems to have made Gabriela capable of beginning to detach herself from the alienating narcissistic identification with her mother and grandmother. By deciding when to start weaning Ana Paula, ignoring Alicia's opinion, she avoided repetition and ensured that the "past stayed in the past". My own presence as observer and companion to the Gabriela–Ana Paula dyad probably reinforced the presence of the third party.

Winnicott (1952) suggested that "there is no such thing as a baby without its mother". It is my contention that "there is no such thing as a baby without its mother, without the mother's mother, and without the mother's mother's mother". Each mother–child pair enforces a maternal lineage criss-crossed with narcissistic bonds and identifications that are unconsciously conveyed from generation to generation.

The observation of the dynamic of the relationship between mother and daughter, mother and grandmother, grandmother and great-grandmother, which revealed difficulties in the maternal line with the processes of differentiation, separation, and autonomy, enabled me to specify my reflections about the complex experience of motherhood, but it also left me with a number of questions. For example, what of projective identifications—of which I was the object—when there is no one to fulfil this important function of mind–womb that embraces them and permits the development of a process of thought into emotional development? The approach used in the pre-clinical setting opened in the process of infant observation is precisely that of fulfilling a function of containing and subsequently giving retrospective meaning (*aprés coup*) to what has been observed. This mental work is sustained by the internal psychoanalytical framework of the observer.

It is also worth asking whether this type of alienating identification, in that it makes the past remain present, supports the validity of certain cultural and social structures that foster the repetition of prejudices, ideals, and models that constrain a woman's development with unnecessary demands that complicate the function of motherhood even further, despite progress in civilization.

A pending task is that of reflecting on the transgenerational transmission of this type of unconscious alienating narcissistic identifications that constrain the conditions necessary for the development of the ego and the unfolding of thought. To make visible the importance of their role in the experience of motherhood is to make it possible to work them through, so that everyone can venture to write their own story.

References

Alizade, A. M. (1999). El sustrato sensual-afectivo y la estructuración psíquica. Sensualidad y afectos. *Revista de Psicoanálisis, LVI*(3): 579–590.

Anzieu, D. (2007). *El yo piel.* Madrid: Biblioteca Nueva.

Aulagnier, P. (2001). *La violencia de la interpretación. Del pictograma al enunciado.* Buenos Aires: Amorrotu Editores.

Benjamin, J. (1991). Father and daughter: identification with difference. A contribution to gender heterodoxy. *Psychoanalytic Dialogues, 1*: 277–299.

Chasseguet-Smirgel, J. (1976). Freud and female sexuality: the consideration of some blind spots in the exploration of the 'dark continent'. *International Journal of Psychoanalysis, 57*: 275–287.

Faimberg, H. (2005). *The Telescoping of Generations: Listening to the Narcissistic Links between Generations.* London: Routledge.

Freud, S. (1921c). *Group Psychology and the Analysis of the Ego. S. E., 18*: London: Hogarth.

Klein, M. (1987). *Envy and Gratitude: A Study of Unconscious Sources.* Philadelphia, PA: Tavistock.

Kristeva, J. (1980). *Desire in Language.* New York: Columbia Press.

Laplanche, J. (1997). The theory of seduction and the problem of the other. *International Journal of Psychoanalysis, 78*: 653–666.

Mariotti, P. (2012). General introduction. In: *The Maternal Lineage: Identification, Desire and Transgenerational Issues* (pp. 1–44). London: Routledge.

Mendoza, J. (2014). Algunas versiones sobre el linaje materno: lo transgeneracional y las identificaciones tempranas en cuatro generaciones de mujeres. *Revista de Psicoanálisis, 14*: 149–160.

Ogden, T. (1987). The transitional oedipal relationship in female development. *International Journal of Psychoanalysis, 68*: 485–498.

Pines, D. (1982). The relevance of early psychic development to pregnancy and abortion. *International Journal of Psychoanalysis, 63*: 311–319.

Raphael-Leff, J. (1993). *Pregnancy: The Inside Story*. London: Sheldon Press.

Raphael-Leff, J. (1994)[1988]. El lugar de las cosas salvajes. In: Moisés Lemlij (Ed.), *Mujeres por mujeres* (pp. 31–44). Lima: Biblioteca Peruana de Psicoanálisis y Fondo Editorial Sidea.

Welldon, E. (1988). *Mother, Madonna, Whore. The Idealization and Denigration of Motherhood*. London: Free Associations Books.

Welldon, E. (2011). Bodies across generations and cycles of abuse. In: *The Maternal Lineage: Identification, Desire and Transgenerational Issues*. London: Routledge.

Winnicott, D. W. (1951). Transitional objects and transitional phenomena. In: *Playing and Reality* (pp. 1–25). New York: Tavistock, 1985.

Winnicott, D. W. (1952). Anxiety associated with insecurity. In: *Through Pediatrics to Psycho-Analysis* (pp. 97–100). London: Hogarth, 1975.

Winnicott, D. W. (1960). Ego distortion in terms of true and false self. In: *The Maturational Processes and the Facilitating Environment: Studies in the Theory of Emotional Development* (pp. 140–152). London: Hogarth, 1965.

Winnicott, D. W. (1969). The use of an object. *International Journal of Psychoanalysis, 50*: 711–716.

Zelaya, C. R., & Mendoza y Soto, J. E. (Eds.) (2006). *La maternidad y sus vicisitudes, hoy*. Lima: Sidea.

CHAPTER EIGHT

Abuse of women: relation to the maternal representation

Vivian B. Pender

Introduction

Abuse of women has many forms and consequences: psychological, economic, political, religious, cultural, and physical. Abuse is unconscious and conscious. It is evident in attitudes, object relations, subjective experience, affective states, and demonstrable behaviors. While different forms of abuse may appear to be distinct from one another, they are not mutually exclusive. Rather, they are interwoven and cumulative in yielding a stereotypic definition of women that can be traced to the first love-object, the mother.

A psychic maternal representation of the mother is universal. Symbolized by the maternal ego, maternal ego ideal, and the maternal superego, it informs the vicissitudes of identity, caretaking relationships, and consolidates bio-psychosocial foundations of all attachments. While responsive and sensitive maternal caretaking is a priority for optimal human development, ambivalence, aggression, and abuse may also play a role. This chapter explores the various forms of abuse and their particular relation to individual and group maternal representations.

Psychological abuse

Psychological abuse arises when there is discordance between a woman's psychic reality and her actual experience reflected by her environment. The potential for psychological abuse arises the moment the sex of a baby is identified. Although fantasies about the female child are ubiquitous, they usually begin in pregnancy, and may be divergent from the reality of the identified sex. In combination with the imagined future woman that the female child will become and fantasies of and about the pregnant mother, universal fantasies of a maternal representation are actualized. At this early stage, potential abuse contained in the maternal representation is first initiated, and later reinforced and cemented.

Balsam (2012) addressed the sexed and gendered body. She iterated that pregnancy is a uniquely female activity. In her psychoanalytic work with women, Balsam addressed women's thoughts and feelings about their bodies, their mother's bodies, and their female analysts' bodies. (I presume that many women analysts understand the importance of their own body, inside and outside, perhaps without acknowledging it.) She addressed the elderly female body, focusing on characteristics such as the aging functions of the internal organs. She connects this with unconscious wishes and defenses concerning the maternal representation. She reconfirms Freud's original idea that the ego is first a body ego and alludes to his theoretical separation of sexuality from procreation as liberating.

Pines (1990) noted that in pregnancy, the intimate relationship between mind, body, affect, and relationships is evident when the body is used unconsciously to avoid psychic pain and conflict. She concluded that a pregnant woman faces two possible experiences: either giving birth to a live baby or effectively destroying the fetus by miscarriage or abortion. She stated, "A mother may thus either facilitate life and motherhood or destroy them both." She reflected on cases where women used sex and pregnancy to resolve or avoid psychic conflict. She illustrated universal maternal ambivalence with several of her cases. These studies suggest that the pregnant woman is subject to a psychological abuse that emanates from her own subconscious, incorporating elements of self-loathing, inadequacy, and inchoate feelings of an emerging deficiency that may have an impact on the female child.

Psychological abuse is transmitted from collective individual maternal representations and insinuated into the mores of large group cultures. In essence, it is a world within which females are considered less capable, less valuable, and, therefore, less worthy as individuals. It appears to be a reaction to, and defense against, the perceived, imagined, and real power of the mother. Weldon (1988) has focused on the mother as the object of denigration. Spivak (2012) emphasized the schizoid experience of being female. "Outside in" and "subaltern" are terms she has used to describe how women are part of the various institutions of our society, but are effectively insignificant and non-essential components lying outside of the institutional machinery. Moeslein-Teising and Thomson-Salo (2013) suggest that the variety of, and investment in, the visual physical adornment of the female body and emphasis on female external body parts represent a universal symbolic denial of reproductive power.

Baruch (1987), Nelson (1967), and Silver (2007) have noted that the power of pregnancy not only affects women. Clinically, male patients can be found to be in awe of and fear the power of pregnancy. They might develop Couvade syndrome, accompanied by some symptoms of pregnancy. For some men, pregnancy has a different meaning. For some, pregnancy can be a demonstration of their own potency and power. Some male patients fear (and wish for) the possibility that they have "made" a woman pregnant. More than once clinical experience has provided evidence of pregnancy envy by male patients. Some men wish they had that reproductive power, evidence of an obvious sense of lack. However, envy of pregnancy has not been as popular-ized as envy of the penis. The focus on the power of external genitalia rather than the potentially higher power of female reproductive organs over life and death is defensively denied.

The psychological impact of abuse on the mother–infant dyad can be profound. Pregnancy appears to be a narcissistic attachment for the mother, since the infant has been part of her, physically and psychi-cally. Ownership of the infant fulfills a narcissistic need for the mother, and, in the best of circumstances, it acts protectively. Ideally, she must identify with the fetus and/or infant as if it were herself in her mother's body and mind. Idealization and omnipotence can be striking narcissistic features in this early dyadic relationship between mother and child. In a position of immense power and dominance over life and death, the infant's mother is vulnerable to narcissistic injury if the child does not fit with her "child ego ideal" or infringes on her own maternal ego ideal. In the face of such narcissism, the child can become the object of the mother's projections or, worse, the object of splitting. In the worst case, the mother conveys disorganization of reality by failing to set limits or by providing a delusional structure. The child is the object of the mother's mind and her ambivalence, always present to a greater or lesser degree. A potentially destructive fantasy, even if merely displaced, cannot be realized until there is an actual pregnancy. In this scenario, all children suffer from some amount of the negative aspects of maternal ambivalence. Influenced by the mother's mental state, anxiety, depression, and personality, the child is the beneficiary of negative quotients that will inform his self-representation and his identification. If these are predominant, he will feel negatively towards himself and his mother (or her surrogates). Importantly, girls will, at some point in their lives, be faced with a similar dilemma, that is, their attitude toward their own potential pregnancies.

Women must constantly balance between two conflicting experiences: their internal reality that each girl and woman experiences privately and the external persona that they are expected to present to the world, particularly from puberty until menopause, around age twelve to around age sixty. The internal reality is the existence of symbolically powerful reproductive organs that most women are aware of consciously. This awareness might only become conscious when they experience the pain and discomfort associated with menarche, monthly menstruation, gynecological diseases, pregnancy, childbirth, breastfeeding, and menopause. Many women in clinical settings speak implicitly about their "inner" feelings, signified by their internal needs and external demands. Externally, girls are clothed in special female attire, they are given female names, restricted to female play, and relegated to female duties, viewed as peripheral to the family line, unworthy of education, subject to sexual indenture, and liable for a dowry. These discordant pressures effectively abuse the maternal psyche and inhibit it from evolving in a more productive way.

Economic abuse

Economic abuse is another form in which women are treated as if they were commodities. Such abuse operates at home and the workplace.

The economic abuse of women is less subtle and more overt than other forms. Such treatment is an extension of attitudes towards the maternal representation imitated and internalized at home and simply carried over to the factory, office, and classroom. Again, women's roles are found to be subordinate, their contributions trivialized, their commitment suspect, and their importance devalued. The metrics of inequality appear readily in the home and in the workplace in the form of pay, promotion, and leave policies. Generally, there is unpaid work at home and unequal pay at work, accompanied by insufficient day care, lack of family leave, and unpaid maternity leave, all coupled with inflexible hours.

Mill and Mill (1851) provided a particularly poignant description of the centrality of the home in the perpetration of abuse of women in an essay entitled "The subjugation of women":

> The most insignificant of men, the man who can obtain influence or consideration nowhere else, finds one place where he is chief and head. There is one person, often greatly his superior in understanding, who is obliged to consult him, and who he is not obliged to consult. He is judge, magistrate, ruler, over their joint concerns; arbiter of all differences between them. The justice or conscience to which her appeal must be made is his justice and conscience: it is his to hold the balance and adjust the scales between his own claims or wishes and those of another. His is now the only tribunal in civilized life, in which the same person is judge and party. (p 295)

In this depiction, it is clear to all what situation is being described. This affirms its persisting applicability to modern times.

In May 2015, the Harvard Business School launched its gender initiative in order to research inequities between male and female employees in the workplace. They found that parity in leadership positions is sorely lacking. Among the 500 top companies that comprise the US Standard and Poors Financial Index, only 4.6% of Chief Executive Officers were female. The study also found that women were less vocal about it and tended to blame themselves. These issues of self-doubt occurred despite the fact that their male counterparts had the advantage of being part of the "club" where men mentor and support each other to ensure success.

The study also looked at the business school's own students. Whereas scores and grades were equal between men and women at the time of entrance, women's grades fell significantly below the men's by the time they graduated. Anecdotes suggested that these young modern men and women exhibited the certain well-established stereotypes. Male peers accepted women if they were attractive ("hot") but rejected them if they were too assertive. Women voiced concern about their "dating cap" (capital) and did not want to do battle with the men who dominated classroom discussions even though it resulted in lower final grades for the women. Men were encouraged to ridicule women and junior faculty. In one year, a third of the junior women faculty resigned, without any protest. Employee discomfort with a woman "boss" was one of the reasons cited. According to the study, even assertive women were not well liked by men or women.

An earlier Harvard Business School survey (2012) of 50,000 adults from twenty-five developed countries found that women with mothers who had worked when they were young had more powerful jobs and higher earnings. In the USA, for example, women who had working mothers earned 23% more than those women whose mothers did not work. Men whose mothers worked were found to spend more time on family and childcare than men whose mothers did not work. These statistics might suggest that mothers mentor their daughters to succeed in the world outside the home whereas they teach their sons to help inside the home. The men studied might have been imitating their fathers who helped at home (or at least supported the idea) while their mothers were working. It might also be interpreted to mean that mothers who have successfully navigated a male oriented workplace have transmitted their own experience to their children. It also suggests that, due to the odds against them, women need more support to be economically successful.

The American Association of University Women (2015) reported that a gender pay gap exists in every state in the USA. Across the range of occupations, including female dominated ones such as primary education, there was lack of parity. Despite equal variables such as title, hours, etc., before age thirty-five, women are paid 90%, of what men are paid. After age thirty-five, the rate drops to 75% for all women. The percentages were even lower, 55–65%, for Hispanic women and women of color.

These data suggest that economic abuse is a feature that invites analytic scrutiny. In the home, maternal functions are resources that include many life sustaining and life progression components. These include organization of reality and when and how to assess another's intentions, mind, and behavior. Reality informs the child what is possible and what is not, what is beneficial and what is harmful. In order to obtain what one needs or desires, reciprocity and negotiation are needed. These resources may be as basic as food and shelter. They are also the basis of empathy, with oneself and with others. Girls who did not receive this kind of attention, or if it was distorted for some reason, are at great risk for not being able to care about themselves, their bodies or their minds. They might neglect ordinary health care, prevention and treatment of illnesses. Their physiological processes might temporarily or permanently change. They might not have an understanding, a concept, or a model of a mind, their own or others. In their maternal representations they might identify with a neglect-ful and/or abusing object and, in identification with the aggressor, become the perpetrator who preyed on them. Without intervention or change, there will be intergenerational transmission of these dynam-ics and relationships that affect working conditions for women outside the home.

The maternal representation applied to the workplace may be equally abusive to women. As defined in these studies, the maternal repre-sentation is passive, receptive, nurturing, resourceful, masochistic, and physically adorned. It is as if there is a social contract that women have in which they, despite their psychological conflict, mutually agree to accept a maternal representation. They do this even though it might damage the fabric of their economic existence. For example, many women have implicitly agreed to perform unpaid surrogate parenting for men. Sometimes, through the use of pornography and prostitution, sex workers, mostly women, have contracted to use their sexuality to enhance male sexual behavior. The wish that women's self-esteem, identification, and self-confidence with a solid ego that can acknowledge and negotiate with her reality, in order to success-fully accomplish her drive, very often remains a fragile hope. More often, her wishes are inhibited at many stages of her life, or, worse, she is abused for being feminine. A difficult task to achieve, most are relegated to being marginalized in both conscious and unconscious ways.

Once again, the maternal representation found in economic abuse can be connected to the original source of all that is needed and desired. Financial, human, and physical resources are necessary for civilizations to continue. Derived from the extended dependency of the child on the mother (or surrogate) for resources, there is competition and hostility. Women, who have traditionally been the "gatherers", continue in many low-income, agriculturally dependent countries to bring water and food to their families. It is analogous to the care-giving roles of women in high-income countries who attend to their families, children or parents. The most prevalent economic factor that interferes with a woman's success and increases her economic vulnerability worldwide is pregnancy and young children. She has been psychologically primed to accept care-taking roles.

Political abuse

Political abuse of women occurs when government policies discriminate specifically against women. In this form of abuse, laws, regulations, and policies are used to exercise political control over women's reproductive freedom, as well as freedom to vote, own land, inherit property, or even to drive a car.

Prior to the availability of oral contraceptives in the USA in 1960, it was principally women who assumed responsibility for unwanted pregnancies, not only the physical burden, but the social one as well. The prospect of such pregnancies thus terrorized women of child-bearing age. Despite the fact that the "pill" was an instant hit due to its effectiveness, eight states banned its sale in 1964 and the Vatican declared opposition in 1968. And while the 1973 US Supreme Court decided in Roe vs. Wade to guarantee a woman's right to choose, abortion remains politicized in the USA's government (US History, 2015).

One need only cite the striking example of Romania under the brutal rule of Ceauçescu. In 1967, he instituted Decree 770, which banned abortion and contraception in a misguided effort to increase the population (although his true motivations are unknown). The use of any practice that inhibited reproduction was considered a criminal state offense. However, instead of mothers choosing to keep their children, infants were abandoned and Romanian orphanages, overrun with large numbers, became infamous for the severe neglect of their wards and the disastrous consequences of proscription of contraception and abortion.

A counter-example is the "one child policy" of China (Rosenberg, 2015). Instituted in 1979 by Deng Xiaoping to limit population growth, it has for decades resulted in forced abortions and sterilizations. Hesketh and colleagues (2005) reported that it was an "an ambitious program of market reform following the economic stagnation of the Cultural Revolution". A voluntary policy that began in 1970 had already resulted in a population decline. However, the law was strictly enforced in urban areas and with government employees. In rural areas, there appeared to be a greater degree of non-registration of female births as well as less rigorous medical treatment of girls who were sick.

> The picture that emerges is that some urban Chinese make the choice to perform sex selection with the first pregnancy, since they are allowed only one child. In rural areas, most couples are permitted to have a second child, especially if the first is female. So if the second (or subsequent) child is female, the pregnancy often "disappears," allowing the couple to have another child in an attempt to have a son. (p. 1171)

Sex ratio imbalances were found in all sectors of China. The authors also noted sex ratio imbalances in many other Asian countries where there is sex-selective abortion and a traditional preference for males.

More recently, in Morocco, the Associated Press reported that twenty-four babies a day in 2012 were being abandoned. It was thought that this was due to a general lack of access to abortion and the stigma of having a child "out of wedlock" or having a child as the result of a rape. Gavalas and co-authors (2015) studied sex selective abortions. They found that

> . . . the number of male per 100 female live births (defined as the sex ratio at birth, SRB) has been shown to be consistently stable in human populations irrespective of time and geographical location. [Worldwide] approximately 105 boys are born for every 100 girls and any significant deviation from this "global average" is considered to be unnatural and is attributed to sex-selective under-reporting of births, sex-selective abortion, sex-selective infanticide or other man-made factors. (p. 363)

They found that in present day Greece,

... the SRB is extremely masculine when the parents originate from the Indian sub-continent and China. The SRB is also unnaturally high (more than 113 boys per 100 girls) in the case of legitimate births born to Greek mothers who are illiterate. These findings are strong evidence that sex-selective abortions are taking place in Greece within population groups with a certain ethnic and social profile. (p. 363)

Reported by National Public Radio (www.pbs.org), Saudi Arabia announced that women would be granted the right to vote in 2015. King Abdullah said that women would also be allowed to run in local elections. However, enormous barriers remain. Separate voting stations for women will need to be constructed. Since utility bills and property ownership are not listed in women's names, voter registration will prove difficult. Last, since they cannot drive or be seen in public in some regions without a male relative, the women's right to vote in Saudi Arabia will not be a reality any time soon.

A singular example of a region of the world where women successfully attained leadership roles is Rwanda since the 1994 genocide (Hunt, 2014). Although hundreds of thousands of women and girls were systematically gang-raped, held as sex slaves, and sexually mutilated, many survived. Since that time, women have become political leaders at all levels of society. After the genocide, the country's population comprised 70% women. Rwanda is the only country in the world to have a female legislative majority. Women constitute 56% of parliament members. Such a critical mass of women in governance in Rwanda is reminiscent of the American Civil War and Second World War periods, when men were simply not available to fill political positions and women assumed many responsibilities previously considered the province of men. These periods, though short-lived, are considered by some to have sparked first and second wave feminism. At present, female majorities in Rwanda's government correlate with its rising gross national product (annual growth rate of 7%), universal education, universal healthcare, and rebuilding the country's infrastructure. Rwanda has moved up in the World Economic Forum's competitiveness index (United Nations Population Fund, 2010). Although much of this is ascribed to President Kagame, the high number of women in leadership is indisputable and cannot be discounted. In 2017, when Kagame finishes his third term, the future of Rwanda's support of women will be at stake. Once freed from oppression and enabled to make political decisions, some women do not wish to return to a time of enforced passivity and even slavery. That said, feminism might blossom in Rwanda if instability in surrounding countries does not overwhelm the possibility.

Political abuse of women is largely related to women's sexual freedom and reproductive rights. One can only speculate as to the causes. In this regard, it is generally related to the maternal representation and its functions. Although access to contraception and abortion is said to enable women's ability to separate sexual enjoyment from procreation, there is some indication that this is precisely the issue. The regression that intimacy includes relates to the maternal representation and the care giving that it involves. Rules of law might not entirely succeed in regulating such intimate human behaviour, but their impact cannot be underestimated. Those who do not abide by "the law" are classified as antisocial. Many women are taught to feel threatened by the law (in Lacanian terms, symbolized by the language of the father figure), even if it conflicts with their instincts and moral conscience. This might be confusing, and perhaps their mothers ultimately protect them by teaching them to abide by the law. Thus, political abuse might be in the interest of survival.

Religious abuse

Religion represents another area of human experience where discrimination against women is deeply embedded. Religion provides a significant and large context for justified and hidden abuse of women. In particular, destructive religious attitudes towards female sexuality, female reproduction, female authority, and the maternal representation are common. A girl's development and future may be determined while immersed in a religious affiliation that is oppressive, controlling, and unquestioned. If God, a male figure, is invoked, it is impossible to contradict His word. Most of the world's religions embrace a divine figure that is male, resulting in a belief system that implicitly reduces women to subordinate status. It appears that the most orthodox and extreme religious factions are usually the most abusive towards girls and women. While the particulars may vary from religion to religion, the effect on girls and women is predictable. Dismissive and abusive attitudes are engendered that undermine female confidence, authority, and independence. This renders female sexuality and reproduction as activities to be controlled.

Tamale (2015) surveyed the world's religions with regard to the features with which their divinities are imbued. She noted that Abrahamic religions define their supreme being as male. Furthermore, the Catholic, Eastern Orthodox, Islamic, and Orthodox Jewish religions allow only males to be their leaders. An exception, Buddhism, while based on a male figure, focuses on freedom from suffering, inner peace, and enlightenment. In contrast, African traditional religions might have neither a male nor a female leader and instead have spirits, divine beings, and symbolic objects that are not usually sexualized. Hinduism has a complex concept of God and includes a feminine form. Shinto, practiced in Japan, is similar in that there is no one God, but, rather, a system of beliefs and traditions.

Trzebiatowska and Bruce (2012) noted that women tended to be more religious than men. They reported that women are more likely than men to pray privately, to worship publicly, and to claim that their faith is important. Over half of the world's approximately seven billion people identify themselves as religious. To emphasize the potential impact of religious abuse, the sheer numbers are dramatic. Younger women referred to themselves as spiritual rather than religious, even though they continue to ascribe to the tenets of the religion.

Brower (2011) showed that some religions openly exploit women and girls. He exposed the practices of a spiritual leader of a fundamentalist church who was eventually arrested for child sexual abuse and statutory rape. He inherited and followed the path of his father in a large cult based on polygamy and pedophilia. Both father and son were reported to have had upwards of seventy wives and, between them, hundreds of children. Several mayors of large cities were reported to be practicing members of the church and authorized illegal marriage ceremonies between young girls and older men. Legitimized by government officials who were members of the church, there was no interference in the abusive practices. Although some women eventually escaped, many have stayed in their "church family" and are exploited to the present time. They are presumed to have Stockholm syndrome, otherwise referred to as capture-bonding.

Amo-Adjei and Tuoyire (2015) studied a large sample of 10,627 women in Ghana. They found a high prevalence of physical and sexual abuse that they related to polygyny and religion. They also discovered a high rate of women's acceptance to being beaten that was justified by an ethnic religious group to which they belonged. The researchers found little questioning of the widespread practice.

Wood and Morton (2012) researched historical sources on witch-hunts. Although not exclusively women, they became the main targets. Witches became, and still are, synonymous with disliked women. For centuries, beginning around 1300 CE, persecutions were common in Europe.

> Though women filled roles as daughters, wives, and mothers, and served as nuns, or prostitutes or midwives, power lay entirely with men—Kings, Popes, the Church hierarchy, the Inquisitor, Courts of Law, the military, the husband in every castle and every hovel in Europe. (p. 8)

In the 1600s, witch trials and executions began in America. Cotton Mather, an ordained minister figured prominently in the Salem Witch Trials. Fueled by superstition about female power, especially in reference to illness in children, the Trials became famous for their discretionary torture and execution of women. Women were construed to be cavorting (a sexual reference) with the devil.

Gilgun and Anderson (2016) interviewed mothers to determine whether religion helped or harmed women who consulted their pastors regarding suspected or learned of child sexual abuse by their husbands. Results varied, with equal numbers of pastors acting helpfully, acting bewildered, and blaming the mother. They noted that, due to the scarcity of such published research, the question of whether religion harms or helps women and families under times of certain kinds of stress remained unanswered.

Pitanguy (2016) has reflected on religious control of sexual and reproductive health and rights. She noted that at the United Nations, various religious groups converge to form a unified ideology. At some points, Islam, Roman Catholicism, and Evangelical Christians have worked together to influence governments to oppose a woman's autonomy to decide on abortion, contraception, and same-sex marriage. They have sought to affect women as much as men by inferring that religious identity will include such ideas and practice.

To the extent that African traditional religions, Hinduism, and Shinto do not embrace an exclusively male divinity, they are less likely to use religion to rationalize abuse of women. In some religions, males offer daily thanks for not being born a woman. The explanation offered for this is that the male is grateful for not having to assume the responsibilities and burdens of a woman. It may be impossible to refute or oppose an unknown and unknowable presence that dictates how women should behave and be treated. Religious abuse is another form of abuse that women as well as men can and will consciously condone. Sometimes arising from fear, ignorance, greed, envy, revenge, or intolerance, the ultimate result is powerful. Religions are very cohesive groups. In most religions in the world, women are excluded from leadership and participation. Men write rules and laws that discriminate against women. It is ironic that women are found to be more religious, given that women are being abused by virtue of their sex by the very religion they embrace.

Cultural abuse

Cultural abuse of women involves sexism. Sexism is defined as discrimination, devaluation, prejudice, or hatred of women. Such misogyny is deeply embedded in the social structures of a particular culture. Sexism is ideological and may be considered as a culture unto itself. Like all cultures, it has a language, jargon, rules, regulations, expressions, expectations, and unconscious unquestioned acceptance. Although the phenomenon of abuse of women is global, the specifics differ from one culture to another. Referred to as intersectionality, different forms of discrimination interact across cultural categories. From one region to another, based on differences in race, ethnic identity, class, etc., women have different experiences.

Benhabib (1992) and MacKinnon (2007) have written extensively about the sexism that affects all women, even though they may be in different social positions, socio-economic levels, developed and developing countries. These feminists claim that cultures construct reality through discourse. Being female and femininity are expressed in language and systems of thought and concepts that are signified by words that reference the totality of the system. According to this theory, signs therefore do not have a fixed meaning, but are assigned meaning by cultures and institutions. Identities, as signs, are socially imposed and restrictive.

Haslanger (2012) has emphasized that modes of sexist oppression are particular for women. These occur in the realms of embodiment and social differentiation. A professor of linguistics and philosophy at the Massachusetts Institute of Technology, she believes that certain assumptions are made about an individual based on the appearance of the body, such as skin color and hair texture regarding race, and female phenotypic characteristics regarding gender. Haslanger notes that the female body is a social construction and can be relatively fixed in cultural practices and structures, for example, in the family.

Germaine Greer, a feminist in the 1970s, controversial for her book *The Female Eunuch*, embraced "women's liberation" rather than women's equality. She thought that men were not any freer to control and decide their fate and equality would just mean assimilation into this kind of life. Pregnancy, she noted, placed women at the mercy of their womb. Having children was a similar impediment in societies that do not value or support pregnancy, parents, or children. In Greer's 2000 publication, *The Whole Woman*, she explored a woman's choices over her body and mind and concluded that women are not given genuine choices to make. Thus, the woman who "has it all" finds herself with less freedom, fewer options, and working harder than ever.

These feminists believe that actual violence against women is the result of a deeply entrenched patriarchal culture that encourages and rewards male physical strength and domination. They assert that most large institutions are structured by masculine ideals: hierarchical in form, valued for aggression and physical strength. In a patriarchal culture, men are likely to use violence, or at least use the threat of violence, to keep their dominant position.

Meltzer and Harris (2008) have noted that the defense against mother's sexuality is a denial resulting in a conflict in the intrapsychic mother representation and the mother–child relationship. However, because procreation brings up images and representations of mother, the "Madonna–whore" complex may be used defensively in order to dissociate and fully enjoy sexual activity.

Birkhead and Møller (1998) have shown that some women have procreation in mind, consciously or unconsciously, when they use their sexual activity to select a mate whose sperm they think contains optimal DNA. A woman may have difficulty separating her innate sexual feelings from how she might use her body. In addition, it might be difficult to separate her feelings from what she has been taught and what she has been inculcated into her thinking.

Spinelli (2005) has provided research that shows the postpartum period, because of the precipitous drop in estrogen and progesterone, is the most mentally vulnerable time that a woman will ever have in her life. Also that female psychological development revolves around cycles and stages of sexual development. She notes that the lack of social, cultural, and economic support may have a significant impact on the diagnosis and treatment of postpartum depression and psychosis. Her research on infanticide demonstrates that many women who murder their newborn infants are indeed suffering from postpartum psychosis. Pregnancy undoubtedly confers a significant psychological, economic, and physical vulnerability on women.

In a private communication (2009), a thirteen-year-old girl from Zambia who did receive primary education reported that when she began menstruating she had to stay home for a week every month because there were no sanitation facilities, no running water, or private toilets at the school. She was also unable to run the few miles to school that she had done earlier. For her, puberty meant that she would be more susceptible to forced marriage, rape, kidnapping, and trafficking.

Devaluation of the female gender role, loss of physical freedom, and greater risk around sexual activity can lead to severe anxiety in adolescent girls. The adolescent girl may also learn to imitate modeled behavior in the use of seduction of the aggressor, a common weapon of the physically weak. The psycho-physiological representation of the inside of the female body may also become a source of pain and violence. It is important to recognize the possible real physical discomfort and pain of monthly menstruation, during first sexual intercourse, pregnancy, and childbirth. It is crucial to remember that while polymorphous perverse fantasies are universal and could be considered the norm, acting out the fantasies in reality is the opposite. Although the behavior might belie a fantasy, it is unknown when intrapsychic mental pressure propels the person to act.

While society in general claims to abhor violence, heroes are often men who are aggressive. In a culture of masculinity, such aggression is predicated on some kind of violent threat or action. Thus, the traditional model of masculinity (superheroes) encourages men to exude an aura of daring and aggression. In contrast, the model of femininity (Marilyn Monroe, Madonna, and Beyoncé) is relative passivity and beauty. Unconscious attitudes based on the maternal representation are reinforced in sexism, language, symbols, and destructive behaviors. Large group cultural definitions of femininity continue to focus on passivity, controlled seductiveness, and nurture. In addition, repeated rejections, painful threats, and aversive conditioning result in learned helplessness. Given in large enough or repeated enough quantities, positive experiences may be avoided, perhaps permanently, even in the face of opportunity. For example, women who are victims of violence and abuse frequently do not access help and relief from their abusive relationships, an allusion to maintenance of the maternal representation (Seligman, 1972; Seligman & Maier, 1967; Shirayama, 2015).

Having little choice, the girl must fit with what is considered "normal" and "natural" in any particular environment. If she does not, psychic conflict may follow. Such adaptation is an important factor in human development. If she does not conform, she risks being labeled with a maladaptive disorder, rejected from her gender culture, and suffer further abuse.

Physical abuse

As Gayatri Chakravorty Spivak, University Professor of Columbia University in New York, wrote in 1993, "Women's body is thus the last instance in a system whose general regulator is still the loan: usurer's capital, imbricated, level by level, in national industrial and transnational global capital" (p. 82).

Physical abuse of women and girls entails threatened or actual physical assault. Sadomasochistic fantasies do not compare to the experience of real violence. Any categorical distinctions that attempt to defend or rationalize the action are purely arbitrary and meaningless. When the perpetrator is a male, it is almost always related to sexual abuse. When the perpetrator is female, for example, a mother beating her child, it might also be related to sexual abuse. Either experience lays the groundwork for future abuse as an adult. Forced intercourse, drug induced sexual submission, prostitution, sex with trafficked persons all occur under duress and, therefore, constitute physical abuse. Infliction of additional bodily harm, such as bruises, broken bones, female genital mutilation, whether as an accompaniment to sexual assault or as a prelude, deterrent, or punishment, compounds the abuse. Whether committed by domestic partners, known relatives, authority figures, or unknown persons, brutality is brutality. Any parsing of the subject is meant to diminish its significance for women and girls. All forms are part of a continuum of abuse suffered by women and ultimately driven by sexual forces.

The World Health Organization (2013) reported that one out of every three women worldwide has experienced physical or sexual abuse. Such abuse can take many forms. It ranges from threats and intimidation to actual physical murder. All subtlety is pushed aside as much of it is conscious and deliberate. Here, we encounter in some parts of the world acid throwing, beatings, breast ironing, bride burning and stoning, corrective rape, dowry death, honor killing, genital mutilation, female infanticide, foot binding, coerced marriage, child brides, enforced prostitution, commercial pornography, genocidal rape, human trafficking, widow immolation, sexual slavery, and murder. In addition to the unconscious forms of subjugation and economic deficiencies, the threat of these later techniques are intended to make the matter clear. Some or all of these forms of abuse are legal in one country or another. As noted, forms of physical and sexual abuse are often differentiated to protect the category of coerced sex. Since some form of prostitution is legal in more than half of the countries worldwide, it needs to be made clear that coerced sex is still abuse. Sex tourism, HIV infection, and other sexually transmitted diseases flourish in countries where prostitution is legal. Nevertheless, it may mean that there are some women who are physically beaten but not raped, but those who are raped always endure violence. Women in every country bear the permanent psychological scars of rape. When other diseases reach this level of prevalence, it is labeled an epidemic. Yet, these actions are not even categorized as crimes unless the victim files a complaint. This abuse can escalate, as evidenced by a recent case in the USA that received widespread publicity. Confirmed by videotape, a high profile football star beating his fiancée unconscious showed that these injustices occur regardless of socio-economic status (*New York Times*, 2014). In this case, the woman submitted that she provoked the incident and the state prosecuted the crime despite the woman's refusal to file a complaint.

The Coalition Against Trafficking in Women, International (2011) has for many years advocated for criminalization of all forms of sexual exploitation and abuse of women. Although sex workers have organized a powerful lobbying initiative, the Coalition noted that "sex work" is not work like any other. It ignores a marginalized population as well as background factors such as poverty, history of childhood sexual abuse, and exploitation. It diminishes the inclusion of violence. It is dissociated from the inequality that women and girls suffer. Unfortunately, there is an organized, wealthy, commercial sex industry that seeks to promote "sex work" as proper work.

Buying sex or paying for sex was found by one researcher to be very common. In a 2011 *Newsweek* online magazine interview with Melissa Farley, founder of Prostitution Research and Education, Bennetts (2011) quoted Farley:

> We had big, big trouble finding nonusers [amongst men]. We finally had to settle on a definition of non sex buyers as men who have not been to a strip club more than two times in the past year, have not purchased a lap dance, have not used pornography more than one time in the last month, and have not purchased phone sex or the services of a sex worker, escort, erotic masseuse, or prostitute. (Accessed October, 2015)

She found that the percentage of men who are non-users according to this definition is approximately 20%. That is to say, that 80% of men fell into one of the categories listed above. Similar reports were published by Indiana University, who found that 69% of men surveyed had used commercial forms of sex.

News media (*USA Today*, 2011; *Huffington Post* (2013) quoted an Attorney General commenting about the annual Super Bowl (US football): "It's commonly known as the single largest human trafficking incident in the United States." The Men's World Cup (international soccer) has also been cited as the largest sex trafficking global event. Each year the US Federal Bureau of Investigation rescues dozens of children and arrests their pimps in whatever city the Super Bowl plays. The US Department of Justice reports that the children are frequently given hormones and dressed up to look older than they really are (Webinar, 2014). Most of the buyers are not known pedophiles. It is the size of these events, the majority of men plus alcohol that is thought to draw traffickers. It is also the complicity of the women who attend and support the events that aids in its perpetuation. Some pimps bring their victims to the location in buses. Some victims have reported having sex with up to fifty male buyers a day.

In 2014, *The Economist* reported on "The economics of prostitution: sex, lies and statistics" and quoted figures obtained from the Urban Institute, a think-tank that investigated the sex trade in eight big American cities. Some pimps, often women, in the southern city of Atlanta were making $33,000 a week. They followed a business plan that imposed rules such as no drugs and no young buyers (who tended to be more violent). A third of the pimps delegated management, training, and recruitment to an experienced prostitute, called a "bottom girl". In this study, although commercial sex was being sold, it seems that there were attempts to control overt violence. One of the conclusions of the report indicated that when other job opportunities are meager, women use prostitution to have an income.

The 2013 documentary film *Tricked* illustrates many of the factors that constitute the commercial sex trade by following the trajectory of a college student into "the life". It also contains footage of the Pimp Ball, held every year in the USA, frequently in a mid-West state, where the pimp winner gets a trophy. There is also a portrayal of a sociopathic pimp, as well as sex buyers, who, in contrast to the pimp, mostly appear guilty upon arrest. The most common risk factors for the victims are childhood sexual abuse and untreated substance abuse. Similar risk factors are noted for being a sex buyer and a trafficker, although more severe in these groups. The 2015 documentary, *Hot Girls Wanted*, portrays the predatory nature of the pornography business, especially in American middle-class white communities.

Institutionalized violence against women is not different from that of institutionalized military violence that pits men in violent combat against men, women, and children. However, state sponsored rape has always been a military tactic. The book, *Military Comfort Women: Sexual Slavery in the Japanese Military During World War II*, conveys the stories of tens of thousands of girls and women forcibly used by the military for sex (Yoshiaki & O'Brien, 1995). More recently, other countries, such as Sudan and the Democratic Republic of Congo, have used systematic rape as a military tool for genocide. As recent as 2012, a US Senate candidate said that in cases of "legitimate rape", women's bodies can somehow block pregnancy (*New York Times*, 2012). Today, very few reports of rape end in a conviction of rape and many victims face barriers in terms of time and the difficulty of the process when attempting to utilize the criminal justice system to seek accountability. According to a 2008 report by the US National Institute of Justice

(2008), most women know their attacker. In 85–90% of sexual assaults reported by colleges, the perpetrator was someone known to the victim; about half occur on a date. The most common locations are the man's or woman's home in the context of a party or a date. The perpetrators may range from classmates to neighbors. Emma Sulkowicz, a college student at Columbia University in New York and daughter of a psychoanalyst, carried a mattress with her during her entire senior year to protest the way in which her reported rape by another student was handled by the authorities. Classmates' (aged 18–21 years) comments on social media varied from support to disbelief. Posters were found at school accusing Sulkowicz of lying.

Non-profit organizations such as the National Center for Missing and Exploited Children reported that one in six runaway children in 2014 were probably sex trafficking victims. Girls, boys, and LGBTQ youth run away from home or are kidnapped. Eighty per cent of sex trafficking victims are women and girls. Childhood sexual abuse and domestic violence, linked and complementary, feed the sex trafficking industry, otherwise known as the commercial sex trade. Known as "pimp radar", traffickers can sense a young victim who has been neglected or abused and seduce her or him with false promises of affection. Contrasted with the sale of arms and drugs, human sex trafficking victims are renewable commodities, that is, they can be used over and over again, with a profit each time they are sold for sex.

Historically, violence against women, mostly perpetrated by men but often instigated by women, has been accepted and even condoned. More than 2,000 years ago, Roman law gave a man life and death authority over his wife. In the eighteenth century, English common law gave men permission to discipline their wives and children with a stick or whip no wider than his thumb. This "rule of thumb" prevailed in England and America until the late nineteenth century. This violence is perpetuated, fostered, and tolerated by institutional practices and social norms and values. For instance, a look at the legal system reveals some of the ways that violence against women has been institutionalized. It was not until the 1870s that courts in the USA stopped recognizing the common-law principle that a husband had the right to "physically chastise an errant wife". In the UK, the traditional right of a husband to inflict moderate corporal punishment on his wife in order to keep her "within the bounds of duty" was removed in 1891. In the more recent past, until 1976, so-called "marital rape" was legal in every state in the USA. In starker terms, a husband had a legal right to force his wife to have sex with him.

Rates of domestic violence were highest in Africa, the Middle East, and Southeast Asia, the World Health Organization found. The numbers were based on data from 1983 to 2010 from eighty-six countries worldwide. More than 600 million women live in countries where domestic violence is not considered a crime. In a 2013 *Lancet* publication, Stöckl analyzed data on more than 492,000 murders in sixty-six countries over twenty years. Nations with the highest rates of murder of women by intimate partners include those in Southeast Asia (about 59%), the Americas (40.5%), and Africa (40%). In combined high-income countries, the rate was about 41%. Fatal violence commonly followed a long history of psychological and physical abuse.

In an extensive study in 1992, Kellermann and Mercy reviewed 215,273 homicides in order to distinguish homicides involving women as victims or offenders from those involving men. Only cases that involved victims aged fifteen years or older were included. The data showed that 77% involved male victims and 23% female victims. Although the overall risk of homicide for women was substantially lower than that of men (rate ratio [RR] = 0.27), their risk of being killed by a spouse or intimate acquaintance was higher (RR = 1.23). More than twice as many women were shot and killed by their husband or intimate acquaintance than were murdered by strangers. Although women comprise more than half the US population, they committed only 14.7% of the homicides noted during the study interval.

Referred to as "domestic violence" as if to minimize its implication, it in fact serves to perpetuate the cycle of abuse of women. By teaching children these values, their moral compass is set in the direction of transmission of violence from one generation to the next to the next *ad infinitum*. It is witnessed, modeled, learned, and emulated by children. In some communities, it is not surprising to hear a male child call a young girl child a "bitch" or a "whore": for example, a five-year-old boy speaking to a three-year-old girl using these terms with a dismissive tone of voice. These boys, emulating the adults around them, have learned that girls can be treated with derision, dismissal, and degradation. Said within culturally defined and accepting roles, both boy and girl were neither offended nor surprised. In the worst of circumstances, the girl child has also learned that her environment accepts her worthlessness, inscribed in epithets and symbols. Her environment includes those to whom she is attached and loves, that is, the authority figures, siblings, and peers. These attitudes are unconscious and, thus, accepted without question. Girls and boys will emulate the words and characterizations that become behavior. It is akin to a linguistic accent, but rather than French or South Boston, it is gendered and sexist. When men (of all sexual orientations) wish to degrade other men, they commonly use feminine terms such as "girly", "pussy", "bitchy", "douche-bag", etc. These derogatory terms refer to female genitals and have reproductive implications. Although sexism is technically illegal in many countries, it is still widely practiced.

If "domestic" violence is not considered a *de facto* crime, then it is implicitly acceptable in the culture in which it exists. Furthermore, there is a contagious factor. Domestic violence is transmitted from one individual to another and from one generation to the next and the next. Fathers teach their sons how to behave around girls and women. In some cases, parents will prohibit physical violence but allow sexual violence. Perhaps perverse, fathers (with the implicit approval of mothers) will help to initiate sexual activity for their sons with a prostitute. Children certainly imitate and seek to emulate their parents, older siblings, and other authority figures. If they witness this violence, then they learn how to practice it and they also learn how to be victims. They inherently love both the perpetrator and the victim. The lack of success (not the lack of activism) in changing the statistics and relative acceptance of this phenomenon may lead to the normalization of violence against women in all its forms. In some families and cultures, violence against the smaller and weaker becomes the norm.

Without treatment or therapy by an enlightened therapist (a new and meaningful relationship), these early developmental issues that involve compulsive narcissistic repair for lost investment and empathy can lead to lifelong bodily destruction as well as destructive relationships and a sense of worthlessness. Sometimes, the psychic destruction is too deep and great; only partial therapeutic benefit can be applied. Notman (1989) and Brody (2005) noted that women with this history are vulnerable and at increased risk for depression and suicide. Narcissistic reparations may be misapplied that involve idealization and modification of the maternal image. Attentiveness to the body surface is manifested in varying modalities. Lemma (2010) commented that tattoos and piercings might be examples of attention to the skin and the unfulfilled infantile need to be noticed and seen. They are frequently a public display and individually unique. "Body art", like other forms of decoration (plastic surgery, cosmetics, hair, apparel, shoes), is a highly cathected narcissistic investment with a high valence. The skin is one of the most primitive sensory organs and signifies connectedness and bodily integrity. The skin encompasses all that is within it. It reflects multiple levels of merging and symbiosis on the one hand and separation and individuation on the other. Modifications are a statement of possession of one's body and the sexual use of the body. Lemma has written about this in more detail, but in my experience, the (usually) young woman reinforces her relationships through a bodily tattoo. Women who are prostituted or trafficked by a pimp are commonly tattooed so that they are made to feel that the trafficker literally owns their body. Of interest in this illegal commercial sex industry is that their "trauma bond" is primarily and substantially psychological and emotional. One reason why some women are vulnerable to becoming and remaining a victim is due to this intrapsychic dynamic. Most victims have the experience of being abandoned, neglected, or abused and misused as a child sexual object. Sometimes, the "best" relationship they have had is one of sexual abuse. Thus, they are easy prey for anyone who offers them (at first or intermittently) a loving relationship. They are spiritually desperate to find someone to care for them, praise them, nurture them, and help them with the real world—in the same way that a mother provides these functions. Girls who do not receive the resources they need from mothers lack the numerous internalized complex maternal functions that they would ordinarily have received. They cannot apply these functions to themselves.

An indicator of the connection between physical abuse of women and the maternal representation is that the majority of these forms of abuse is inflicted in familiar surroundings such as home, by a relative or close person, or have to do with physical attractiveness, sexual enjoyment, sexual reproductive organs, and reproductive capacity. Many are crimes of passion. Freud suggested that women who are sexually attractive are despised and devalued by a certain category of men who cannot integrate intimacy and sexual desire. He further described this difficulty as a pathogenic fixation on a mother or sister substitute, "the child's primary object-choice." According to Freud, writing in 1912(d), there are men for whom there is a need for a debased sexual object, that is, a prostitute. The prevalence and long-standing cultural acceptance of prostitution and pornography may attest to this need for women primarily to be degraded. Being called female is an insult to most men. Corbett (2009) noted the term "destructive masculinities", that is, those that are primarily based on violence and degradation of women.

Conclusion

The sheer pervasiveness of abuse of women is breathtaking. The long history of abuse of women in so many sectors poses a threat to all human beings. Sometimes, it is deemed criminal but never brought to authorities; sometimes, abuse is legal and promoted. Even when it is illegal, it is denied, disavowed, and ultimately accepted. Despite the complexity of individuals, the maternal ego and maternal ego ideal are universal in the psyche. The first impact on the body-ego, the maternal ego is ideally "good enough" and contributes to the internalized maternal ego ideal. In psychoanalysis, we find that the source of all power is the maternal image, a condensation of maternal ego and ego ideal that are defined by possession of valued resources to sustain life, comfort, and desire. Since human children have a prolonged dependency, they rely on the power of the maternal ego for individual and group survival. At its best, the maternal ego is benevolent, generous, empathic, the organizer of reality, and conveyor of good moral judgment and values. The maternal ego manifested by maternal function both shares in and observes the child's development.

However, when witnesses realize the intense power of the dyad that is the original source of dependency, a reaction begins and confines, suppresses, and sometimes intentionally destroys the maternal function. The witness may also desire the power and may, thus, intervene and triangulate. Although it begins with the individual dyad, it is subsequently sustained by group dynamics. In reaction to this universal fear, the defense is institutionalized in such organizations as government, religion, business, and academia.

The pre-oedipal mother to the dependent child either gives her resources or withholds them, in varying quantities and qualities. This invaluable capacity of women, their reproductive potential, may be imagined and believed to give them dominance over such things as life, death, and continuation of the species. Although women are not a homogenous group, they are predominantly viewed to be in this role. Girls are either fantasized as little future women or are prepared to be women who potentially have enormous power. In this perspective, violence against women can be traced to a primary source, mother or the maternal representation in the individual psyche. A universal phenomenon, the maternal image, shaped by many factors, is endowed with love, attachment, aggression, and power. In relation and opposition to this maternal image, there is ambivalence and dependency. Helplessness gives rise to desire and frustration. Universal maternal ambivalence combined with a sense of denigration might lead mothers to exert their power. Adding this to the relationship of child and mother, the possibility for negative affects and outcomes increase. It is as if there were a universal desire and wish to control, restrict, and manipulate female sexual behavior and reproduction because it is condensed with the singular creative power of childbirth. There is a universal myth about one's own birth as well as myths about childbirth that reside in individual and group psyches. This results in the critical vulnerability to violence that is intended to destroy women's sexuality. Abuse of women is almost always sexual in nature, directed at sexuality and involving reproductive potential. It is deeply entrenched in all forms of abuse: psychological, economic, political, cultural, religious, and physical. Is it possible that Freud led the psychoanalytic community away from a positive understanding of female sexuality, rather instead portraying the female body as dark, frightening, and unknown? Has psychoanalysis instead emphasized sex and aggression, mostly from a male perspective, rather than a subjective model of relational psychoanalysis?

In summary, psychological, economic, cultural, religious, political, and physical abuse of women is so pervasive that there is little surprise when one hears about it. It is based on sexual violence. It is an indication of how cellular and ego-syntonic it is in every culture. As women's rights and freedoms increase, the greater is the backlash and violence against them. The majority of abuse of women is aimed at their sexuality, evidence of the conflict that arises when need and desire confront the lack of resources to fulfill wishes. As symbolized by her maternal representation, a mother is desired as the exclusive source of primal devotion. It is imagined that from her springs all that is necessary and wished for in life for pleasure and survival. In many symbols and fantasies, these resources reside in women and this then becomes the roots of psychological, economic, religious, political, cultural, and physical abuse of women.

References

American Association of University Women (2015). The simple truth about the gender gap. www.aauw.org/research/the-simple-truth-about-the-gender-pay-gap/ (accessed October 2015).

Amo-Adjei, J., & Tuoyire, D. (2015). Do ethnicity and polygyny contribute to justification of beating women in Ghana? *Women's Health*, 1: 1–18.

Balsam, R. (2012). *Women's Bodies in Psychoanalysis*. New York: Routledge.

Baruch, E. (1987). A womb of his own. *Women's Health*, 13(1–2): 135–139.

Benhabib, S. (1992). *Situating the Self: Gender, Community, and Postmodernism in Contemporary Ethics*. New York: Routledge.

Bennetts, L. (2011). The growing demand for prostitution. http://www.newsweek.com/growing-demand-prostitution-68493 (accessed October 2015).

Birkhead, T. R., & Møller, A. P. (Eds.) (1998). *Sperm Competition and Sexual Selection*. London: Academic Press.

Brody, S. (2005). Psychiatric and characterological factors relevant to excess mortality in a long-term cohort of prostitute women. *Journal of Sex Marital Therapy*, 31(2): 97–112.

Brower, S. (2011). *Prophet's Prey: My Seven-Year Investigation into Warren Jeffs and the Fundamentalist Church of Latter-Day Saints*. New York: Bloomsbury.

Coalition Against Trafficking in Women, International (2011). http://catwinternational.org/Home/Article/59-presentation-to-un-special-seminar-on-trafficking-prostitution-and-the-global-sex-industry-postion-paper-for-catw-part-two (accessed October 2015).

Corbett, K. (2009). *Boyhoods: Rethinking Masculinities*. New Haven, CT: Yale University Press.

Freud, S. (1912d). On the universal tendency of debasement in the sphere of love. *S. E., 11*: 179–190. London: Hogarth.

Gavalas, V., Rontos, K., & Nagopoulos, N. (2015). Sex ratio at birth in twenty-first century Greece. *Journal of Biosocial Science*, 47(3): 363–375.

Gilgun, J. F., & Anderson, G. (2016). Mothers' experiences with pastoral care in cases of child sexual abuse. *Journal of Religion and Health*, 55(2): 680–694.

Greer, G. (1970). *The Female Eunuch*. London: MacGibbon & Kee.

Greer, G. (2000). *The Whole Woman*. New York: Random House.

Harvard Business School (2012). www.hbs.edu/news/releases/Pages/having-working-mother.aspx (accessed October 2015).

Harvard Business School (2015). Harvard Business School launches gender initiative. http://www.hbs.edu/news/releases/Pages/hbs-launches-gender-initiative.aspx (accessed October 2015).

Haslanger, S. (2012). *Resisting Reality: Social Construction and Social Critique*. Oxford: Oxford University Press.

Hesketh, T., Lu, L., & Zhu, W. X. (2005). The effect of China's one-child family policy after 25 years. *New England Journal of Medicine, 353*: 1171–1176.

Hot Girls Wanted (2015). http://www.imdb.com/title/tt4382552/ (accessed October 2015).

Huffington Post (2013). www.huffingtonpost.com/2013/02/03/super-bowl-sex-trafficking_n_2607871.html (accessed October 2015).

Hunt, S. (2014). The rise of Rwanda's women. *Foreign Affairs*, May/June: 150–156.

Kellermann, A. L., & Mercy, J. A. (1992). Men, women, and murder: gender-specific differences in rates of fatal violence and victimization. *Journal of Trauma, 33*(1): 1–5.

Lemma, A. (2010). *Under the Skin: A Psychoanalytic Study of Body Modification*. London: Karnac.

MacKinnon, C. (2007). *Women's Lives, Men's Laws*. Cambridge, MA: Harvard University Press.

Meltzer, D., & Harris, W. M. (2008). *The Apprehension of Beauty: The Role of Aesthetic Conflict in Development, Art, and Violence*. London: Karnac.

Mill, J. S., & Mill, H. T. (1851). *The Enfranchisement of Women*. London: The Westminster Review.

Moeslein-Teising, I., & Thomson-Salo, F. (2013). *The Female Body: Inside and Outside*. London: Karnac.

Nelson, J. (1967). Anlage of productiveness in boys: womb envy. *Journal of the American Academy of Child Psychiatry, 6*(2): 213–225.

New York Times (2012). Senate candidate provokes ire with legitimate rape comment. www.nytimes.com/2012/08/20/us/politics/todd-akin-provokes-ire-with-legitimate-rape-comment.html?_r=0 (accessed July 2015).

New York Times (2014). Ray Rice domestic abuse case offers questions for prosecutors. www.nytimes.com/aponline/2014/09/12/us/ap-fbn-rice-video-prosecutor.html (accessed July 2105).

Notman, M. T. (1989). Depression in women: psychoanalytic concepts. *Psychiatric Clinics of North America*, 12(1): 221–230.

Pines, D. (1990). Pregnancy, miscarriage and abortion. *International Journal of Psychoanalysis*, 71: 301–307.

Pitanguy, J. (2016). Women's human rights and the political arena of Brazil. In: E. Chesler & T. McGovern (Eds.), *Women and Girls Rising: Progress and Resistance Around the World* (pp. 105–119). New York: Routledge.

Rosenberg, M. (2015). China's one child policy. http://geography.about.com/od/populationgeography/a/onechild.htm (accessed October 2015).

Seligman, M. (1972). Learned helplessness. *Annual Review of Medicine*, 23(1): 407–412.

Seligman, M., & Maier, S. (1967). Failure to escape traumatic shock. *Journal of Experimental Psychology*, 74: 1–9.

Shirayama, Y. (2015). Opposite roles for neuropeptide S in the nucleus accumbens and bed nucleus of the stria terminalis in learned helplessness in rats. *Behavior and Brain Research*, May 16, epublication (accessed October 2015).

Silver, C. B. (2007). Womb envy: loss and grief of the maternal body. *Psychoanalytic Review*, 94(3): 409–430.

Spinelli, M. G. (2005). Neuroendocrine effects on mood. *Review of Endocrine Metabolic Disorders*, 6(2): 109–115.

Spivak, G. C. (1993). *Outside in the Teaching Machine*. New York: Routledge.

Spivak, G. C. (2012). *An Aesthetic Education in the Era of Globalization*. Cambridge, MA: Harvard University Press.

Stöckl, H. (2013). The global prevalence of intimate partner homicide: a systematic review. *Lancet*, 382(9895): 859–865.

Tamale, S. (2015). Crossing the bright red line: the abuse of culture and religion to violate women's sexual and reproductive health rights in Uganda. In: E. Chesler & T. McGovern (Eds.), *Women and Girls Rising: Progress and Resistance Around the World* (pp. 144–159). New York: Routledge.

The Economist (2014). The economics of prostitution: sex, lies and statistics. http://www.economist.com/news/united-states/21599351-laying-bare-supply-and-demand-oldest-profession-sex-lies-and-statistics (accessed October 2015).

Tricked (2013). The Documentary. http://www.imdb.com/title/tt2246924/ (accessed October 2015).

Trzebiatowska, M., & Bruce, S. (2012). *Why Are Women more Religious than Men?* London: Oxford University Press.

United Nations Population Fund (2010). Statistics for Rwanda. epublication. www.unfpa.org/search/node/rwanda%20statistics (accessed October 2015).

US History (2015). The fight for reproductive rights. www.ushistory.org/us/57b.asp (accessed October 2015).

US National Institute of Justice (2008). http://www.nij.gov/topics/crime/human-trafficking/pages/international-discussions.aspx (accessed in October 2015).

USA Today (2011). Child sex rings spike during Super Bowl Week. http://usatoday30.usatoday.com/news/nation/2011-01-31-child-prostitution-super-bowl_N.htm (accessed October 2015).

Webinar (2014). Human trafficking: training healthcare. www.healthcare againsttrafficking.com (accessed October 2015).

Welldon, E. (1988). *Mother, Madonna, Whore: The Idealization and Denigration of Motherhood.* London: Free Association Books.

Wood, R., & Morton, L. (2012). *Witch Hunts: A Graphic History of the Burning Times.* Jefferson, NC: McFarland.

World Health Organization (2013). apps.who.int/iris/bitstream/10665/85241/1/WHO_RHR_HRP_13.06_eng.pdf?ua=1 (accessed October 2015).

www.pbs.org/newshour/rundown/in-saudi-arabia-women-can-now-cast-a-vote-and-run-for-office/ (accessed October 2015).

Yoshiaki, Y., & O'Brien, S. (1995). *Military Comfort Women: Sexual Slavery in the Japanese Military During World War II.* New York: Columbia University Press.

CHAPTER NINE

Atrocities against mother and child re-presented in the psychoanalytic space

Sverre Varvin

Introduction

In the past century, civilians increasingly became targets in inter-country wars, totalitarian regimes, and internal wars. This trend continues in this century. The basic unity in all societies, the family in its different forms, is, thus, increasingly under attack in these war zones with serious consequences for the mental health and the development of its members.

Families' experiences that their close ones are wounded, molested, raped, and tortured under conditions of upheaval and massive uprooting: in 2012, around 23,000 human beings were forced to leave their homes each day due to war, conflicts, and persecution, a number that has increased in 2014 and 2015. There is, furthermore, a gender bias in today's atrocities. Women become targets in ways that are devastating not only for themselves but also for their children. This includes rapes, trafficking and prostitution, imprisonment, torture, and so forth. Women are targeted for many reasons: to humiliate the male, to destroy procreation, to fuse one's genes into the enemy, and to serve soldiers. Under these circumstances, assaults on women have destabilizing consequences for the family/group and society as a whole.

We have now the worst refugee catastrophe since the Second World War with more people fleeing atrocities and poverty than perhaps ever before. In 2015, there are more than sixty million refugees worldwide, a rise from 51.2 millions in 2014 (Flyktninghjelpen, 2014; Varvin, 2015). This catastrophe has been, and is, handled badly by the world community and more and more people are brought into unbearable situations with extreme suffering—and progressively more people die during their flight.

Traumatising experiences are abundant. When one member of a family or group is traumatized, the whole group is affected: wives when husbands are tortured, children when mothers are raped. The horror is often beyond description and millions live with unspeakable experiences that will affect coming generations.

Psychoanalysis may provide a space for these experiences to be contained and, at least to a certain degree, be put into a human context. That is why we offer therapy for traumatized persons, not only to help the one identified as being traumatized, but also to help the group and the family contain such experiences in a time dimension that, at least to a certain degree, can make the past less insistent and damaging. This type of work has repercussions also on a societal level, in that narratives are created that counteract inhuman, repetitive, destructive tendencies. Salient problems concern psychoanalysts' capacity to contain (not many work with these patients) and also the capacity of psychoanalysis to comprehend and understand atrocities of this magnitude. The last point concerns questions of theory, to which I shall return.

In this chapter, I present material from psychoanalytic work with two women who had been exposed to severe traumatizing experiences, and try to show how they struggled to create psychic space and narratives that made it more possible for them and their close ones to go on living.

Responses to traumatization

Trauma is a word that does not really capture the experiences I shall describe. The word "trauma" implies something static and reified, like a "thing" in the mind and its use tends to divert attention from the dynamic and reorganizing processes in the traumatized person's mind, body, and relations to others that occur after being exposed to atrocities. These are processes that depend on the level of personality organization, on past traumatizing experiences, on the circumstances prevailing during atrocities, and, most importantly, on the context that meets the survivor afterwards. It is the person's own responses to atrocity and, more importantly, the responses of others and societies that, to a large degree, determine the fate of the traumatized person and her group. Research has convincingly confirmed the importance of the response to the traumatized person afterwards, beginning with Hans Keilson's seminal work on Jewish child survivors after the Second World War (Gagnon & Stewart, 2014; Keilson & Sarpathie, 1979; Simich & Andermann, 2014; Ungar, 2012).

Psychoanalysis is one such societal response, both in its practical therapeutic form and as a comprehensive theory for understanding the mind's relation to the body and the context.

Traumatization and its responses

Traumatized persons struggle with mental and bodily pain that is difficult to understand and difficult to put into words. The pain may be expressed as dissociated states of mind, as bodily pain, and other somatic experiences and dysfunctions, as overwhelming thoughts and feelings, as behavioural tendencies and relational styles, and as ways of living. The effects of both early and later traumatization may show itself in many diagnostic categories where the symptoms characterizing PTSD is only one form. Manifestations related to traumatization in the psychiatric illness picture may be depression, addiction, eating disorders, personality dysfunctions, and anxiety states (Leuzinger-Bohleber, 2012; Purnell, 2010; Taft et al., 2007; Vaage, 2010; Vitriol et al., 2009).

What is common for these manifestations are deficiencies in the representational system related to the traumatic experiences; those experiences are painfully felt and set their marks on the body and the mind without, however, being inscribed in the mind's life narratives. They are not (or are deficiently) symbolised in the sense that they cannot be expressed in narratives in a way that would allow meaning to emerge that can be reflected upon. The traumatic experiences remain in the mind as dissociated or encapsulated fragments that have a disturbing effect on mood and mental stability (Rosenbaum & Varvin, 2007). Experience becomes deprived of emotional meaning.

As a rule, extreme traumatization (such as rape and torture) eludes meaning *when* it happens and also precludes forming an internal third position whereby the person, in his or her own mind, can create a reflecting distance from what is happening and what has happened. The inner witnessing function, so vital for making meaning of experiences, is attacked during such extreme experiences (for example, torture and other severe maltreatment), impeding the individuals from being able to experience on a symbolic level the cruelties they undergo. When the external witnessing function that can contain the pain also fails, the traumatized person is left alone. The result is often that these experiences remain as fragmented bits and pieces that can express themselves only in bodily pain, dissociated states of mind, nightmares, and relational disturbances. The traumatized person will try to organize experiences in unconscious templates or scenarios that are expressed in different, more or less disguised, ways in relation to others and self.

When working psychoanalytically with traumatized patients, the analyst inevitably becomes involved in these unsymbolized, fragmentary, and, as a rule, strongly affective scenarios related to the patient's traumatizing experiences. This happens from the first encounter with the patient and is mostly expressed in the non-verbal interaction with the patient. It might take a long time before these manifestations may be given a narrative form that, in meaningful ways, can be put into a historical context that relates to traumatic and pre-traumatic experiences. To achieve this end implies hard and painful emotional work by the patient, and also by the analyst.

There is increasing evidence that psychoanalytic therapies are helpful for traumatized persons in comprehensive ways, in that this approach may help to address crucial areas in the clinical presentation of complex traumatization (complex PTSD) that are not targeted by other current, so-called empirically supported, treatments, such as the many exposure techniques that are offered. Psychoanalytic therapy has a historical perspective and works with problems related to the self and self-esteem, with enhancing the ability to resolve reactions to trauma through improved reflective functioning, and it aims at internalization of more secure inner working models of relationships. A further focus is work on improving social functioning. Finally, and this is increasingly substantiated in several studies, psychodynamic psychotherapy tends to result in continued improvement after treatment ends (Schottenbauer et al., 2008).

Patients with complex trauma often live in difficult social, economic, and cultural situations and, thus, treatment needs to be integrated with rehabilitation procedures and often with complicated somatic treatments. This holds true for many traumatized refugees, but also for complex family-based traumatization. Treatment and rehabilitation of the traumatized will, therefore, often need to be conducted by a team, and when and how to implement psychoanalytic therapy has to be carefully evaluated and, furthermore, will need constant support from the team and social services.

Trauma and the social context

For these unsymbolized and insufficiently symbolized experiences to approach some integration and be given some meaningful place in the individual's mind, they need to be actualized and given form in a holding and containing therapeutic relationship. This implies that the analyst must accept living with the patient in areas of the mind that are painfully absent of meaning and, at times, filled with horror.

As a rule, however, this is not sufficient: without acknowledgment of the traumatic events at the societal, cultural, and political level, the individual and the group's work with traumatic experiences might be extremely difficult. Without this affirmation, the traumatized person's feeling of unreality and fragmentation connected with the experiences may continue.

This was the case for many after the Second World War in the West, where the official slogan to a large degree was that one must go on living and put the past behind one. In Norway, this had devastating and often fatal consequences, not only for concentration camp survivors (Eitinger, 1965) but also for many sailors serving in warships who had endured the extreme hardship of being constantly attacked and torpedoed by German submarines. (Askevold, 1980).

Similar situations have developed in many countries or regions. China is one example, as a result of the adversities that have been so prevalent in the country's history over the past two centuries. Yu Hua describes, in the novel *Brothers*, how the individual and collective consequences of the extreme atrocities perpetrated against neighbors and fellow citizens during the cultural revolution seemingly were forgotten in the service of managing life and survival (Yu, 2009).

One of the most difficult to handle contributors to personal suffering in massive social traumatization in the Cultural Revolution, genocides (Rwanda, the Balkans, Kampuchea), and now in the Syrian disaster is the helplessness experienced when observing close ones, especially children, being maltreated and killed and not being able to prevent this or protect the victims. This underlines the importance of Niederland's seminal insights on survival guilt (Niederland, 1968, 1981), a theme that was very much in the background in the trauma literature for many years. It was, however, highlighted very clearly by the young people who survived the Utøya massacre on 22 July 2011 in Norway (Varvin, 2013a).

The dynamic and structure of extreme traumatization

How trauma affects a person depends on the severity, complexity, and duration of the traumatizing event, the context, the developmental stage, the way in which traumatization affects internal object relations; for example, whether earlier traumatic relations are activated (Opaas & Varvin, 2015) and the support and the treatment offered after the event.

Phenomenology of traumatization

Being traumatized is experienced in both children and adults as something unexpected that should not happen and creates a situation where they feel a profound helplessness and a sense of being abandoned by all good and helping objects. This profound feeling of helplessness and being abandoned may be carried over into the post-trauma phase, where the survivor, to a greater or lesser degree, and depending on the circumstances, might develop a deep fear of an impending catastrophe where he or she will be helpless and where nobody will help or care. An inner feeling of desperation and fear of psychosomatic breakdown with fear of annihilation might ensue and much of post-trauma pathology can be seen as a defence against this impending catastrophe.

This impending catastrophe reflects the early fear of breakdown experienced in infant life (Winnicott, 1991). Post-trauma anxieties are deep, comprehensive, and may best be understood as annihilation anxiety (Hurvich, 2003) or nameless dread (Bion, 1962).

Human created traumatization influences internal object relations scenarios in different ways. Early traumas that bear more or less similarity to the present traumatization may be activated, so that the present trauma is imbued with earlier losses, humiliations, and traumatic experiences. Even early, safe-enough relationships may be coloured by the later traumatizing relationships when, for example, a too authoritarian father may be fused with a torturer, thus almost destroying the good enough aspects of this relationship (Varvin, 2013b). Unbearable losses may cause the traumatized person to forever seek a rescuer or substitute in others, as happened with patient B, to be presented later.

Complicated relations to the traumatizing agent, the circumstances, and other relations involved may be actualized in the transference. Identification with the aggressor is well known (Hirsch, 1996). In a recent work, Henningsen described the phenomenon "concrete fusion" (*konkretistische Fusion*), which refers to the situation where the traumatized person internalizes the traumatizing object and a part of the self fuses with this traumatizing object in order to keep the object inside, and, in this way, avoid the complete object loss that characterized the traumatizing experience. This merged self–object relation may become split off and kept more or less encapsulated, hidden in the personality, and might appear during later crises or traumatization and it could be actualized in the transference relationship in therapy (Henningsen, 2012).

The traumatized person, thus, internalizes important aspects of the traumatizing scenario in the form of a self–object relation which might be more, or often less (as in concrete fusion), differentiated and/or fragmented and, in different ways, self-negating. As we shall see, the actualization of these may, in the analytic process, take dramatic forms.

Relation and symbolization

One salient task in psychotherapy with traumatized patients is to enhance a meta-cognitive or mentalizing capacity that can enable the patient to deal more effectively with traces and derivatives of the traumatic experience. This implies helping the patient out of mental states characterized by concreteness and lack of dimensionality.

Mental traces of traumatic experiences are "wild" in the sense that the person has no capacity to organize and deal with them; he has no inner container in relation to an inner empathic other that can help give meaning to experience (Laub, 2005). They are fragments of thoughts, feelings, and bodily sensations without an organizing ego and there is no third position from where the subject can have distance from, relate to, and possibly reflect on, the experiences. They are presented to the mind in a way from the "outside" and experienced as alien and threatening.

The ego meets an overwhelming abundance of stimuli and impressions. The regulating functions of the mind break down and the processes of the psychic apparatus are pushed towards states of extreme anxiety and catastrophe (Rosenbaum & Varvin, 2007).

There is an experience of loss of internal protection related to the internal other—primarily the loss of the necessary feelings of basic trust and mastery. An empathic internal other is no longer functioning as a protective shield and the functions that give meaning to experience might no longer work. Attachment to, and trust in, others might be perceived as dangerous, reminding of previous catastrophes. Relating to others, for example in psychoanalytic psychotherapy, might be felt as a risk of re-experiencing the original helplessness and the feeling of being left alone in utter despair. Withdrawal patterns might be the consequence, creating a negative spiral, as withdrawal also means the loss of potential external support (Varvin & Rosenbaum, 2011).

Thus, the effects of trauma may be longstanding and complex. They may affect several dimensions of the person's relations with the external world and cause disturbances on the bodily–affective level, on the capacity to form relations to others and the group and family, and on the ability to give meaning to experience. The last is dependent on the social and cultural existing or non-existing meaning-giving functions which, under normal circumstances, provide affirmative narratives; for example, stories told by elders, scientific explanations, psychological theories and political acknowledgment, and leaders' acknowledging the historical circumstances of the atrocity.

The traumatized person is living with historical experiences that are not formulated, but are painfully and non-verbally represented in the body and in the mind. The task of therapy is to allow these experiences to emerge in the transference relationship so that words and meaning can be co-created, even if the experiences themselves, by all human standards, are cruel and devoid of meaning. The cultural and societal dimensions are, thus, not outside the psychic space, but an integral part of ways of experiencing self and others. The intention to humiliate often has a gender based cultural background that becomes part of the inner traumatic experience. This has consequences for analytic work. Raping a woman to humiliate the husband and destroy familial stability places the woman in a doubly humiliating position, but will also leave the man in an extremely difficult situation that might be impossible to overcome. This is one dynamic behind the tendency to be silent about such atrocities.

However, such atrocities become actualized in the therapeutic relationship as actions, unbearable countertransferential feelings, and they might become present in most disturbing ways. This might happen when the analyst is drawn into relational scenarios where he or she becomes part of the emerging trauma-related scenes that, hitherto, the patient has struggled with alone.

Actualization and enactment, thus, might be an opportunity for these scenarios, at least to a certain degree, to be symbolised and reflected upon, which I try to show in the case presentations.

Actualization, projective identification, and enactment

The traumatized patient will, from the start of therapy, involve the analyst in unsymbolized and unconscious relationship, where the patient communicates by acting out and, in this way, presents important aspects of her traumatic experiences (Varvin, 2013c). In this way, what is called trauma, but which, in fact, is the patient's reaction to, and struggle with, the repercussions of her experiences, will be present from the beginning of the contact. Treatment of "the trauma" is not something that comes later when a trauma narrative is told, as is believed by exposure therapists.

What the patient communicates touches the analyst and might hook on to unconscious, not worked through material on his or her side, resulting in action that, at first sight, is not therapeutic: what is called countertransference enactment (Jacobs, 1986). These enactments on the part of the analyst may, however, be a starting point for a possible process of symbolization and making conscious of these implicit experiences (Scarfone, 2011).

It should be underlined that enactment actually involves a collapse in the therapeutic dialogue where the analyst is drawn into an inter-action where she or he unwittingly acts, thereby actualizing uncon-scious wishes of both him/herself and the patient. It may be a definable episode in a process with more or less clear distinctions between the pre-phase, the actual moment, and the post phase but might be part of a prolonged process in therapy (Jacobs, 1986) or both, as was the case with the clinical material to be presented. Enactments appear, thus, as an unintentional breakdown of the analytic rule of "speech not act" and could imply a new opportunity for integration or could hinder the analytic process.

Enactments can come as a total surprise but can also be identified in, for example, fantasies and thoughts and feeling states on what has gone before (Jacobs, 2001). Most often, it is a surprise and it is only afterwards that it is possible to look at what happened and then, if things go well, be able to understand which processes were at work.

In the context of traumatization, enactments may represent a possibility for symbolizing material related to traumatic experiences. Scarfone holds that

> remembering is not, when it works, a simple act of "recalling" or "evoking". It implies the transmutation of some material into a new form in order to be brought into the psychic field where the functions of remembering and integration can occur. (Scarfone, 2011)

Enactments, thus, can, in connection with traumatization, be seen as actualization of relational scripts or scenarios where unconscious, unsymbolized material is activated both in the patient and in the analyst. This is often seen as an unavoidable part of the analytic inter-action and outcome depends on the analytic couple's ability to bring the enactment into the psychic field.

The pressure is usually understood as starting from the patient, although mutual or reciprocal pressure may be seen (McLaughlin, 1991; McLaughlin & Johan, 1992) where the analyst's conflicts reinforce the patient's tendency to act. An unconscious fantasy is actualized in the transference, the pressure is mediated via projective identification, and the analyst "acts in" due to unresolved countertransference prob-lems.

I try briefly to illustrate aspects of these processes with material from the treatment of two severely traumatized women.

The body's unbearable pain

The patient, A, came from a middle-class family in a large city in an Asian country. She was the only girl and had three brothers. Her mother was somewhat modern and supported her in her struggle to get an education. Father, much older than mother, was strictly religious and conservative.

Her experience was to be raised in the crossfire of the conflict between the mother's and the father's view of what was appropriate for a girl. According to tradition, girls should not have an education and, at the most, attend Qu'ran School, something she felt was deeply unjust. She pursued her intention to get an education with a stubbornness that undoubtedly was inspired by father's attitude.

She experienced two episodes of sexual assault between the ages of seven and nine years, which she described as very frightening and potentially traumatizing.

She developed into a person who took care of other people's problems, and she was extremely afraid of offending or hurting others. She had few friends.

After high school, she was educated as an assistant nurse, and worked in the poorer part of the city, where she became aware of the enormous poverty and suffering in her country. While working in a legal social organisation, she met her husband, who held a leading position in a political movement. They had two children, who were eleven and thirteen years old, respectively, at the start of treatment.

Shortly after her children were born, the political climate deteriorated, and mass arrests began. Her husband and several members of his extended family were arrested. Eight of them were soon executed. Her husband survived, but was badly tortured.

Soon afterwards, she was arrested with her two small children, then four months and two years old. A and her two children spent two years in prison, and some of their experiences were beyond human understanding and, for her, beyond words to describe. She was gradually able to talk about them during therapy, but she gave the impression that much was too difficult to recount.

She could not talk with her husband and others in her family, as she did not want to cause them pain. Her husband had experienced too much himself in prison and suffered from prolonged periods with sleeping problems, nightmares, and somatic pain. A and her husband were separated for a long time after she was released from prison, as he lived clandestinely and later fled.

AAI-classification (Adult Attachment Interview (Crittenden & Landini, 2011)) demonstrated an avoidant (insecure) attachment pattern with compulsive care giving. Mentalizing capacity was low at the start of therapy.

A described a childhood where she repeatedly felt rejected by her father. Her coping strategy was compliance and caregiving in the sense that she tried to see things from her parents' and other's perspectives and to avoid confrontation. This way of dealing with oppression proved useful for her while in prison and might also have helped her during the period of persecution after she was released.

Trauma story: a short summary

First, they were in a prison in a small town for about a year. A and her two children had to live in a small cell, less than one square meter in size, she said. As it was impossible to stretch out when sleeping, she developed a technique of bending her legs backwards in order to rest and to give the children more space. At the beginning of therapy (about ten years later), she was still obliged to sleep in that position to get some rest. Food was scarce and hygienic conditions were poor. At a time when her youngest child was about to die of hunger and thirst, the guard brought contaminated milk that instantly made the child extremely sick and brought him nearer to death. For extended periods, she had to stand, hooded, against the wall, not allowed to sit or take care of the children, who had to crawl on the floor. They could hear the screams of people being tortured, and A was hit while the children watched.

They were then moved to a larger prison in a central city. Here, they were placed in a large, overcrowded cell. She had to curl up to give space to the children and to her fellow prisoners. The fellow prisoners were regularly tortured, and bleeding and maltreated persons were a common sight. Many had their toes or fingers cut off, some became lame, and some were killed in front of A and the children. The following is part of a conversation between therapist (T) and patient (P) from Session 1.

P: Yes, because there we have seen so much, too much, we had never expected that human beings could do things like that.

T: So you have many bad experiences inside you.

P: Of course.
(Pause, ten seconds)

T: You were thinking about something from prison.

P: Yes, it was in the middle of the night, they had fetched someone from the cell where I was and they raped her. . . .
(Pause, ten seconds)
    Yes, we were all in the same room, and they came, one, two, or three men could come. They were covered all over with black clothing so we could not see. We could not see anything of those people, they were all covered. And in every cell we were about seventy at the time. And then they came, placed themselves in the middle of the room, turned around several times pointing, and then [they would] suddenly stop, and the finger pointed at one of us. The others of us had almost stopped breathing while this man turned around—now it will be me, by coincidence. When one was pointed at, we others could breathe again, but we were desperate for the person who had been selected. Because we did not know [their fate]. Is it torture or execution? (Pause.) And I remember my friends; they were fetched at four o'clock in the morning for execution and we were not allowed to get up and say our thanks and say goodbye. And it was like that, if the fellow prisoners took my children on their laps, they got whipped.

T: For taking your children on their laps? (The therapist is openly shocked.)

P: Yes, they accused us of having a kind of contact with each other.

I cite this passage at length because it also described the paralysing fright that became a part of her personality. She said during the follow-up interview, "Before I was afraid of everything, all the time. Now it is totally changed. I will never forget you." She added that she had not been aware that it was fright.

She described further how these experiences had affected her children, especially the older one, and her struggle to help them afterwards. She saw how he (the older child) afterwards, in identification with the perpetrators, played torture games with other children. She claimed to have succeeded to a large extent, together with her husband, in helping the children in a positive way through their complicated childhood. From all the descriptions during therapy, this seemed to be largely true, but both children had psychic problems and her younger child developed a serious immune deficiency disease in his teenage years.

During the five years she stayed in her home country after being released from prison, she and her family were constantly harassed. She was several times taken for "interrogation", as it was called, sometimes for days, sometimes for months, and maltreated. She was harassed on the street and was constantly afraid of being killed. Members of her family were also taken for interrogation. The police sadistically took her in every time they knew there was some celebration in the family. She tried to work, but was constantly plagued by weakness and pain. In addition, she was often, because of her low status as an ex-prisoner, not paid for the work. Her main objective was to survive and to take care of the children. However, inside she was desperate. "I wanted to die," she said. The pressure was enormous; she felt so weak at times and had so much pain that she was not able to stand up or walk—"I had to crawl." She said that this was in many ways worse than being in prison. There, she knew what to expect. In this period, she lived in constant fear of the unexpected.

When she understood there was a real danger that her children might be taken away from her and that she herself could be put in prison for a long time, she decided to flee. As is often the case, she could not say farewell to her closest family. A perilous escape brought her and the children to Norway, where her husband waited for them.

The oppression did not stop after they had fled. Family members in the home country were constantly harassed because of their exiled members, which represented a constant source of pressure and pain for her and her husband. In addition, the embassy kept exiles under surveillance, reporting on their activities to the authorities in the home country, and punished their families in different ways. Thus, precautions had to be taken so as not to cause suffering for the family.

Psychoanalytic psychotherapy aims to work with internal anxieties and, especially with traumatized persons, one of the main objectives is to help develop a sense of inner safety. When the external situation is still dangerous, although not necessarily in terms of the patient's own personal safety, this creates deep worries and anxieties, especially in a person from a culture with a strong family orientation. Under these circumstances, the patient must feel confident that the therapist acknowledges and cares about the safety of the patient's extended family as well as that of the patient.

Since A's arrival in Norway, she had had numerous physical ailments: pain in different parts of her body (back, chest, stomach, legs, and headache), breathing problems, and recurrent urinary tract infections. She had also developed an intractable thoracic kyphosis.

She suffered from intrusive memories and nightmares relating to traumatic experiences, extreme anxiety, and depression. She gave an impression of extreme sadness.

Treatment process

The psychotherapy was conducted face-to-face in a total of 165 sessions. The first year of the therapy was with an interpreter. The patient expressed the desire at the beginning of the therapy to "learn enough Norwegian to express myself". When she decided to do without an interpreter this was, at least partly, motivated by mistrust.

The analyst formulated the focus of the psychotherapy in the following way: ". . . to find what happens in you when you get pain, when you become sad or dreary, and if there can be ways you can work with yourself to feel better in your body without having to take medicine" (which she did not want to do) (Session 1).

The instruction given at beginning of therapy was an invitation "to try to say whatever comes to your mind", with an additional explanation of the meaning of this related to her cultural beliefs-. This was, as could be expected, a rather difficult task for her. Having been interrogated numerous times, this invitation naturally evoked resistance. One main aim was to help her to talk in general and in particular about difficulties regarding both the current situation and her past experiences. She often behaved in a passive way, expecting to "get treatment", which was related to her cultural tradition (doctors give treatment) but also to her helplessness and feeling of non-agency in relation to her pain.

She often regressed into a passive–aggressive position, demanding tha her therapist should "make her well". "When will I be well, doctor?" and "When will the pains go away?" were recurrent questions. The transference implications of this demand, putting the therapist in the difficult position of being the helpless helper, and thereby preparing the ground for disappointment, were obvious, and proved difficult to clarify.

She sought a variety of somatic treatments while in therapy (often when disappointed by, or mistrusting, the therapist) and even managed on one occasion to persuade a surgeon to perform an operation, which had no positive effect.

The therapeutic process could be divided into three phases, as listed below.

1. *The rapprochement phase* (sessions 1–18): the first verbalization of traumatic memories and the establishment of a preliminary alliance. The immediate effect was a spontaneous improvement in her depression and some of her somatic problems.
2. *Resistance and mistrust* (sessions 19–90). In this phase, she had many somatic complaints, very often openly distrusted the therapist, and she quit therapy twice.
3. *Phase of autonomy* (sessions 91–165). Here, she was able to make mental connections on her own and work with what frightened her in her daily life, and, thus, gained considerable autonomy.

I focus on some aspects of the transference–countertransference relation.

She involved the analyst in unsymbolized relationship, communicating by projective identifications, action, and affective pressure (Varvin, 2013b). The effects of her overwhelming experiences were, in this way, present from the beginning.

Her way of relating and communicating was intense and activated the analyst's unconscious material on his side, resulting in unintended, unconscious countertransference enactments.

I shall try briefly to illustrate aspects of these processes with A.

After the long period of resistance and mistrust where her fright of again being humiliated became a major focus, things loosened up and she began to link present fears with her prison experiences and other atrocities. This resulted in increased inner freedom and also a more autonomous life. She began to see friends, moved around in the city more freely, and even learned to drive a car. She realised that she had been frightened of almost everything at beginning of therapy and a process started where she could identify what made her afraid and the roots of her fears. For example, she panicked when her husband touched her ears. This she could connect with the time in prison when she was hooded and had to "watch" her children with her ears. She experienced anxiety when hearing voices from the radio, reminding her of the messages in the prison from the loudspeaker, giving the names of those who would be tortured. The color black made her almost paralyzed: the connection to the black-clothed men in the prison became clear when the analyst wore a black jacket.

An enactment episode ran as follows: she came to the session complaining of intense back pain and demanded to lie on the couch. When the analyst moved his chair closer, feeling encouraged by her increased freedom in the consulting room and hoping for a closer contact, she became stiff, full of anxiety and silent. It took some sessions to clarify that the scene represented a seduction situation, reminding her of assaults she had experienced in the prison. The analyst's wish for closeness, after long and frustrating resistance and aggression from the patient, represented for her a violent, sexual approach. The unconscious roots of the analyst's wish, and the not very cautious way it was acted out, was material for self-analytic work.

Summary

She brought her experiences from her prolonged and complex trau-matizing experiences into the consulting room and involved the analyst in scenarios of distrust and attack that were difficult to under-stand and emotionally hard to contain. A marked change occurred when she was able to realize that she was afraid, that something she experienced here and now made her stiff with fright. This was a start-ing point for a historicizing process in which gradually she was able to make connections between present fears and earlier experiences, as described above. This was an amazing process in which she seemed to have internalized the analyst's constant efforts to contextualize her present fears. In this process, she increasingly insisted on making these connections by herself. Furthermore, she started to relate to her pre-trauma childhood experiences. She gradually realized that she had experienced her life as entirely filled with anxieties where there were almost no "safe points" which she could relate to, none anchoring in earlier safe enough relational experiences that could have given her at least some feeling that the world could be safe. One example demonstrates this: her fear of the color black brought memories of a strict and quite cold grandmother. When reflecting, she realized that the memories were "colored in black" and she remembered her experiences when grandmother took her for the weekly baths at the village's public bath. At the end of the bathing rituals, she was taken to a deep well in a rather dark place. She remembered she had been afraid, but realized that that the blackness had generalized and colored the memories of grandmother. When this was sorted out, other good memories appeared. Washing was seen in a different context and, in that way, her childhood gradually "became better". I think this part of her work with the past demonstrated the retroactive (*nachträglich*) work of extreme traumatization and especially how it activates early fears of breakdown and how psychoanalytic therapy worked retroactively to reorganize memories from early parts of her life.

Loss and trauma: a case story

B, a woman in her late thirties, came to Norway as a refugee from a Latin American country nine years before treatment. She reported a relatively happy childhood, being loved by father and mother and her siblings, and she had managed to get an education as well. She was married and was working as clerk when she was arrested because of her husband's participation in a non-violent political organization. At the time of her arrest, she was pregnant, in the last trimester. She was maltreated physically (including beatings on her pregnant womb) and psychically (threats, seclusion, etc.), and suffered from malnutrition and lack of proper medical care when she became ill. Her husband was arrested at the same time and was tortured to death some months later. She was allowed to go to a public hospital to give birth, and an escape was arranged for her shortly thereafter. While she was living clandestinely, her child died of an unknown disease, probably caused by the torture, maltreatment, and lack of adequate medical care during her stay in prison.

After the death of her child and husband, she lived clandestinely for about a year before she fled from her country under difficult circumstances. During this time, she experienced additional serious traumas. When she arrived in Norway, the authorities did not believe her. She was put in prison and sent back to a third country, where she had to live under very poor conditions for some time and where she also experienced serious traumatization. Later, she was again allowed entrance to Norway with help from human rights organizations.

She arrived in Norway severely depressed and suicidal and had serious eating problems in addition to post-traumatic symptoms and psychosomatic symptoms. In the years in Norway, she suffered almost continuously from nightmares, re-experiencing, avoidance behaviour, somatization, and psychosomatic illness and recurrent depression. In spite of this, she managed to settle and achieve a considerable degree of integration in the community. She lived alone and had friends. but no intimate contact with men. Her life in exile was characterized by high levels of activity, lots of helping others, and little time for herself, seemingly reflecting a need to act rather than feel.

B had, to a large extent, mourned her husband, for example, performing grief rituals on his birthday. The loss of her child was not a problem she presented when seeking therapy and it remained ignored during the first part until it emerged in a quite dramatic way in a session after a week's break in the treatment.

A key session

She arrived on time at the session, out of breath as she had been running, believing she was late. Her first remark was "I lost the bus" (a common expression in Norwegian when arriving late for the bus, but also indicating the theme of loss). In the first part of the session, she spoke in staccato manner, evoking a strong need in the analyst to help and support her.

She talked about her loneliness during the break, the need to have someone to lean on, to trust, and who could be close. The analyst affirmed her feeling of loneliness; something that set in motion a counter movement where she referred to a "progressive" friend who maintained that one could easily do without the support of a family. Her own family and her close relation to them and also her ambivalent feelings towards them had been a theme throughout the therapy. In this section of the session, the analyst's interventions also became intellectual, with a lack of affective resonance. The analyst, in this way, joined the patient in an enactment attempting to ward off painful material.

Then a shift occurred when the analyst remarked, remembering her earlier clearly stated affection for her family, that they, her family, surely would have liked her to have a family. She then became silent for some minutes and finally said, crying, "Yes, I have been thinking if I had my daughter, she would have been thirteen years old and . . ."

She cried a lot and seemed distant, obviously re-experiencing scenes from the past. Then, haltingly, in short sentences and after encouragement, she told about the birth of the child, how happy she had been when she heard the child cry. It felt like a victory. Also, the dangers came to her mind and she was frightened and desperate in the session. She did not manage to stop crying even as she left.

This was a breakthrough of memories, or, rather, memory fragments, which came as a surprise for the patient (and for the analyst). It was a re-experiencing, like a film, of the trauma scenario, a broken narrative.

She was physically ill during the night and when she came the next day she was still quite affected, and it gradually became clear what had happened before and during the previous sessions, which, as it appeared, represented an actualization of the drama when she lost her child.

Three consecutive nights before the key session, she had had the following dream, which she recounted, realizing the connection with her child's death:

> "And then suddenly I get all . . . I feel I, I got like . . . I had . . . I did not tell you, I dreamt for three nights [before the key session] that I cried . . . I was very narrow in my throat and, and had like saliva around my mouth. It's like a . . . then I thought like, what is it that makes me feel? I don't get enough oxygen and . . . like heavy breathing. When I, eh, was in the middle of crying, when I woke up."

She then could narrate how the child died. She was living clandestinely in poor conditions. Her child got fever and had more difficulties in breathing. In the end, the baby died in her arms of lack of air (asphyxia). Her despair and grief were abruptly curtailed by the dangerous circumstances, which demanded that she moved on. Her baby was buried in haste and the harsh tone taken by her comrades prevented any emotional reactions in her.

We can now reconstruct aspects of what happened in her therapy. She had a markedly positive, almost idealizing, transference towards the analyst. In the break, she had felt utterly lonely and this had evoked in her unconscious memories of her child, as well as other persons she had lost (her husband, and also her father when she was in exile). In the session she came out of breath with a feeling of loss (expressed in her first remark: "I lost the bus"). The countertransference was characterized by a desperate wish to help, but then a felt helplessness occurred that resulted in distancing and intellectualization on the analyst's part.

In hindsight, it was possible to identify several episodes earlier in the therapy where the theme of loss had come up and also where dead children had been mentioned. This had obviously been an attempt by the patient to bring what was possibly her most painful experience into the therapy, but she then backed away and either intellectualized or dropped the theme. The analyst had colluded with this and also avoided the theme of loss, which had clear connection with the analyst's own problems and some unresolved issues concerning his own losses.

The theme of loss became, however, more acute for her in the break preceding this key session. She had obviously, during this time, partly unconsciously, lived through and been occupied with her tragic loss and identified with her dead child and, through projective identification, the analyst got the role of the helpless helper, pushing him to act according to the role assigned to his part. This interpretation was supported by analyst's subjective countertransference reactions (i.e., feeling solicitous but helpless).

The relative abstinence in the session allowed her to start symbolizing her traumatic loss. The dream was obviously the signal of an unconscious preparation for re-experiencing the death of her child, in which she gave voice to the part of herself identified with the child trying to survive.

As the theme of loss was elaborated, B began to integrate the loss of her child with her other losses—her husband's death, her mother's death some years ago, and also other deaths. Thus, the emergence of the loss of her child brought with it memories of other losses, which she then worked to integrate and mourn during the rest of the therapy.

Needless to say, this was a hard and laborious process also for the analyst, who had to work on his own unresolved issues. I would not claim that it was completed, but the treatment did make a difference in her life; she was no longer depressed and had less somatic pain and, more importantly, she started a new way of life. She was no longer the tireless helper; she took time to care for herself and relax and she managed to establish a relationship with a man.

Conclusions

The work with A result in a remarkable improvement in a very sick woman. She remained, however, disabled and not able to work. She managed, nevertheless, to live a freer life with an increased capacity to care for her children and relate to her husband.

B functioned better and was less incapacitated by post-trauma problems, even though she did not live a good life. Treatment resulted in marked improvement also for her.

Common for both were the development of a psychic space where past and present were more clearly distinguished, the achievement of greater autonomy and freedom to make choices, and markedly better relational functioning.

I started with a general description of the situation for traumatized refugees, the hardship they have undergone, and the commonly hard conditions in exile. In addition, it should be mentioned that our and others' research generally show high level of psychic suffering and low quality of life for this group (Opaas & Varvin, 2015; Opaas et al., 2015; Rees et al., 2011; Steel et al., 2002; Vaage et al., 2010).

The central question is: what help do severely traumatized persons need and what place does psychotherapy have in addition to other somatic and rehabilitation efforts.

I have here focused on psychotherapy, which is the treatment of choice for psychic post-trauma problems. There is, furthermore, an obvious need to clarify our theories on traumatization. The word "trauma" seems to me, as mentioned earlier, rather useless and its common use obscures more than clarifies. The effects of extreme traumatizing experiences can best be understood as complex responses that involve the whole personality which must be understood in its historical context (Oliner, 2014).

We have, in our research, identified a subgroup with restricted response to traumatization with lamed affects, poor affect regulation and tolerance, bodily symptoms, and impaired relational capacity (Opaas et al., 2015): a situation deemed by many not suitable for psychoanalytic approaches. A had experienced most of the hardest traumatizing experiences in prison, after prison, and during flight. She was clearly constricted, with a low mentalizing capacity, a high level of suffering, and fulfilled criteria for personality changes after extreme traumatization (*ICD-10* diagnosis F82.0). She improved, however, during therapy and was able to use a psychoanalytic space for developing her mentalizing capacity. (Technique was, of course, modified.) B. had a different starting point in that her personality was more integrated and her warding off of traumatizing experiences had been, in a way, more successful.

A and B had different paths to recovery, or partial recovery, demonstrating that being traumatized must be studied and understood in its specificity.

Both treatments demonstrate that:

1. Time is an important parameter and that too short treatments, often recommended now, that are terminated in a phase of resistance, could be devastating.
2. Work in and with transference and countertransference is essential, confirming later research on the treatment of personality-based pathologies (Høglend et al., 2006, 2008).
3. The analyst/therapist needs to be involved in trauma-related scenarios
4. Countertransference enactments may bring forth unsymbolized material.
5. Increased symbolization and mentalization is possible in a long enough therapeutic process.

The most important aspects of relational traumas are non-verbal and only partly symbolized. Traumatized people experience a partial foreclosure, that is, parts of the symbolic is undermined, contrasting with a more total undermining of the symbolic function in psychosis. Foreclosed signifiers are not integrated in the subject's unconscious, so they tend to re-emerge from outside, in "the Real". Another way of saying this is that they appear as beta-elements and sometimes also as bizarre objects through, for example, hallucinations. In this way, the treatment of severely traumatized patients has similarities with the treatment of psychosis. Furthermore, the traumatized patient has the experience that language is perverted during torture and other atrocity situations, so he or she has learned to rely on non-verbal aspects of communication. The fact that so much of the focus in interpersonal relations with severely traumatized patients relies on the non-verbal dimension might explain, to a certain extent, why psychoanalytic therapy works with people from other cultures where the patient's and the analyst's mother tongues are different. As Erikson stated poignantly many years ago, regarding communication with exiled and immigrants, they do not "hear what you say, but 'hang on' to your eyes and your tone of voice" (Erikson, 1964, p. 95). Apart from this, one must underline that psychoanalytic therapy is, in itself, a culturally sensitive approach.

Massive traumatization creates destabilization of the basic structures of human relationships:

- in the dimension of intimate relationships where intrapsychic and interpersonal functions concern regulations of emotions, primary care, basic identity, and so forth;
- in the dimension of the individual relations to the group where identity and developmental task are negotiated;
- in the cultural or discourse dimension, where different discourses are established that give meaning to, and stabilize, relations and developments on the individual and group levels.

Therefore, treatment of the traumatized patient can only with difficulty work in a social/cultural setting in which traumatization is not acknowledged and worked with at other levels in society.

References

Askevold, F. (1980). The war sailor syndrome. *Danish Medical Bulletin, 27*: 220–224.
Bion, W. R. (1962). *Learning From Experience*. London: Heinemann.

Crittenden, P. M., & Landini, A. (2011). *Attachment. A Dynamic Maturational Approach to Discourse Analysis.* New York: W. W. Norton.

Eitinger, L. (1965). Concentration camp survivors in Norway and Israel. *Israel Journal of Medical Science, 1:* 883–895.

Erikson, E. H. (1964). Identity and uprootedness in our time. In: E. Erikson (Ed.), *Insight and Responsibility* (pp. 81–107). New York: Norton.

Flyktninghjelpen (2014). Flyktningregnskapet. Alt Om Mennesker På Flukt Verden Over. Ed. http://www.flyktninghjelpen.No/Arch/_ Img/9179288.Pdf: Flyktninghjelpen. Norway Refugee Council.

Gagnon, A. J., & Stewart, D. E. (2014). Resilience in international migrant women following violence associated with pregnancy. *Archive of Women's Mental Health, 17*(4): 303–310.

Henningsen, F. (2012). *Psychoanalyse mit traumatisierten Patienten. Trennung, Krankheit, Gewalt.* Stuttgart: Klett-Cotta.

Hirsch, M. (1996). Forms of identification with the aggressor – according to Ferenczi and Anna Freud. *Prax. Kinderpsychol. Kinderpsychiatr, 45:* 198–205.

Høglend, P., Bøgwald, K., Amlo, S., Marble, A., Ulberg, R., Sjaastad, M., Sørbye, O., Heyerdahl, O., & Johansson, P. (2008). Transference interpretations in dynamic psychotherapy: do they really yield sustained effects? *American Journal of Psychiatry,* [Online], 165.

Høglend, P. A. S., Marble, A., Bøgwald, K. P., Sørbye, O., Sjaastad, M. C., & Heyerdahl, O. (2006). Analysis of the patient–therapist relationship in dynamic psychotherapy: an experimental study of transference interpretations. *American Journal of Psychiatry, 163:* 1739–1746.

Hurvich, M. (2003). The place of annihilation anxieties in psychoanalytic theory. *Journal of the American Psychoanalytic Association, 51:* 579–616.

Jacobs, T. (1986). On countertransference enactments. *Journal of the American Psychoanalytic Association, 34:* 289–307.

Jacobs, T. (2001). On misreading and misleading patients: some reflections on communications, miscommunications and countertransference enactments. *International Journal of Psychoanalysis, 82:* 653–669.

Keilson, H., & Sarpathie, R. (1979). *Sequentieller Traumatisierung bei Kindern.* Stuttgart: Ferdinand Enke.

Laub, D. (2005). Traumatic shutdown of narrative and symbolization: a death instinct derivative? *Contemporary Psychoanalysis, 41:* 307–326.

Leuzinger-Bohleber, M. (2012). Changes in dreams: from a psychoanalysis with a traumatised, chronic depressed patient. In: P. Fonagy, H. K., M. Leuzinger-Bohleber, & D. Taylor (Eds.), *The Significance of Dreams* (pp. 49–88). London: Karnac.

McLaughlin, J. T. (1991). Clinical and theoretical aspects of enactment. *Journal of the American Psychoanalytic Association, 39*: 95–614.

McLaughlin, J. T., & Johan, M. (1992). Enactments in psychoanalysis (Panel report). *Journal of the American Psychoanalytic Association, 40*: 827–841.

Niederland, W. G. (1968). Clinical observations on the "survivor syndrome". *International Journal of Psychoanalysis, 49*: 313–315.

Niederland, W. G. (1981). The survivor syndrome: further observations and dimensions. *Journal of the American Psychoanalytic Association, 29*: 413–425.

Oliner, M. (2014). *Psychic Reality in Context*. London: Karnac.

Opaas, M., & Varvin, S. (2015). Relationships of childhood adverse experiences with mental health and quality of life at treatment start for adult refugees traumatized by preflight experiences of war and human rights violations. *Journal of Nervous and Mental Diseases, 203*(9): s. 684–695.

Opaas, M., Hartmann, E., Wentzel-Larsen, T., & Varvin, S. (2015). Relationship of pretreatment Rorschach factors to symptoms, quality of life, and real-life functioning in a three-year follow-up of traumatized refugee patients. *Journal of Personality Assessment, 98*(3): 247–260.

Purnell, C. (2010). Childhood trauma and adult attachment. *Healthcare Counselling and Psychotherapy Journal, 10*(2): 9–13.

Rees, S., Silove, D., Chey, T., Ivancic, L., Steel, Z., Creamer, M., Teesson, M., Bryant, R., McFarlane, A. C., Mills, K. L., Slade, T., Carragher, N., O'Donnell, M., & Forbes, D. (2011). Lifetime prevalence of gender-based violence in women and the relationship with mental disorders and psychosocial function. *Journal of the American Medical Association, 306*: 513–521.

Rosenbaum, B., & Varvin, S. (2007). The influence of extreme traumatisation on body, mind and social relations. *International Journal of Psychoanalysis, 88*: 1527–1542.

Scarfone, D. (2011). Repetition: between presence and meaning. *Canadian Journal of Psychoanalysis, 19*: 70–86.

Schottenbauer, M., Glass, C. R., Arnkoff, D. B., & Gray, S. H. (2008). Contributions of psychodynamic approaches to treatment of PTSD and trauma: a review of the empirical treatment and psychopathology literature. *Psychiatry, 71*: 13–34.

Simich, L., & Andermann, L. (2014). *Refugees and Resilience*. Dordrecht: Springer.

Steel, Z., Silove, D., Phan, T., & Bauman, A. (2002). Long-term effect of psychological trauma on the mental health of Vietnamese refugees resettled in Australia: a population-based study. *Lancet, 360*: 1056–1062.

Taft, C. T., Kaloupek, D. G., Schumm, J. A., Marshall, A. D., Panuzio, J., King, D. W., & Keane, T. M. (2007). Posttraumatic stress disorder symptoms, physiological reactivity, alcohol problems, and aggression among military veterans. *Journal of Abnormal Psychology, 116*: 498–507.

Ungar, M. E. (2012). *The Social Ecology of Resilience. A Handbook of Theory and Practice*, New York: Springer.

Vaage, A. B. (2010). Long-term mental health of Vietnamese refugees in the aftermath of trauma. *British Journal of Psychiatry, 196*: 122–125.

Vaage, A. B., Thomsen, P. H., Silove, D., Wentzel-Larsen, T., Van Ta, T., & Hauff, E. (2010). Long-term mental health of Vietnamese refugees in the aftermath of trauma. *British Journal of Psychiatry, 196*: 122–125.

Varvin, S. (2013a). Ideologiens galskap eller galskapens ideologi. *Matrix, 30*: 156–173.

Varvin, S. (2013b). Psychoanalyse mit Traumatisierten. Weiterleben nach Extremerfahrungen und kompliziertem Verlust (Psychoanalysis with the traumatised patient: helping to survive extreme experiences and complicated loss). *Forum der Psychoanalyse. Zeitschrift für klinische Theorie und Praxis, 29*: 372–389.

Varvin, S. (2013c). Trauma als Nonverbaler Kommunikation. *Zeitschrift für psychoanalytische Theorie und Praxis, 28*: 114–130.

Varvin, S. (2015). *Flukt og eksil.* Oslo: Universitetsforlaget.

Varvin, S., & Rosenbaum, B. (2011). Severely traumatized patients' attempts at reorganizing their relations to others in psychotherapy: an enunciation analysis. In: N. Freedman, M. Hurvich, & R. Ward (Eds.), *Another Kind of Evidence. Studies on Internalization, Annihilation Anxiety, and Progressive Symbolization in the Psychoanalytic Process* (pp. 226–243). London: Karnac.

Vitriol, V. B., Ballasteros, S. T., Florenzano, R. U., Weil, K. P., & Benadof, D. F. (2009). Evaluation of an outpatient intervention for women with severe depression and a history of childhood trauma. *Psychiatry Services, 60*: 936–942.

Winnicott, D. W. (1991). Fear of breakdown. *Psyche, 45*: 1116–1126.

Yu, H. (2009). *Brothers.* New York: Pantheon E Books.

CHAPTER TEN

Machismo and the limits of male heterosexuality

Isaac Tylim

A couple of years ago, while visiting Tibet, going from monastery to monastery, I established a dialogue with a rather jovial Tibetan monk. His English was simple, but we were able to communicate fairly well. While talking about my South American origins, he, to my amusement, declared: "many macho-man there." I am inclined to believe that the meaning of the word "macho"—along with South American soccer teams—ought to be the most widely known Latin American reference.

Machismo is a term commonly associated with Hispano/Latin American cultures. It is a derivative of "macho" and connotes a quality or attribute of masculinity. Machismo is an attribute reserved to describe a way of organizing the world and sexual differences from the clear and rigid buttress of dichotomic thinking. In the world according to machos, there are machos and there are *hembras*; men with *cojones* and sissies without them.

Machismo has been linked to patriarchy, chauvinism, colonization, oppression, religious institutions, and persecution. It is an ideological web that tends to infiltrate all levels of the social matrix, exerting a profound impact on men's and women's psychosexual and psychosocial development.

Machismo may be considered a stereotype of masculinity, a perverse solution to the ambiguities that surround the differences between the sexes and a desperate attempt to ward off castration anxiety. I shall go back to this at a later point.

What are the origins of machismo in Latin American cultures? What can a psychoanalytically informed exploration of the phenomenon of machismo teach us about the nature of masculinity and its impact on women and their daughters—as well as on men and their sons?

Following the discovery of America, the European *conquistadores*, in pursuit of golden chimeras, destroyed the soul of ancient civilizations. The atrocities perpetrated by those men who, in the second half of the fifteenth century, crossed the Atlantic in search of a passage to India have been veiled by a slew of official stories. This had, and continues to have, the effect of erasing large portions of Meso and South America history.

The invaders systematically attacked autochthonous religions, languages, and customs, causing major psychological and cultural ruptures. The effects of these ruptures have endured for centuries in institutionalized transformations capable of perpetuating the power of the invader's authority.

The newcomers to American shores, while invested in desecrating the cultures they conquered, made it their mission to plant the seeds of European ideas in the non-Christian land. The Europeans came to the New World with an ideological system ready to be imposed on those they saw as being without faith. Their colonization fused the cross, the sword, and the crown in a devastating plan to take possession not just of land or other objective or material goods, but also of the subjectivity of its inhabitants.

The Spanish *conquistadores* managed to leave the indigenous and mestizo populations in what the Mexican Nobel Laureate Octavio Paz refers to as "the labyrinth of solitude." In this labyrinth, Mexicans were forced to survive "between myth and negation, fantasy and reality, deifying or idealizing certain historical periods, obliterating others". Latin American crucial problem according to Gabriel Garcia Marquez "has been a lack of conventional means to render our lives believable. This, my friends, is the crux of solitude" (from Garcia Marquez's Nobel Prize acceptance speech in 1982).

A version of history based on the colonizer's macho power was thus imposed. The fate of the Aztecs seemed to have foretold the fate of most indigenous groups in Central and South America. The colonizer's imposition of order was sustained by subjugation and systematic humiliation of the other. Men could be killed and women raped with impunity. The Inquisition, a tribunal run exclusively by men, further affirmed the ruling male-centered ideology.

While the Inquisition persecuted all those who refused to accept the mandate of the Catholic Church, it is interesting to note that a large number of those who were burnt at the stake were priests who were not just common-or-garden heretics. Schons, Sor Juana Ines de la Cruz's biographer, cited by Paz (1995), attests that Spaniards—secular men and priests alike—who emigrated to "New Spain" tended to be promiscuous, fathering numerous children and refusing to recognize them as their offspring. The sexual escapades of these powerful men were so rampant that a 1668 newspaper obituary for a handsome archbishop suggests that the deceased was a very virtuous man because he was able to maintain his virginity to the end of his life on earth (Paz, 1995, p. 106)!

Contemporary machismo in Latin American is the living legacy of colonization. Colonization provided a relatively safe setting to enact a kind of perverse male sexual liberation among the ruins of the colonized countries. The apparent male sexual liberation that took place in the New World, well away from the restrictive European mores, generated versions of machismo that still prevail in Latin countries, spanning socio-economic, educational, and generational barriers.

In my reading of the phenomenon, machismo reflects the prevalence of a centralized cultural commodity imported by the Spanish *conquistadores*. The *conquistadores* often invoked their self-assumed right to domination under the blessing of a punitive and male controlled administration, aided by a church that was also male dominated. There were no women on the Inquisition tribunal that questioned the erotic sub-text of Sor Juana Ines de la Cruz's poetry.

Machismo relies on a binary system that defines masculine traits in opposition to feminine ones. In other words, macho supremacy in Meso and South America has defined social discourse in terms of one member of the pair being idealized while the other was being marginalized.

Machismo freezes the interplay between opposites, and the play between the sexes ceases to be free. The power of the man is justified by describing it as "man's nature", which causes women to be seen as objects rather than subjects. Macho men lead privileged existences at the top of the hierarchy, just as conquistadors did. The non-macho complementary link in the binary system is often ignored, used, and/or abused, and always controlled.

How can we translate machismo to a psychoanalytic language? As stated above, in machismo one encounters a stereotype of masculinity constructed around a defense against softness and vulnerability. Machismo may be viewed as a reaction formation against unaccept-able passive longings and the concomitant universal wish to return to the pre-genital mother. The idealization of the father's potent phallus serves as a buffer against the threat of de-identification and dissolu-tion. The dominant culture provides the costumes and the props necessary to stage a scenario where male/female, passivity/activity, master/mistress, upper rank/lower rank are sustained and protected by the social and political order.

Psychoanalytic theory affirms that the discovery of sexual distinc-tion is a decisive and formative point in the development of both males and females. The early realization that a boy has something that the girl does not have influences psychosexual development, facilitat-ing or hindering the structuring of human desire. Male and female sexuality are achievements of differentiation that may be attained through a partial resolution of the ambiguities attached to the ques-tion of the differences between the sexes. Anchored in constitutional bisexuality, undifferentiated sexuality is ruled by the demands of the pleasure principle. Elaborate omnipotent and grandiose fantasies emerge in an attempt to hold on to a position in which the reality of the differences between the sexes may be denied.

Psychoanalytic theory has built its foundations on the tensions that erupt between elusive biological concepts and psychological ones. Psychoanalysis has taught us how human sexuality flourishes in the domain in which biology becomes absorbed and transformed by fan-tasy, that striking interaction between mind and body. Through this adventurous journey from the soma to the psyche, sexuality ceases to be a recapitulation of a predicted set of events, and may be concep-tualized instead as a stage for multiple and various creative transfor-mations.

Freud needed to prove his theory that the discovery of the anatom-ical differences between the sexes was decisive in the psychosexual development of both men and women. Castration anxiety in boys and a sense of inferiority and penis envy in girls were the expectable consequences of his theory. The culminating point of development, that sought-after resolution of the Oedipus complex and the establishment of the primacy of genitality and heterosexuality, might have skewed Freud's thought. A prisoner of the prevalent Victorian morality of his time, Freud did not investigate what was there prior to the shock of discovery of the anatomical differences between the sexes, leaving unexplored the dyadic mother–child relationship. In so doing, he neglected to acknowledge the role of the mother, generating a phallocentric theory with serious consequences for the psychoanalytic theory relating to both masculinity and femininity.

The early notion of constitutional bisexuality is often relegated to the background in favor of binary concepts that accentuate oppositions at the expense of similarities or symmetries between the sexes. A dichotomy between what constitutes masculinity and what constitutes femininity has provided an illusory, pseudoscientific bedrock to a theory of psychosexual development which has at its end-point the attainment of heterosexuality and perpetuation of the species. Thus, from a few basic oppositional terms—male/female, active/passive, heterosexuality/homosexuality, a theory of what constitutes masculinity and femininity was built. Addressing male and female sexuality seems to be a tentative way of organizing thoughts about the sexual behaviour of men and women. This way of thinking simplifies and makes pseudoscientific the wide range of human sexual experience, both internal and external. Dichotomies applied to subjective experience became politicized and moralized in ideologies that attempted to explain the complexities of human sexuality, reducing it to "natural" masculinity or "natural" femininity.

Feminist reading of Freudian theory has pointed out how, in that system, being male, active, and heterosexual was assumed to be superior to being female, passive, and homosexual. However, in reality these dichotomies actually do not hold, and the black and white approach to human sexuality is more an aspiration than a fact.

Naturalizing the sexes, that is, an attempt to convert assumptions about sexuality into facts, curtails access to knowledge not just about differences, but also about one's own origin.

The reading of macho culture in the USA has a different take. "Macho man" in the USA used to evoke an immediate image of the Village People, a pop band that dominated the gay scene in the late

1970s and through the 1980s. They contributed to the transformation of hyper-masculinity into camp, or a neo-sexual (McDougall, 1980), neo-macho man.

The Canadian psychoanalyst George Zavitzianos (1972) coined the term "homeovestism" in referring to those perverse scenarios where the individual—unlike a transvestite—dresses up in specific clothing that might be worn by a person of the same sex. The intention is to shore up their threatened femininity or masculinity. Men dressed up like cowboys in boots and hats *à la* John Wayne may be considered "homeovestites". One is dealing here with a masquerade of masculinity (Kaplan, 1987) to cover up gender anxieties and the fluidity associated with the differences between the sexes.

Zavitzianos distinguishes homeovestism from transvestism in the sense that the former represents an identification with the idealized phallic parent of the same sex, needed to overcome an unconscious identification with the castrated mother, while the latter represents a wish to strengthen the identification with the castrated mother and to simultaneously repudiate that wish. Could the macho man image be regarded as a variety of homeovestism?

Gender is related to peer formality and represents an internalized notion of a gender norm that is constructed rather than biological or innate. Society's regulatory and repressive discourse sustains gender construction. Gender as a performative act connotes a theatrical aspect (Butler, 1988). As Butler says, men and women "act" their gender. However, there is a significant difference between playing a role on stage and playing one's gender off stage. In the former, the difference between fiction and reality remains clearer, while in the latter—as is the case with machismo—the demarcation between fiction and reality becomes blurred. The psychological and socio-political side-effects of acting gender is manifested in scenarios of power and domination.

Like all gender constructions, machismo maintains itself through a repetition of gender performance. This repetition has a compulsive quality that aims at protection the gender construction thus created. The threat of women's power nurtured the resurgence of the old macho man, reflected in the increased violence in films (Schwarzenegger), music (Eminem), and radio shockers (Howard Stern). September 11 set the stage for the return of the old macho man under a cloak of patriarchal vitality embodied by Giuliani, Rumsfeld, and Bush. Our *zeitgeist* is filled with males who operate in the realm of what might be referred as "hallucinatory machismo." To the macho man, the world is a battlefield, and brutality is considered the core of maleness. It is transmitted through the generations, from fathers to sons.

Although machismo by definition is a homophobic ideology, its real opposite is not homosexuality. The macho man may be contrasted to what Limentani (1993) refers to as the "vagina-man." Limentani coined the term as a counterpart to the notion of the phallic woman. An exploration of the characteristics of the so-called vagina-man might shed light on the psychodynamics of macho man, and, in this manner, the gap between psychoanalytic discourse and cultural heritage may be bridged.

Vagina-man is a heterosexual man who is capable of sustaining long-lasting relationships with powerful women, being, at times, somewhat promiscuous. Confident in his masculinity, he is not threatened by his partner's masculine side. The vagina-man has managed to integrate masculine and feminine aspects with a modicum of success. Sexual experimentation with boys in childhood or adolescence had no significant sequelae for the vagina-man.

According to Limentani, in the course of psychoanalytic treatment of a vagina-man, the analyst is bound to unveil a repressed fantasy, "a secret wish to be a woman, associated with a profound envy of everything female" (p. 274). From a different angle, I would like to call attention to the clinical observation that because the vagina-man is comfortable with both masculine and feminine pulls, he is less likely to sexually abuse his daughter.

Over the years, I have had the chance to note a shift in the way male analysands deal with their fear of castration and bisexual conflicts. Sexual liberation and contemporary gender bending has made it easier for these heterosexual patients to bring into consciousness hitherto denied or repressed wishes to identify themselves with women. This type of femininity within masculinity is entirely psychic. Their passivity does not seem to interfere with masculine traits, and they manage to exist at the limits of heterosexuality.

Conversely, the macho man, although capable of sustaining relationships with women, tends to split the object into mother and whore. The splitting permits the coexistence of two opposite sets of ego and affective states without contradiction. The duality of mother–whore is condoned by a political and religious cultural discourse. It is as if the macho man resides on different islands at the same time, reflecting the fragmentation of the ego and a lack of integration between opposites.

The macho man abhors his feminine side, projecting it on the woman who embodies his own denigrated passive longings. In this regard, the macho man resembles the Spanish conquistador. The latter's marginalization and exploitation of the native populations of colonized lands mirrors the marginalization of all that reverberates with passivity. Moreover, their promiscuity is conducive to fathering children by a number of women whom they colonize and rule in more than one household. Overall, the macho man is more capable of abusing his daughters than his vagina-man counterpart.

The macho man becomes involved with women in order to disown his own fear of castration. The tension between fantasies of submission and control is externalized in what Jessica Benjamin (1988) has elaborated as sadomasochistic scenarios that reproduce the Hegelian master and slave dialectic.

The macho man is invested in denying his dependency on the woman so as not to be confronted with his dependency on her. Objectification serves to own and exert control, crushing equality in the relationships between the sexes.

The macho man, like his counterpart, the "vagina-man", may have had casual homosexual encounters during his development. However, unlike the vagina-man, who seems capable of integrating those encounters into his own narrative with apparent ease and without major conflicts, the macho man tries to eject those experiences, exiling them to a remote psychic island. Homophobia is the result of projection and disavowal of those unacceptable longings that challenged machismo's reliance on binary illusions.

Poverty, high infant mortality, and unstable or tyrannical governments continue to erode Latin countries. Well-established institutions and modes of relating between the sexes resist change. Despite recognized advances promoted by feminism and the higher visibility of women in the workforce, machismo has maintained its status as one of the most devastating legacies of the Spanish colonization.

The international recognition granted to Latin American literature, cuisine, soccer, tourist destinations, and fashion does not match Latin countries' repetitive aborted attempts to promote social and political change in the arena where the sexes collide.

Machismo has not been eradicated, despite the new global order. Macho-man stereotypical models of masculinity are perpetuated by the media and passed down from generation to generation. While, in developed countries, masculinity has been under siege for quite a while, the siege does not seem to have had a significant impact on developing or Third World countries. The decentralization of the macho role requires a decentralization of prevailing macho ideologies, something akin to an ending of the colonizer's mentality. In the realm of masculinity, the macho man/colonizer needs to become more at ease with that which Freud deemed unanalyzable: his fear of passivity. Positive results would largely depend on the macho man's ability to analyze, work through, and accept the limits of his own heterosexuality.

McDougall has written on the subject of neo-sexual solutions (1980), distinguishing them from perverse scenarios. Neo-sexual solutions are strategies used in the service of resolving ambiguities and anxieties related to the reality differences, that is, the differences between the sexes. Neo-sexual, to McDougall, means suffering from narcissistic injuries stemming from the realization that anatomy is destiny. Despite bisexuality being the bedrock of human sexuality, biology imposes limitations that the neo-sexual attempts to deny by asserting "I have no need of the opposite sex to have sex." At the other end of the spectrum, the term perversion, once dominant in psychoanalytic discourses, has been reserved for those sexual practices that involve exploitation, overt aggression, or non-consensual sexuality (e.g., rape, sexual abuse of children). Would machismo qualify as a reversal of neo-sexual solutions? Is machismo an attempt to ward off a widespread cultural trend that announces the dawn of new versions of masculinity?

The new masculinities

The world is a small place nowadays. Globalization and cyberspace have brought developing countries (a euphemism for Third World countries) closer to the First World. The works of Isabel Allende, Miguel Asturias, Jorge Luis Borges, Carlos Fuentes, Mario Vargas Llosa, Gabriel Garcia Marquez, Octavio Paz, Juan Ruffo, and many more literary figures have become permanent residents on Barnes and

Noble's overcrowded shelves; some of the most upscale New York restaurants serve sophisticated nouveau Cocina Latina; Brazilian and Argentinian soccer players have become celebrities. Who has not heard about the Mayan ruins? Evita and Frida Kahlo are the subjects of the entertainment industry and the art world. Cyberspace does not recognize geographical barriers.

What makes a man? What makes a woman? Do transgender individuals have different brain chemistry? Is machismo the result of hardwiring that the male cannot escape from? Burkett (2015) has recently suggested that transgender narratives might reinforce old stereotypes of constituted femininity or masculinity and, in this manner, bring back binary ways of conceptualizing gender and sexual differences-.

The representation of masculinity and femininity by the media often acts as a barometer of cultural changes. A "new wave" that focuses on alternative depictions of both masculinity and femininity suggests significant challenges to traditional stereotypes.

Representations of sexual differences are encoded in mainstream, commercial films, television sitcoms, fashion, and advertising that reaches the most remote corners of the world. Whether accentuated or denied, sexual differences lead to the exposure of the ideology of desire and the demystification of categorical or "natural" ways of thinking about human sexuality and about what is to be considered masculine or feminine.

Historically, the film industry, television, and advertising campaigns have displayed a double standard regarding the representations of women and men. It is a well-known fact that while women's nudity was accepted and even expected, men's was to remain off limits. This state of affairs began to change in the last two decades. Males on the screen or on advertising boards have began to show more skin and muscle. Softer, if not weaker, men are now commonly seen on both large and small screens. These men are often unable or unwilling to make important decisions in their life, at times trapped in a type of objectification once applied to women. Along with these changes on how men are represented, the penis has become more visible. It is interesting to note that the explicit frontal shot of a nude man in the opening scene of *Basic Instinct* was not censored, allegedly because the man was dead.

Traditional images of masculinity have been challenged as much as, or perhaps even more than, those of their female counterpart. The change is so pronounced that cultural critics are now referring to a "re-creation of masculinity." Threat not withstanding, today's films and media expose the male nude body almost with the same regularity as females. Objects of desire were in the past the domain of female representations. Not any more. Men are increasingly seen as objects, pin-ups—think of Sylvester Stallone nude on the cover of *Vogue*, or Bruce Willis naked, as a pregnant man mimicking at the time his pregnant wife, who also appeared pregnant and nude on the cover of a previous issue of the same magazine.

It is also possible to address the question of differences and similarities by analyzing the way women and men are impersonated in films (Bell-Metereau, 1993). Anxiety about gender roles is mirrored by changes in representation, not just of men and women, but also in the changes in representations of male and female impersonators. While, in the 1960s, impersonations tended to be humiliating (*I Was a Male War Bride*), misogynistic (*Some Like it Hot*), or psychotic (*Psycho*), from the mid 1970s onwards the viewer was able to observe a more sympathetic representation of impersonators (*The Rocky Horror Picture Show, La Cage aux Folles, Victor-Victoria, Tootsie, The Crying Game, Mrs. Doubtfire*).

Bell-Metereau regards cross-dressing as a reference to the relationship between authority and freedom: male or female impersonators explore differences and similarities by opposing institutionalized binarity in matters of sex and gender. In Almodovar's *All About my Mother*, Lola, the father, appears as the signifier of the rupture with binary categories. Masculine and feminine, maternal and paternal merge. Esteban's father (Lola) seems to have regarded fatherhood as a burden. To reject fatherhood may be interpreted as act of rebellion and, at the same time, an affirmation of a new, post-Franco radical freedom marked by a deep intolerance towards categories that create a dichotomy between the genders.

Masculinity, transmasculinity: he, she, or V

Postmodern and queer theoretical discourse addressed alternative perspectives of what constitutes masculinity in contemporary culture.

The violent constitution of masculinity, the fluidity of gender roles, the creative and original ways in which transvestites and transgender individuals (women to men) display masculinity offers food for thought regarding the construction of gender and their respective stereotypes.

A video interview with Buck Angel, a performer and activist, is one of the most salient examples of a new version of masculinity. Buck Angel has delved into the changes that shaped her transition from woman to man. Buck Angel was born female, "but I was a boy"; this migration to masculinity is referred to as "trans-masculinity."

Muscular, well built, and acting "like a man," Buck Angel believes that "just because you do not have a penis doesn't mean you are not a man."

The body is involved in libidinal architectures that are creative attempts to work out solutions for desire. To many men and women, the body seems to betray the gender divide, cracking the binary system. The overall message is that sexuality is not about anatomical differences, but about something more complex than penises and vaginas. In order to understand human sexuality and grasp a deeper approach to gender, it is imperative to return to the body. This translates into the need to move away from cultural constructions of gender that impose and prescribe how the bodies of males and females ought to be libidinized.

The question of how gender is encoded in verbal or written language might lead to interesting reflections. Language is a minefield for the politically incorrect pedestrian. Is a trans-masculine individual described as "he" or "she"? Transgender characters in narratives often feel confused due to the author's discomfort with referring to them as he or she.

Language tends to mirror the binary system. To transcend it, it may be necessary to declare masculine and feminine pronouns obsolete.

Justin Bond, transvestite author of *Tango*, a memoir of his childhood infatuation with women and his wish to become one, proposes loving the masculine while not injuring the feminine. Even in language, as a child, "I longed to be both Fred Astaire and Ginger Rogers." Justin is in favor of replacing he or she with a new pronoun: V. In V, each side of the V recognizes the two sexes. V (Justin, or V instead of he or she) criticized the *New York Times* for not adapting the new terminology when reporting on trans-masculines or transvestites.

Gender inequalities in caregiving

"Equality between men and women cannot be achieved without a theory of gender as sexed and a rewriting of the rights and obligations of each sex, qua different, in social rights and obligations" (Irigaray, 1993, p. 85).

Well-established institutions and modes of relating between the sexes resist change despite recognized advances promoted by feminism and the higher visibility of women in the workforce. With only a few exceptions, North or South, developed or developing countries seem to have maintained double standards as far as the division of labor is concerned. Old stereotypes and constructed versions of what are masculine or feminine occupations are not easy to eradicate. Those stereotypes survive with detrimental effects on the fate of men, women, and the communities they serve.

Gender stereotypes are based on a binary system that defines masculine traits as being in opposition to feminine ones. For centuries, male supremacy has defined the social discourse regarding gender-specific activities, caregiving being considered a woman's job. The latter promoted unfair inequalities, freezing the sexes in a play between opposites, as if there is something that is essentially masculine or essentially feminine with regard to, say, plumbing or child rearing.

Although in the past two decades we have become more accustomed to same-sex parents, homebound husbands, or women working on construction sites, men remain at the periphery of caregiving functions. Grandparents raising grandchildren, parent-like children or adolescents, first generation children mediating for their immigrant parents, yes; average adult men staying at home to care for a sick family member, rare.

In many places across the globe, men continue to lead privileged existences as masters of the work market, while the non-manly complementary link (women) remains relegated to an auxiliary role, the stereotype of the female nurse to the male physician, the homemaker to the commuting man.

Gender inequalities are embedded not only in action, but also in language. Linguistic codes perpetuate differences, designating the male as having a higher occupational status. For instance, in French, the male physician is *médecin*, while the female is *doctoresse*, where the suffix "esse" signifies lower status. Adding an "e" to *médicin* to form the feminine refers not to the subject, but to the medical practice. In other terms, things and words are sexed. So, the masculine is the doctor as a man, the feminine word for the same profession is a tool (Irigaray, 1993).

In caregiving, one encounters a stereotype of masculinity constructed around male defensiveness against softness and vulnerability, attributes associated with stereotypical femininity. Gender inequality in the context of providing and nurturing the sick may be regarded as a reaction formation against culturally imposed, unacceptable roles. Male and female idealization of masculinity serves as a buffer against the threat of incursion into what is ambivalently regarded as women's territory: caregiving.

It would take a long excursion into child psychosocial development to expose the roots of the male's discomfort with caregiving functions. A possible etiology of male bias could be traced back to the male's childhood resentment at his early dependency on female caregivers. While the female counterpart will strive to identify with mother, the male child will build a barrier in an attempt to separate and attain a masculine identity. It would appear that to be male, one must fight off the wish to be a caregiver. In this way, macho man is born.

The macho man abhors his feminine side, projecting it to women who, in general terms, are ambivalently admired and devalued for their devotion to others. The macho man may become involved with women in order to distance himself from the position of caregiver.

Is men's reluctance to operate as caregivers a function of deep, unacknowledged envy/admiration for women's capabilities to do it all? Perhaps it is, in many cases. Yet, psychological motivations notwithstanding, advances in the medical field imply that people will be living longer. Moreover, increased urbanization, with concomitant dissolution of family units and the decrease of intergenerational sharing of responsibility for sick members of the family, calls for the need to share the burden generated by caregiving.

Raising male awareness of ideological, political, and economic implications of sex differences might be the right way to move toward a new culture of differences. In this vein, gender equality in caregiving will not only be a case of restoring justice, but a practical step for the wellbeing of individuals, families, and communities alike.

Occupy masculinity

For centuries, machismo reduced masculinity to stereotypes, but seems today more ready to admit its limits. As prisoners of gender constructions, and forced to join in a masquerade, males were prone to replay rigid performances in the theater of the sexes. In so doing, they were deprived of access to other dimensions of being.

Contemporary males are increasingly aware of the toll they had to pay under the yoke of that "old masculinity," and are calling for its abandonment.

The "new masculinity" may be viewed as a liberating movement determined to unlock the gate of femininity within masculinity. The time for "Occupy Masculinity" has arrived. "Occupy Wall Street" was demanding fairer distribution of wealth. Occupy Masculinity will, one hopes, allow the creation of space for the complexities and fluidity of what it means to be male in the twenty-first century.

References

Bell-Metereau, R. (1993). *Hollywood Androgyny*. New York: Columbia University Press.

Benjamin, J. (1988). *The Bonds of Love*. New York: Pantheon Books.

Burkett, E. (2015). What makes a woman? *New York Times, Sunday Review*, 6/07/15, pp. 1, 6.

Butler, J. (1988). Performative acts and gender constitution: an essay on phenomenology and feminist theory. *Theater Journal*, 40: 519–531.

Irigaray, L. (1993). *Je, Tu, Nous. Toward a Culture of Differences*. New York: Routledge.

Kaplan, L. (1987). *Female Perversions*. New York: Anchor Books.

Limentani, A. (1993). To the limits of male heterosexuality. In: D. Breen (Ed.), *The Gender Conundrum. Contemporary Psychoanalytic Perspectives on Femininity and Masculinity* (pp. 273–285). London: Routledge.

McDougall, J. (1980). *Plea for a Measure of Abnormality*. New York: International Universities Press.

Paz, O. (1995). *Sor Juana de la Cruz o Las Trampas de la Fe*. Barcelona: Six Barral.

Zavitzianos, G. (1972). Homeovestism: perverse form of behaviour involving the wearing of clothes of the same sex. *International Journal of Psychoanalysis*, 53: 471–477.

CHAPTER ELEVEN

Women and activism: a long history, a complex problem

Adrienne Harris

Introduction

For the past few years, I have been working on the problem of human trafficking under the auspices of an International Psychoanalytical Association Committee that is constituted as a non-governmental organisation (NGO) to the United Nations. This work proved to be a bridge to my past work in feminist activism, in anti-war work and in other projects on the health and status of women. This essay has several agendas. First, I look at the continuities and discontinuities of work in support of vulnerable and politically and socially challenged women. Second, I look at the conflicts among women and between men and women that make work on human trafficking, in particular, very difficult and very challenging.

Finally, I look at some emerging trends in the politics and activism around human and child trafficking, changes that make trafficking both more visible and identifiable and, thus, potentially more open for political action.

Thirty years ago, in 1983, I made a radio documentary for the Canadian Broadcasting Corporation. It was broadcast over a three-week period and looked at women's peace movements over nearly a century and across different countries. The series was called *Woman as Peacemaker*. At that moment, there were strong initiatives for peace coming from women's groups in North America, in Europe, and in Israel and the programs brimmed with the voices of confident women describing the enormous potency of activism that, for most, had been life transforming. Inevitably, I found that looking at women and peace activism was both a political journey and a personal one.

The documentary took a historical look at women's peace activities around both world wars and in the reaction to nuclear threats. There was, even then, a sharp distinction between the women's peace politics emerging out of a general analysis of power and political oppression and a women's peace politics that stressed the role of motherhood, the naturalness of mothering, the innate skills for peace that women apparently possessed as the motivator for working for peace. Somewhere in the middle of the past century, one could begin to see that these peace movements played the mother card strategically rather than exactly authentically. Women Strike for Peace would be a good example. Actually filled with women who were active in the world and in politics, its use of maternal stereotypes was like wonderful political theatre.

However, it is one of the grounding ideas in this chapter that perhaps the strategic use of motherhood was also a trap, presaging some splits in feminism that were hugely costly for the movement in the 1980s. We have just seen a version of these wars and splitting in the feminist responses to Caitlin Jenner, scolded for wanting to be sexy.

Huge changes in the underpinning ideologies came with feminism. Women became interested in power and in a view of gender that was fluid and culturally driven, never innate or simply biological. These movements and the identity politics that followed them branched widely into a range of activities particular to women: reproductive health, violence against women, human trafficking (called the white slave trade in First World World War parlance), and many projects of anti-imperialism.

Ynestra King and I edited a book on some of this history, *Rocking the Ship of State* (1983). The history gives a rich picture of a burgeoning interlocking of movements: one cherished value crossing many differences was an interest in cooperating and working collectively.

But this scene that lived in many feminist venues nationally and internationally was not without its conflicts and difficulties. One key area involved sex. The so-called sex wars of the 1980s pitted woman against pornography (WAP) and sexual exploitation against women who wanted to speak and agitate for expanded and expanding experiences of sexual life: puritanism or morality *vs.* freedom or exploitation. These conflicts proved to be impossible to contain and these battles, one might truthfully say, shredded the woman's movement, sometimes side-swiping and sometimes engaging questions of race, class, and culture along with questions of sexuality and gender identity (Chateauvert, 2014; Duggan & Hunter, 2014).

Flash forward three decades and I find myself deep at work with a group of colleagues who are developing bridges between mental health and psychoanalysis on the one hand and, on the other hand, humanitarian aid and global problems, some of them around women and children. We begin to work on human trafficking and I have an unsettled feeling of *déjà vu.*

But that is not exactly correct. It is a repetition and also a new situation in which there are new tools for analysis. I feel this personally, but it is also true collectively. Psychoanalytic, psychodynamic thinking, not initially a strong feature of identity politics and early feminism has made all our understandings more complex. Now examining the experience and reach of human trafficking, there is more complexity to thinking about consent, more self-critique regarding the moralizing and anxiety-driven aspects of the new ideas about sexuality and freedom. There is more self-analysis of persons involving in healing and helping.

Critics of the humanitarian aid movements refer to this group of projects very dismissively as the "rescue" industry (Agustin, 2007; Moore, 2015). Those of us in these endeavors can be increasingly thoughtful and self-aware of the complex agendas, personal and political, in being a healer or rescuer. This entire thought, powered at base by psychoanalytic ideas, makes any political action a subject of enormous self-analysis. In just the way that analysts are increasingly urged to examine their countertransference to patients and clinical situations, similarly, men and women working to oppose or stop human trafficking must be self critical as well as critical.

So, to inquire as to my own shift from a more exclusive interest in sexual freedom to a concern for sexual exploitation, I would see both the scale of the problem of a global program of trafficking in persons and a more fine-grained analysis of the force of power and coercion on sex workers across the board. One tendency in thinking of sex workers is to make a distinction between escort systems, adult entertainment, more bourgeois forms of sexual exploitation, and the trafficking of low-income countries' women and children (Grant, 2014; Stoller, 1991, 1993). Increasingly, I am not so comfortable with these distinctions. But, equally, these distinctions are important to appreciate and think through (Butler, 2004).

Psychoanalysis, and psychoanalysis in conjunction with social theories like feminism and queer theory, requires any of us who work in opposition to sexual exploitation to think through our own motives and anxieties. Sexual behavior and sexual fantasy are so thoroughly policed and managed that one has to be ready to examine what aspects of our concern for trafficking has some repressive agenda with regard to sexuality. The modern work within psychoanalysis on sexuality (Dimen, 2003; Laplanche, 1999; Saketopoulou, 2015) expands our appreciation of the powerful experience of excess and enigma in all sexual experience. Understanding human trafficking will require thinking about the power of sexuality, its currency and potential for wonder, for addiction, and for psychic labor alongside thinking about exploitation and enslavement. In this way, human trafficking may be different even as it is overlapping slavery. Slavery did have sexual trafficking and exploitation folded into other projects for which slaves were entailed and used (Davis, 2014).

Inevitably, considerations of human trafficking take us to the question of consent. Psychoanalytic thought places consent in question. In a model of human functioning in which unconscious experience is ubiquitous and unquenchable, neither consent nor refusals are entirely straightforward. In the current crises around rape and assault on college campuses, this matter continues to be difficult to think through and plan for. College campuses are sites of primarily entitled and enlightened persons. Even there, or particularly there, these questions of freedom and respect and sexual action remain unsettled. How much more crucial and difficult, then, is it to consider consent in the context of poverty, coercion within families, and the vulnerability to danger and control by others?

What is not so fully discussed in regard to any sex work is the role and presence of early sexual trauma in sex workers and trafficked persons. In a Webinar conducted at Weill Cornell Medical College, committees of the American Psychoanalytic Association and the

International Psychoanalytical Association, a number of people—in the medical field, and in law enforcement, and from the world of trafficking—spoke to the visibility of trafficking (it is not a hidden crime) and to the risk factors, which overwhelmingly include histories of sexual abuse and substance use (UNODOC Global report, 2013).

In this sense, the decades since this issue was first engaged by feminists have seen a great shift in our appreciation of trauma (be it sexual, physical, war related, or occupational). In the Webinar on Human Trafficking, a young woman in her mid-twenties described being drawn into prostitution and herself linked this to her own history and the identity-undermining effects of sexual abuse. In the past decades, within all mental health work, there is an increased attention to the effect of trauma, its erosion of self-esteem, its link to heightened vulnerability in any victim, and also our continued difficulty in noticing the devastation to children and to families and to subsequent generations.

Over several years, I have worked to understand and find a mode of organization to work effectively on this issue. Even as I have understood more, what I have felt primarily and fundamentally defeated by is the question of advocacy and prevention. Why can we not develop a political movement to eradicate trafficking? Human trafficking is a criminal enterprise on a global scale, with staggering financial resources. It compromises and destroys the lives of millions of women and children. Why are we not more activated and therefore active?

To some extent, some of the struggles centered around whether sex work was best thought of and organized around in terms of labor issues rather than slavery and exploitation. This tension exists into the present. The introduction of a psychoanalytic perspective might, in fact, disrupt this polarity, asking that we consider the issue of previous trauma as a precursor to trafficking and as adjunct to, and emergent from, it.

Trafficking

There is first of all the sheer scale of what is occurring. Children, women, and men are trafficked for work (forced labor and sexual exploitation) (UNODC Global Report on Trafficking in Persons, 2013). From one set of statistics in the UN report of 2013, it is estimated that

12.3 million persons are trafficked for forced labor and 20.9 million for sexual exploitation. Women and children are 55% of the forced labor force and 98% of the persons who are sex trafficked. Children are over-all 20% of the persons trafficked for sexual exploitation, but in several regions (Vietnam and West Africa, children are close to 100% of the population of persons trafficked). One striking detail from the UN Trafficking in Persons Report: children being prostituted are often required to use steroids which may make them look older and also contribute to being physically able to have sex with more partners. These steroids are bought by the children from the very meager pay-ment they receive. In the Webinar on Human Trafficking, doctors and law enforcement officers (law enforcement officers included FBI staff and a Department of Justice Assistant United States Attorney) spoke about the important process of identifying both those at risk for being trafficked and those already kidnapped or coerced into prostitution.

Over and over again as the day went on, one saw that human traf-ficking is not a "hidden crime" exactly. It is, if anything, hidden in plain sight. Women and children who are being trafficked are marked by many signs: obedience to the people they are with, histories of infections, unhealed fractures, gynecological diseases of many kinds, STDs, tattoos that mark possession and possessor. Probing more psychiatrically, one finds histories of sexual abuse and violence, poor self-esteem, runaway history, vulnerability to manipulation, and neglect. At one point, from the law enforcement side, it was estimated that most "missing" children who are reported are, in fact, children who are being/have been trafficked.

If we cannot agree how to marshal a mass movement of opposition on the scale of nineteenth century anti-slavery and abolitionist move-ments, we can at least keep our eyes open. We also have increasingly clear signs of who uses situations where trafficked persons are work-ing. On average, 80% of men and many fewer women report having used at least one of the following during any given year: brothels, lap dances, strip clubs, online pornography, and escort services.

This increased visibility will make it harder to screen out the pres-ence of trafficking and the damage caused by it. This was one of the phenomena that worked in anti-slavery organizing. David Brion Davis (2014) an important Civil War historian, argues that it was the visibility of slaves with voices, heard through both writings and speaking, which began to put a human face on the inhumanity of enslaving persons. This is beginning to happen: Girls Educational and Mentoring Services (GEMS) and other grass roots organizations are beginning to open this window into the world of trafficking.

It is impossible to learn about trafficking in persons without understanding the vicarious traumatization at all levels of help and engagement. The emphasis I am putting on "vicarious" traumatization only underscores the incredible difficulty of getting help of a genuinely useful kind to the primary victims of human trafficking (Boulanger, 2013).

Human trafficking functions as a global network: countries from which people are trafficked, countries that are the agents of transmittal, and countries that consume what has been trafficked. The latter would be the high-income countries: us. People are recruited mostly from the low-income countries, from Africa and the Far East. There are groups and countries that primarily organize and manage the transporting of trafficked people to the points of "consumption." The high-income countries consume workers and sex workers of all genders and ages.

At a 2013 meeting of the American Psychoanalytic Association, UN members and NGO members involved for decades in political and humanitarian work on the problem of human trafficking came to talk to a discussion group organized by the IPA in its role as an NGO to the UN, chaired by Vivian Pender. Psychoanalysts listened and reacted. We could easily feel, and be collaborative on the matter of, vicarious traumatization, the degree to which workers in these areas are indelibly marked by what they hear and see. This got through to people. UN participants were taking notes, nodding.

If our group has learned anything (and begun slowly to convey what we have learned), I believe it is that people doing the work of humanitarian aid and support of trafficked persons usually carry a lot of vicarious trauma themselves. A young lawyer described the task of watching child pornography in order to decide what was litigable or criminal. Because of the sensitivity of the materials and the delicacy of developing legal cases, this young woman watched this material in quite isolated and depressing circumstances. She describes hours spent in front of a video screen and seemed almost surprised and ashamed at being so haunted by the film material. Certainly, she had nowhere to process, and recover from, the images that had invaded her mind and body. I think if we understood and applied ideas about dissociation and fragmentation to a variety of humanitarian projects, we would see the massive amounts of vicarious traumatization that, even with some significant programs beginning or already in play, remains inadequately treated. I think there is a plausible ethical and clinical role we can play in this regard. About this aspect of work on human trafficking, I feel relatively confident and we have many colleagues with expertise to offer us in this regard.

The Super Bowl

In the 2014 meeting of our group at the American Psychoanalytic Association, many of the same workers, joined by FBI and law enforcement representatives, focused on trafficking here in the USA. The discussion centered on the sites of mass concentrations of persons as sites for trafficking, and named the Super Bowl.

It is a generally reported statistic/finding that athletic events like the Super Bowl and events that attract a huge audience of attendees or supporters routinely draw people being trafficked and their managers/pimps. The Super Bowl is considered to be the single event annually in the USA generating the most instances of trafficking. Added to the problem, there is always the conflict about which agencies of the state intervene here: criminal justice or humanitarian aid.

Despite working for some time to educate ourselves, our committee members and the listening discussion group were deeply unsettled. How do we process that one of the most classic, iconic American celebrations is also a major opportunity for large scale sex trafficking? The "problem" of the Super Bowl brings up one of the most difficult and problematic aspects of work on trafficking. One thread of opposition to trafficking has tied these practices to masculinity, and to men generally. This has fractured feminist reactions to working on human trafficking and seems to many to be singularly counterproductive for mass support against these practices, whether it is occupational or sexual exploitation that is involved.

To add to the complexity of the problem of combating human trafficking, a new statistic presents itself. Over 30% of the persons who carry out the trafficking are women, often those who have themselves entered the system of slavery as trafficked persons. On the one hand, this works against a very damaging gender polarity in analyzing and combating human trafficking. On the other hand, the conflating of victim and perpetrator makes intervention and genuine rehabilitation much more difficult.

Since the majority of consumers are men resident in high-income countries, there is the added problem of conflict across gender lines, a conflict that radically constricts activism. I had an unpleasant experience of this when I criticized online what I felt was an unthoughtful presentation of an article on human trafficking around the Super Bowl in 2014. This touched a raw nerve for many men, and the fallout went in multiple directions. Not exactly going viral, but the opposition to any critique of sports was striking and, to me, very unsettling.

The idea that the Super Bowl was a potent attractor of human trafficking was distinctly unpopular on the list server to which I posted it. What then occurred was an outburst of emails and communications insistently lauding the heavenly sport of football, the excitement of the Super Bowl, the glorious team spirit, our guys, etc., etc. It seemed to me, in the deepest sense of that term, hysterical.

But, in a way that was all too familiar from long ago struggles, this also seemed to turn organizing against trafficking into gender war. There is nothing "natural" about the conjunction of large scale sporting events and sex or gender. Large scale political events, or concerts, any event with a mass audience collecting in one venue, is increasingly and very systematically a venue for trafficking. What is consistent across many such situations, regardless of the gendered makeup of an audience, is the deep denial about how pervasive and ubiquitous, how hidden in plain sight, this matter of sex trafficking is. We practice this denial in many different settings, from labor conditions in low-income countries, through the globalizing of child care, through the most current exposure that is the danger to mostly undocumented and certainly ill-paid workers doing manicures and beauty work for women.

These sentiments of determined and impassioned protection are, and have been, central to many sports journalists' essays on the question of head injuries and their importance in football. Football is religion, flag, life, and manhood. The US National Football League (NFL) has been steady in its denial until very recently. I felt that the issue surfacing and being acted out was at the heart of my worries about work in activism in relation to trafficking. To the degree that concern about trafficking constituted an assault on football, it began to seem to be akin to an assault on the most basic and fundamental masculinist values in modern life. It has seemed hopeless.

Then something happened that gave me a way to shift perception. Around the 2015 Super Bowl, a series of articles and reports appeared on the matter of head injuries and their long-term consequences for football players. A tide is turning in the sports and popular press. People who love football are, in varying states of agony and upset, turning away from the game. A writer quoted a friend's reaction to his essay on the dangers of football head injuries with a poignant sentence, "Don't take this away from me" (Hruby, 2012).

There was a statistical window on to the consequence of the violence in the modern game. One report calculated the potential loss of earnings and health and life span for players with head injuries. On average, players stay approximately six years in the NFL; one out of every three players are estimated to have dementia and brain injury to some degree. Close to 80% of players, post-NFL career, are bankrupt or in financial trouble within two years of retiring. Do the math (Belson, 2014).

The indifference of owners and fans to this unmistakable pattern is stunning but unquestioned by almost all commentators on the matter of the dangers of professional football. It is cynically assumed by all that if there is any headway to be made in this struggle, it will be the outcome of lawyers and lawsuits, not political action or humanitarian protest.

So, I pair the public response (the most neutral term would be apathy) to human trafficking and to football injuries, as they are emblematically linked and lived out at the Super Bowl. The Super Bowl is, in a sense, an equal opportunity destroyer: men and women of a particular class and color (usually) are at significant risk. I think this is a matter to publicize and agitate about. In fact, just as the consciousness around head injuries and sports is beginning to make inroads into public consciousness, so is the scale of human trafficking. There are public advertisements at many sporting events warning of the danger of trafficking. It is becoming more visible.

Pornography

As I have explored and tried to understand and to find a route to action (singly and collectively) around human trafficking, I have found myself drawn to think about pornography, that old and divisive topic of the early women's movement. This phenomenon has transformed radically with the rise of the internet. As clinicians, I and many others see people who found themselves addictively engaged with online pornography. Again, the specter of social control and social repression beckons. What exactly is wrong with pornography? How is it different from other sexual or romantic scenes (cinema, soap operas, entertainment) in which people perform, or enact, sex for money. Is consent different? Are work conditions different?

When we consider internet pornography clinically, we are primarily concerned with the impact on, and meaning for, the viewer. What is being deadened, sequestered, flattened, and avoided in the consumer who is quite addicted to watching pornography? We examine the defensive intentions of such viewing. Cole is one of the few psychoanalysts who has considered the acts of viewing from a psychoanalytic perspective. He considers first of all the experience of watching internet pornography through the lens of cultural theory and philosophy as well as psychoanalysis:

> In *Screening Sex* (2008), Linda Williams develops a bidirectional and mimetic theory of filmed sexual acts, whether hard-core porn or mainstream romance movies, two ends of a continuum evocatively called screened sex (pointing toward what is revealed on and what remains behind a screen). One motive driving her theory explicitly is to complicate the simple, mimetic theory, one that can see porn as at the least corrupting and in the most extreme instances inciting action in an otherwise innocent and passive audience. For Williams, watching porn invites, even demands, an interaction not only because of the technological innovation that so radically alters our relationship with any text or image in the age of the digital media but also because of the kind of relationship that porn sets up, depicting as it does acts that culminate in an involuntary physical response, the orgasm. This model begins with how we imitate behaviors we see in the environment because of a correspondence we feel inside ourselves with that which we come into relation outside of our bodies. Because our nervous system responds in an involuntary way this can be thought of as an "innervation" (Williams, 2008, p. 20). But Williams builds on this "a model for taking in energy through motoric stimulation that extends back toward the world, for taking energy from the image back into the self" (p. 20). Williams's theory rests on a refined and complicated version of mimesis in which we do not merely imitate the filmed images we view but where our bodies are porous receptors for the

sensory stimulation conveyed by those images. It is almost as if the viewer were a sexual partner along with the performers. Here we can read an explanation for porn's reach into the genitals of its users. Williams's theory even makes room for a nearly curative effect of porn. The viewer's imagination, captivated by an image, imaginatively entering the scene herself, might benefit from the new erotic possibilities she encounters there. (Cole, 2011)

Williams is giving a careful account of the experience of watching with a very careful attention to the experience of the watcher. Cole makes this situation more complex by thinking of the subjectivity of the performer and its impact on the subjectivity of the viewer. In other words, he thinks as a psychoanalyst.

When we watch pornography, we do not only watch sexual acts. We watch people who are at work to present these acts to us in a commercial product. In his 1936 essay, "The Work of Art in the Age of Its Technological Reproducibility: Second Version," Walter Benjamin describes the difference between watching a performance that takes place in real time and space and the effect of viewing a film on the audience. As a mechanically reproducible artifact meant to produce a profit, a film or video is made in order to achieve maximum distribution. This kind of document or artifact of human expression is no longer valued because of its relation to an original or because it is itself "authentic" and we in the audience are not in the presence of an authentic original, though what we witness cannot, we believe, be faked. So the effect of a film or video on a viewer is different from the effect a live performance has. The mediating presence of a camera fundamentally changes the relationship between the audience and performer. Although we in the audience may identify with the character(s) the position we occupy is more like that of the camera. It is with the camera that we are in closest relation, and so we arguably more nearly resemble a critic than an actor. This is where I locate porn's "strange invitation." The degree of our sense of contact with a performer depends on the skills of porn producers, but the viewer's relation is that of an outsider, not a participant. Watching a video requires an adjustment, a negotiation between the observing and evaluating role of critic of what is depicted and one's willingness to become involved with the images, allowing them to enter one's mind and body. (Cole, 2011)

I want to push this set of observations further into a consideration of the experience of the performer. Stoller's (1991) paper on the experience of sex workers stressed the alienation and dissociation of their accounts of the work. Is this the outcome of pre-existing trauma, the effect of the work on the person producing and performing sexual acts, or some interaction between the two states. If trafficked persons are vulnerable and also have histories of abuse, how does this state make them liable to be recruited to pornography? Does the experience of performing in pornography exacerbate trauma and its effects?

I am concerned here that we consider the pornography worker's subjectivity as well as the viewer's. This is particularly important when the performer is a child. Again, statistics are a source of conflict among people thinking and writing about trafficking and pornography. Estimates of the presence of child pornography on the internet were at 20% in 2003 (IMEC) and a number of researchers note the presence of increasingly violent and graphic child pornography with prepubescent children (under twelve). Some of this material is commercial, some amateur and individually made. Commentators on this industry have urged those of us considering these phenomena to be sensitive to the specifics within cultures and settings and the variation in how and why these products appear and are disseminated.

I want a critical and public space in which we consider the impact of performing pornography on persons, both young and adult, coerced or consenting, and interwoven with this the impact on the viewer of these scenes both in regard to their violence and in regard to the dissociated and potentially traumatized state of the performer. Cole was able to push his own reactivity to pornography (he was bored) into another realm of observation. His boredom masked his anxiety.

I think of Goldberg's (2008) work on the impact on the psyche of modern forms of alienation and the counter-catastrophic personality. Following these ideas, I would suggest that pornography is one among many portals through which dissociation is culturally transmitted (Ritter, 2015). There are, of course, many mechanisms that produce and sustain social alienation, but considering the producing, performing, and consuming of filmed pornography may contribute to our anxieties about working to stop trafficking. Traumatic dissociation is contagious. The contagion is spread through a variety of forms. internet pornography might be important because of its ubiquity, its wide and increasing presence, in all its forms and settings. It is striking to me that most critical energy and clinical work on pornography has centered on the impact on the viewer, without a full exploration of the state of the producer/performer and its mimetic transfer into audiences, singly or en masse.

It is likely that political action and consciousness-raising about trafficking will have its most intense traction where child trafficking is concerned. There is no legal status of "consent" for underage children. While there have been debates about when such consent would be morally feasible, it is unlikely to be set below twelve.

Yet, there is evidence that child pornography is increasing in amount, extent, and graphic violence. To work on this problem will require people across a variety of disciplines identifying risk factors and children at risk. Given the hidden nature of pornography production, the identification of children at risk is particularly important. Finding sites of intervention, such as schools, street life, public spaces, clinics, and ERs, and realizing that this problem is more visible than we have liked to imagine is crucial.

Is there any social issue that contains this much contradiction? Extreme need and the seriousness of the exploitation and danger to persons, interwoven with anxiety and resistance to thinking or acting, is a dominant feature of the public and social response to the issue of trafficking. Sex seems to me to be one important stumbling block here. Sexuality is, at one and the same time, so private and so socially dominated and regulated.

I close by framing the question of women and child trafficking in the more general context of violence against women. As with trafficking, this question of violence specifically directed against women must be asked globally. Rape and brutality against women is a constantly threatening and fast accelerating act of warfare and revenge that accompanies and drives warfare at every imaginable level, often sanctioned by military and governing leaders in combat and post combat situations.

It is easy to notice and protest against this terribly increased violence against women where punishment is always sexualized in rape, whatever else is done. Recently, Ian Buruma (2015) wrote an account of the year 1945, at the end of the Second World War, after "peace". Titled *Year Zero*, in it he recounts the turmoil, hunger, social violence, and vengeance both in Europe and in the Pacific countries that had been at war. In every country and context he examined, sexual violence (rape and murder) against women was considered appropriately retaliatory, necessary, an entitlement of the conquerors, and was often officially sanctioned. And it was not solely sanctioned by Stalin. It is tempting to try to "other" these terrible crimes and assaults and, certainly, the memory of these practices and this violence becomes erased (except in the singular and collective unconscious).

It might be a necessary step in thinking of trafficking as both global and criminal to also think of trafficking in the context of sexual violence against women. There is a war on women.

Conclusion

It remains curious, but more deeply alarming and confusing, that human trafficking presents such powerful challenges in terms of organizing mass public protest and activism. Trying to find a pathway through conflicts among women, between men and women, has proved to be overwhelmingly difficult. I suspect that the fact that sex is at the core of trafficking is an element in this intractable problem. In addition, these conflicts are on the liberal end of the social and political spectrum.

I conclude with a series of questions, questions we need still to be asking and answering. Does it demoralize women to be helped (the role of the "rescue industries")? Is work involving the sexual use of the body different from other kinds of work? How? Is the global and criminal intricacy of this problem part of its intractability? Another related question involves the isolation and control of trafficked persons. Is the trafficked person fatally distanced from his or her community and family?

What are the links between trafficking and pornography and how might these links be analyzed and serve as grounds for activism?

References

Agustin, L. M. (2007). *Sex at the Margin: Migration, Labor Markets and the Rescue Industry*. New York: Zed Books.

Belson, K. (2014). Brain trauma to affect 1 in 3 players, NFL agrees. *New York Times*, September 12.

Boulanger, G. (2013). Fearful symmetry: shared trauma in New Orleans after Hurricane Katrina. *Psychoanalytic Dialogues*, 23(1): 31–44.

Buruma, I. (2013). *Year Zero: A History of 1945*. New York: Penguin.

Butler, J. (2004). *Precarious Life; The Powers of Mourning and Violence*. London: Verso.

Chateauvert, M. (2014). *Sex Workers Unite: A History of the Movement from Stonewall to Slutwalk*. New York: Beacon.

Cole, G. (2011). A strange invitation: on the ordinary problem of pornography. *Studies in Gender and Sexuality, 12*: 254–267.

Davis, D. B. (2014). *The Problem of Slavery in the Age of Emancipation*. New York: Alfred A. Knopf.

Dimen, M. (2003). *Sexuality, Intimacy, Power*. Hillsdale, NJ: Analytic Press.

Duggan, L., & Hunter, N. (2014). *Sex Wars: Sexual Dissent and Political Culture* (10th Anniversary edn). New York: Routledge.

Goldberg, P. (2008). Catastrophic change, communal dreaming and the counter-catastrophic personality. Paper presented to the 4th EBOR Conference, Seattle, WA, November 1.

Grant, M. G. (2014). *Playing the Whore: The Work of Sex Work*. New York: Verso.

Harris, A., & King, Y. (Eds.) (1983). *Rocking the Ship of State*. Boulder, CO: Westview Press.

Hruby, P. (2012). Why I broke up with football. SportsonEarth.com. August 30.

Laplanche, J. (1999). *Essays on Otherness*. London: Routledge.

Moore, A. E. (2015). The American rescue industry: toward an anti-trafficking paramilitary. Truth-out.org.

Ritter, A. (2015). Theories of trauma transmission following Ferenczi: survivor syndrome and transgenerational phantoms. Paper presented to the International Ferenczi Conference, Toronto, May 7–10.

Saketopoulou, A. (2015). On sexual perversions' potential to act as portal to unformulated mental states. In: A. Lemma & P. E. Lynch (Eds.), *Sexualities: Contemporary Psychoanalytic Perspectives* (pp. 205–218). New York: Routledge.

Stoller, R. (1991). Eros and polis: what is this thing called love? *Journal of the American Psychoanalytic Association, 39*: 1065–1102.

Stoller, R. (1993). *Porn: Myths for the 20th Century*. New Haven, CT: Yale University Press.

UNODC Global Report on Trafficking in Persons (2013). www.unodc.org/documents/Global_Report_on_TIP.pdf

INDEX

campus, 35
corrective, 180
culture of, 36
fantasies of, 37
fictional representations of, 35
gang-, 172
genocidal, 180
legitimate, 182
marital, 183–184
myth of, 36
state-sponsored, xvi, 182
statutory, 174
systematic, 182
victims, 30
Raphael-Leff, J., 145–146, 148, 150
Reene, K. J., 99
Rees, S., 214
religion, 2, 22, 61, 69, 93, 173–176,
    187, 245
    Abrahamic, 174
    African traditional, 174–175
    autochthonous, 222
    Buddhism, 174
    Catholic, 21–24, 174–175, 223
    Eastern Orthodox, 174
    Evangelical Christians, 175
    fundamentalists, xvii
    Hinduism, 174–175
    Islamic, 174
    Orthodox Jewish, 174
    Shinto, 174–175
Reynolds, C. R., 111
Rich, K., 69
Richards, A., 68
Ritter, A., 249
Robbins, T., 72
Roiphe, K., 136
Rontos, K., 171
Rose, J., 67–68
Rosenbaum, B., 196, 200
Rosenberg, M., 171
Rossi, A., 110
Rowley, H., 18, 23–26
Roy, J., 68

Rudnytsky, P. L., 67
Ruth, R., 101, 110

Saketopoulou, A., 240
Salas-Wright, C. P., 109
Sarpathie, R., 195
Sasaki, A., 113
Scarfone, D., 202
Schiller, B.-M., 136
Schottenbauer, M., 197
Schumm, J. A., 195
self, 19, 21, 27, 63, 101, 134, 151, 196,
    199, 201, 247 see also: denial,
    object
-actualization, 31, 53
-analysis, 239
-analytic, 209
-assertion, 132, 134–136, 138–140
-assumed, 223
authentic, 28
-aware, 239
-censoring, 53
-concept, 80, 115
-confidence, 169
-critical, 239
-critique, 239
-defense, 7
-definition, 134
-development, 141
-discovery, 52
-doubt, 10, 167
-effacement, 16
-employed, 153
-enhancement, 135
-esteem, 99, 106–107, 130, 169, 196,
    241–242
-experience, 101
-expression, 20, 132, 135, 140
false, 19–20, 22, 26–27, 70
fear for, 136
-hood, 43
-knowledge, 50
-loathing, 2, 164
-negating, 199

private, 70
-protection, 31
-psychology, 101
-reflective, 104
-regard, 107
-regulation, 94
-reliance, 141
-representation, 166
sense of, 94, 131, 136, 147
split, 20
true, 11, 20, 36–37, 50, 52, 55
wrong, 20
Seligman, M., 179
Selten, J., 108
separation, 25, 91, 96, 104, 106, 110,
    115, 119, 149, 157, 159, 186
    see also: anxiety
-autonomy, 154
bodily, 147, 154, 157
experience, 150, 157
-individuation, 94, 101, 149,
    157–158
major, 26
maternal, 112
phase, 151
physical, 80
recent, 43
theoretical, 164
sexism, xvi, 17, 20, 28, 40, 176, 179,
    185 see also: conscious
sexual(ity) (passim) see also: abuse,
    behavior, desire, fantasy,
    identity, object
action, 240
activity, 39, 99, 177–178, 185
agency, 30, 35–36
approach, 209
assault, xvii, 97, 180, 183, 203
bi-, 224–225, 227, 229
bodies, xvi, 63, 136
burgeoning, 131, 136
choices, 15, 39
coming of age, 48
conditioning, 38

consensual, 229
development, 36, 178
differences, 159, 221, 230
disappointment, 15
discrimination, 3, 5
distinction, 224
enjoyment, 37, 173, 186
equality, 93
escapades, 25, 223
expectation, 63
experience, 35, 63, 225, 240
experimentation, 227
exploitation, 19, 180–181, 239–242,
    244
exploration, 36
feelings, 177
female, xvii, 35–38, 59, 68, 173–174,
    188, 224–225
forces, 180
freedom, 25, 173, 239
gratification, 26
harassment, 38
health, 175
hetero-, 225, 227, 229
homo-, 225, 227–228
human, 224–225, 229–230, 232
imposition, 37
indenture, 166
indiscretions, 25
inexperience, 39
infant, 149
initiation, 36, 54, 70
intercourse, 178
knowledge, 36
liberation, 223, 227
life, 26, 39, 239
loneliness, 18
masculine, 137, 224
mutilation, 172
nascent, 36
needs, xvi
neo-, 226, 229
orientations, 185
parade, 33